Books are to be returned on or befor
the last date below.

Na
Sc
an

National Standards and School Reform in Japan and the United States

Edited by
Gary DeCoker

Foreword by
Susan H. Fuhrman

Teachers College, Columbia University
New York and London

Published by Teachers College Press, 1234 Amsterdam Avenue, New York, NY 10027

Library of Congress Cataloging-in-Publication Data
National standards and school reform in Japan and the United States / edited by Gary De-Coker.
    p. cm.
    Includes bibliographical references and index.
    ISBN 0-8077-4200-7 (pbk. : alk. paper) — ISBN 0-8077-4201-5 (cloth : alk. paper)
      1. Education—Standards—Japan. 2. Education—Standards—United States.
      3. Curriculum change—Japan. 4. Curriculum change—United States. 5. Comparative education. I. DeCoker, Gary.

LB3060.87.J3 N38 2002
379.1'58'0952—dc21   2001052825

ISBN 0-8077-4200-7 (paper)
ISBN 0-8077-4201-5 (cloth)

Printed on acid-free paper

Manufactured in the United States of America

09 08 07 06 05 04 03 02   8 7 6 5 4 3 2 1

Contents

Foreword

National Standards and School Reform in Japan and the United States comes at an opportune moment for American readers. Virtually every state has been engaged in standards-based reform for about 10 years. Policymakers are designing and redesigning expectations for student learning using national standards proposed by professional associations as models. They are developing and implementing assessment systems that attempt to measure achievement of expected outcomes and accountability systems that offer rewards and sanctions attached to progress on assessments. In the fall of 2001, Congress was in the final stages of producing an Elementary and Secondary Education Act that requires states to test at certain grade levels and that links federal funding for disadvantage students to certain minimal progress in student performance. We do not have formal national standards as does Japan, but we have an increasing standards-driven environment and are experiencing a nationalization of education policy in many ways. Are there lessons American policymakers and educators can learn from Japan, where national standards have long been established?

Gary DeCoker and his colleagues confirm many of our images of Japanese education. The picture of the Japanese curriculum as both richer and more focused than ours has animated many American reformers who see high Japanese achievement and its standards-based system as strongly related. Americans are also inspired by the idea that since the question of "what is to be taught" has been settled by national standards, Japanese teachers are free to focus on "how to teach" in a way that leads to more thoughtful and effective pedagogy. The chapters in this book provide rich descriptions of Japanese curricula, materials and teacher practices that support these characterizations. Japanese science texts for example, include more problem-solving activities, experimental activities, in-depth coverage, connections to daily life, and well-sequenced activities than do our textbooks. They even have better visuals. Teacher manuals in mathematics are heavily content-focused, providing an overview of the relevant content and goals. They also stress pedagogical content, explaining the typical level of knowledge at the relevant grade and how the concepts to be learned can build on what has been taught before and connected to what the students will learn in the future. Japanese teachers engage in instructional research, and teacher professional development focuses on improving instruction in specific subjects, with teachers working together to devise and perfect "study lessons."

As admirable as these aspects of Japanese education seem to Americans, many educators here discount the possibility of emulating them. Some assume that their depth and richness are only possible because of Japan's national curriculum. Because the Ministry can impose a focused, parsimonious set of standards, the argument goes, Japan escapes all the uncertainty about curriculum that leads to the kind of diffuse, superficial textbooks and scattershot in-service programs that we have in the United States. Our decentralized system is blamed for a lack of depth, frequent repetition, and the lack of challenge in the American curriculum. One of the most valuable contributions of this book is the much more nuanced, textured view of Japanese education policymaking and implementation than is captured by the oft repeated conception of an all-powerful Ministry of Education. While the Ministry does promulgate a Course of Study, and no correspondingly powerful central authority exists in the United States, we learn that the Ministry does face many limits and must negotiate many audiences in seeking to have influence. Textbooks, for example, are not simply reflections of the national Course of Study; rather, teacher-authors and ordinary teachers who critique the books are very influential. Teacher collaboration around lesson development cuts across districts and prefectures, providing a powerful horizontal force that mediates the implementation of the national curriculum. And, the increasingly powerful private sector—*juku* or supplemental education providers and influential elite private schools—limit the Ministry's influence.

Realizing that Japan's educational system is not as centralized as some Americans might have thought still does not mean, however, that Japanese practices are easy to emulate in a different cultural context. Many factors of Japanese society, such as its deep peer culture which undergirds teacher collaboration, are central to the operations of the school system. DeCoker and colleagues are careful to point out the limits on our ability to import educational reform approaches from Japan while at the same time providing many valuable lessons. We learn, for example, that many districts rotate teachers among schools, which is perhaps one way to deal with the inequity in teacher assignments found in many large American cities. Readers will find many other examples of Japan doing things differently that provoke thought and make us question our own practices. *National Standards and School Reform in Japan and the United States* teaches us much more about Japanese education than most Americans know; in the process we learn a great deal about our own system as well.

Susan H. Fuhrman

Acknowledgments

THIS BOOK STARTED as an afterthought. At the end of a letter written to Tom Rohlen, I added a sentence casually stating that someone should attempt to pull together some of the recent research on Japanese textbooks. A few days later, the telephone rang. Tom, in his charitable and supportive manner (we had only met once), suggested that we hold a conference on the topic and offered to help me search for funding.

Our grant proposal gained the support of the Spencer Foundation, and their funding allowed us to bring a group of people from Japan and the United States to a 3-day conference at Green Gulch Farm Zen Center, north of San Francisco, in November 1998. The peaceful environment, vegetarian cuisine, and helpful staff created the perfect atmosphere for our work.

Along with the chapter authors of this book, additional people participated in the Green Gulch conference. Some wrote papers; everyone contributed to the discussion that helped create this volume. Edward Beauchamp, Kazuko Behrens, Kyoichi Ito, Richard Rubinger, and Hiroshi Usui attended. Mark Lincicome wrote a paper, but his schedule did not permit him to join us. Samuel Coleman and Akane Zusho became chapter co-authors when they made contributions subsequent to the conference.

I would like to thank all of the participants for their enthusiasm, hard work, and timely responses to my seemingly endless queries. In addition, I should thank Jackie Hill, who first suggested the idea for this project at a Midwest Japan Seminar meeting in 1995, John Singleton, whose book *Learning in Likely Places* supplied a model for this project, Jeff Mirel, whose suggestions and encouragement helped me though the final stages, and Ohio Wesleyan University Provost William Louthan, who provided support at a crucial time in the project.

Lastly, I would like to acknowledge my gratitude to the editors at Teachers College Press, especially Susan Liddicoat and Aureliano Vázquez. When I first began assembling the papers, I felt that the experience had helped me learn a great deal about Japanese education. After working with such fine editors, I now realize that I have learned just as much about the editing process. Each of our chapters, and the book as a whole, is much improved because of their editing skills and analytical ability.

What Do National Standards Really Mean?

Gary DeCoker

T HE EDUCATIONAL SYSTEMS of most industrial nations include national curricular guidelines. The U.S. educational system, in contrast, still relegates curricular decisions to state and local governments. Pointing out this difference, some educational reformers in the United States imply its significance in explaining the low achievement levels of U.S. students on many international tests, while others view it as a source of creativity and vitality in American education. The way in which national standards may in fact affect educational achievement or teaching practice, however, remains difficult to gauge. Given that the United States has nothing approaching national standards, researchers can only speculate about the impact of a move to a more centralized educational system.

This book attempts to move beyond speculation with a study of the Japanese educational system. The authors begin with the premise that the U.S. and Japanese systems of education are fundamentally different, but that these differences do not preclude making comparisons and drawing insights. By describing the interplay of various constituencies in Japan's centralized system, we hope to help American educators and policymakers consider issues that may apply to education in the United States.

In Japan, the national government's control of curricular standards is enhanced by a government textbook-approval process. For that reason the textbook, as the embodiment of national standards, is a place to begin in understanding the way Japan implements its national curriculum. Most of the comparative research on Japanese textbooks, however, has focused on textbook content and teaching methods. This project, conceived more broadly, attempts to provide a comprehensive study of the articulation of national standards in Japan from the development of the standards at the Ministry of Education (MOE)* to their implementation in the classroom.

U.S. IDEOLOGICAL DEBATES

Since the discussion of national education standards by former presidents Bush and Clinton in the early 1990s and the renewed enthusiasm for achievement testing by President George W. Bush, Americans have been debating the federal government's role in determining the curriculum of the nation's schools. To date, however, this debate consists of more passion than reason. Politicians and educators on both sides of the political spectrum continue to oppose national standards, but their arguments often rely less on logic than on hyperbole. The political right warns us of Washington bureaucrats who will dictate a specific curriculum and steal control of the local schools. The political left presents a parallel warning that such a curriculum could become dominated by right-wing zealots or religious ideologues. But despite the fervor for the subject, or perhaps because of it, politicians and the educational community have yet to explore the issue of national standards in any depth. Instead the political center seems to be finding growing support for federally mandated state standards and testing, a process that shifts the difficult decisions out of the federal arena and creates a pastiche of standards documents and tests.

The debate over the national standards clearly illustrates the problem: People can't agree on the content of the curriculum. This lack of agreement results in the writing and rewriting of curriculum guides and courses of study at each level of government. Over the last decade and a half, national professional organizations, state curriculum committees, local teachers, and other groups have spent countless hours producing hundreds, perhaps thousands, of standards documents. In turn, publishing companies, attempting to produce textbooks that appeal to the national market, struggle to incorporate the new documents, and as a result, continue to expand textbook content. While other countries develop national standards that give focus to their curricula, the United States continues to produce additional standards documents and resulting textbooks that favor breadth over depth of coverage. Textbooks might contain something for everyone, but they satisfy no one. Still, by default, the process by which they are

---

Editor's note: In January 2001, many ministries and agencies of the Japanese government were merged and renamed. The Ministry of Education, Science and Culture became the Ministry of Education, Culture, Sports, Science and Technology. In this book, the authors use the term Ministry of Education (MOE).

produced and marketed has become the means by which Americans create national standards.

One might argue, and some people do, that the vigorous debates over the nation's school curriculum are an indication of a healthy, functioning democracy. But in practice democracy often becomes chaotic and unfocused. When local communities debate the merits of various curricula, they are attempting, in theory, to select for themselves what best fits their unique circumstances. But their search quickly moves the local debates into the broader national arena. Textbook companies, political action committees, and politicians have a way of "nationalizing" the local debates. And the local schools and their teachers are left with the same ambiguities and either-or positions that dominate our national debates. They may appear to have choices, but the menu becomes the same across the country. A few textbook companies dominate the nation's educational marketplace, and their books lack a coherent curricular vision (Schmidt, McKnight, & Raizen, 1997). The increased use of state proficiency tests has shifted some influence from publishing to testing companies. In many cases, however, the same companies produce textbooks, tests, and test-preparation materials.

INSIGHTS FROM JAPAN

Since the publication of *A Nation at Risk* in 1983, U.S. politicians have promoted the need for educational reform by citing the low scores of American students on international achievement tests. Comparing international test results between countries is a very complicated process. While there is recent evidence of improvement in the standing of American students on some sections of these tests, the overall perception of the U.S. public is that American students lag far behind their international counterparts. Throughout the past decade and a half, Japan's educational system has been held up as a model for the United States. School uniforms, time-on-task, the number of schools days a year—the list of admirable qualities of Japanese education seems endless. And it's always changing. American politicians and policymakers at all levels continue to put forth the supposition that the supposed failure of American education and the success of Japanese education arise from whatever happens to be the latest insight.

Unfortunately, many of the statements by politicians and the media simplify the carefully nuanced work of comparative researchers and present it out of context (LeTendre, 1999). Their goal is not to describe Japan; instead, they hope to promote a specific educational reform in the United States, using Japan as a lever. The net result is that the American public is left with the feeling that education in the United States is sorely lacking compared to that in Japan. And many American educators, tired of hearing about it, simply dismiss the entire comparative enterprise.

Ironically, throughout the years of American infatuation with education in Japan, Japanese dissatisfaction with their system has increased. In some cases, the Japanese educational establishment's response has been to move away from the very policies that many Americans seem to admire. For example, Japan's Ministry of Education has taken steps to broaden the high school curriculum, reduce the emphasis on entrance examinations, and create a 5-day school week. Both countries seem to be moving in opposite directions, and the old images that each country has of the other are no longer accurate.

Despite the calls for reform on both sides of the Pacific, distinct differences in the two educational systems remain. The most obvious is the centralized Japanese system and the decentralized approach in the United States. Skeptics of comparative research begin and end with this point, arguing that we cannot learn anything from a system that is so different from our own. To make this argument, however, given the dominance of the centralized approach throughout the world, is to reject any understandings that might come to Americans from comparative education. Even though the United States is one of the few industrialized countries with a decentralized educational system, we cannot conclude that the country has nothing to learn from abroad. Such a xenophobic view is not supportable in any modern institution.

JAPAN'S IDEOLOGICAL BATTLES

One of the enduring U.S. images of Japanese education is the faceless bureaucrat in Tokyo extending his reach to every classroom throughout the 47 prefectures (equivalent to U.S. states) that make up Japan. This image, probably originating in the military's manipulation of Japanese education during World War II, depicts Japan's Ministry of Education in charge of every aspect of the educational system, leaving Japanese teachers little flexibility. But national standards do not by definition result in a lack of teacher freedom and involvement. In fact, as some of the authors of this volume point out, Japanese teachers in many ways have more freedom and are more involved precisely because of the national system. Japan's national system also does not guarantee that the government will be able to move the educational system at will. Even with its control over the curriculum, the Ministry of Education often finds its policies significantly altered by the time they reach the classroom. Some of the changes come from adjustments made by teachers and administrators; others result from supplementary educational institutions such as *juku** that react in ways that often conflict with the ministry's intent. In addition, the pace of change in Japanese society today sometimes makes the ministry seem like a dinosaur from another era, slowly reacting to change as its influence lessens.

In the United States, debates over education policy are framed in national terms with international ramifications. American reformers often argue that we need to improve education in order to keep up with overseas economic competition. As a nation we perceive pressure from abroad when we feel insecure about our international standing, such as after the Soviet launch of Sputnik in 1957 or during the U.S. economic recession of the late 1970s and early 1980s. In Japan, however, outside pressure has occasionally come directly and forcefully from its neighbors. Every 10 years or so, when the Ministry of Education publishes its revised curriculum guidelines and publishing companies develop new textbooks, Japan's Asian neighbors carefully read the sections dealing with international issues, especially the events of World War II. The standards and textbooks, they assume, reflect the national government's position and offer insight into subtle power shifts that might preclude a change in foreign policy. Domestic issues also result in conflict in Japan. For the entire postwar era, for instance, the Ministry of Education's attempt to incorporate Japan's national flag and anthem into school events and ritual has been resisted by some citizens, and until recently the Japan Teachers' Union (JTU) has almost instinctively rejected many of the ministry's reform proposals. The ministry's ability to censor textbook content, too, has been debated in the courts for most of the postwar era.

Historians and social scientists in Japan and abroad have long studied the conflict that is inherent in Japan's centralized educational system and its national curriculum (Hein & Selden, 1999; Thurston, 1973; Yoneyama, 1999). Citing the national government's authority to set curriculum standards and approve textbooks for classroom use, they describe a pervasive ideological clash between the government and various educational constituencies. Conflict, many researchers argue, comes from the struggle to change or resist the policies of the Ministry of Education. The authors of this book do not deny the importance of the conflict model, but we also believe that adherence to this top-down interpretation of Japanese education has produced a simplistic picture of power relations and movements for change.

The chapters that follow identify more complex and subtle power rela-

---

**Editor's note*: In Japanese, the plural of most nouns can be formed without the addition of an "s"; thus, both "an institution such as a *juku*" and "institutions such as *juku*" are correct, depending on the context.

tions involving actors whose initiatives help to shape or reshape Ministry of Education policies. They reveal the dynamic nature of Japan's educational system by describing the influence of outside forces and the fluid, interactive processes that affect educational policy. Some authors argue that the ministry has in fact lost control over the educational system; others point out that in some ways the ministry, following Japan's current climate of deregulation, has been actively relinquishing control. In any case, by taking a more syncretic approach, we hope to open new viewpoints. Our goal is to help the reader better grasp the intricacies of Japan's educational system and better understand the ramifications of a national system as it might evolve in the United States.

MAJOR THEMES OF THE BOOK

Educational Reform: Top-down, Bottom-up, and the "Soft Middle"

Most observers assume that a centralized system of education results in a top-down reform process. Built into the hierarchical structure of Japan's educational system, however, are "feedback loops" that allow information to move back and forth across national, prefectural/municipal, and local governmental levels. Although the Japanese educational system has a rigid structure, a "soft middle" level allows for modifications to take place in policymaking and in implementation, especially through the work of prefectural and municipal curriculum specialists. Japanese teachers, too, have a voice in policymaking, standard setting, and textbook writing, and many of Japan's "top-down" reforms undergo a transformation in the gradual process of implementation. As a result, Japan's educational system, from the policy level to the classroom, seems more integrated than does the U.S. system. The Japanese system also seems more stable and resistant to "quick-fix" reforms. Of course, in a rapidly changing society, this stability can be both an asset and detriment. Many Japanese view educational reform efforts as too little, too late. And some reforms bring unintended consequences when they meet the dynamic private sphere of supplementary education.

The Private and the Public Sectors: Separate or Intertwined?

Japan's public educational system, in many ways, appears aging, inflexible, and trapped by the past. Its values of stability, equality, and national economic mobility seem contradictory to the parental desire for new approaches that might propel their children in the race for personal success.

When we include the private sector, however, Japan's educational system looks dynamic. Viewed together, the two sectors work in a symbiotic relationship: The public sector, following a uniform curriculum through Grade 9, allows for the outward appearance of equity, while the private sector, in its parallel curriculum of supplemental study, allows for the reality of a competitive world where students strive to get ahead. The Ministry of Education's *Course of Study* serves as the guideline for both the public system and the *juku* industry.

In the United States, on the other hand, private schooling often appears opposed to the public system. Tax credits, vouchers, charter schools, and other attempts to introduce change in the U.S. system originate from the perceived failure of the public system. Success in the private sector often means a shift in support away from the public schools. Japan's national system, in contrast, seems to offer a structure where the roles of the public and private sectors remain intertwined, but not necessarily at odds. Viewed positively, schools offer the standard fare, and *juku*, using the dynamics of the educational marketplace, fill in the gaps for students with unmet needs. Of course, in their quest for profit and market share, *juku* marshal their enormous resources toward marketing and prey on the anxiety of parents, only some of whom are willing or able to pay the tuition and fees. In both countries, the private sector has only begun to exert its influence. Japan's Ministry of Education, perhaps fearing its own loss of control over the educational system, is exploring ways to regulate the examination-preparation *juku* without having to grant them school accreditation. In contrast, freedom from government regulation and the educational bureaucracy is one of the reasons American reformers cite for moving public funds to the private sphere through vouchers and charter schools.

Textbooks and Teachers' Editions: Tools or Crutches, Assets or Detriments?

Japanese national standards offer publishing companies a common structure for the development of their textbooks. As a result, innovation takes place in the method of presenting content, rather than in the selection of content. And for Japanese teachers and parents, the national standards become specific, long-term criteria by which to judge the quality of textbooks and teaching. The United States lacks such a national context. Japanese teachers, operating within a stable system of standards and textbooks, work together to perfect their lessons by developing creative variations of existing approaches. The U.S. conception of creativity, on the other hand, encourages teachers to reinvent the curriculum every few years, and the best teachers tend to develop unique curricula and approaches. In Japan, teachers' manuals provide a level of detail far beyond those in the United States, where ready-made lessons are less valued. To some observers, national standards and precise manuals might seem restrictive to both teachers and students, but within this context, Japanese teachers, especially in the early grades, develop student-centered ways to help their students explore the content within a defined area. In other words, creativity in Japan happens within a structure. American teachers and their students, thinking of structure as an impediment, view creativity as something that happens outside the existing framework. An American teacher might work to invent a new unit or new approach to bring to the classroom and reinvigorate the students. A Japanese teacher, on the other hand, will likely work with colleagues to progressively refine existing experiments that help students understand the content.

National Standards, Teacher Professional Development, and Classroom Practice

Recent research points to the extensive network of teacher professional development in Japan (Lewis & Tsuchida, 1998; Shimahara, Chapter 7, this volume; Stigler & Hiebert, 1999; Yoshida, 1999). Teachers, oriented to curricular and educational reforms through peer relationships, collaborate around lesson development. In the United States, on the other hand, teachers do not have a shared context, nor a culture of sharing. As a result, most teachers, viewing their job as personal rather than collaborative, practice teaching as an art where techniques and teacher-made materials are kept secret. In Japan teaching is a craft where techniques and materials are shared. Similar to Japan's tea ceremony and other traditional arts, in the craft of teaching, past approaches are reduced to a meaningful collection of wisdom that over time becomes the accepted authority. In the United States the art of teaching allows little room for past wisdom as it looks ahead to the creation of something new. American debates over new teaching approaches, however, often become simplistic and ideological. The battles over the teaching methods in reading and mathematics, for instance, focus more on images and terminology—phonics versus whole language, basic math versus problem solving—than on a teacher with a classroom of students. In the end many teachers, having been left out of the debate, react by rejecting reforms that are presented to them as absolutes. Instead they continue to draw on the best of both sides—some phonics along with good literature; some computation exercises along with abstract problem solving. In Japan, however, innovation in teaching methods comes from the teachers themselves in their collaborative lesson-development work. These new methods are described by a vocabulary of teachers and evaluated by their classroom efficacy in reaching a well-defined set of goals.

Breaking Down the Stereotypes

The chapters herein describe the Japanese educational system as complex, dynamic, and full of vitality, a depiction that serves to break down the stereotype, found on both sides of the Pacific, that Japan's system is one-dimensional, rigid, and stagnant. In many ways, the images you get in both countries depend on where you look. Differences exist in Japan between elementary and secondary education, between college-preparatory and terminal high schools, between the public schools and *juku*, between the open-ended national standards and the specific lesson plans of most text-books and teachers. Historical legacies, too, become sources of stereotypes. Japan's national system began just over a century ago in response to a loosely defined set of private initiatives in the early modern period. Later, especially in the prewar era, control tightened at the top. But a lot has happened since then to open up the system to influence from below. Despite lingering images of conflict from recent Japanese history, most notably the resistance of the Japan Teachers' Union, conflict cannot serve as the single, defining characteristic of the system.

The authors hope to advance understanding of the Japanese educational system among American educators and policymakers, and through comparisons with that of the United States, illuminate implicit and unquestioned aspects of U.S. educational organization and practice.

REFERENCES

Hein, L., & Selden, M. (Eds.). (1999). *Censoring history: Citizenship and memory in Japan, Germany, and the United States.* Armonk, NY: M. E. Sharpe.

LeTendre, G. (1999). *Competitor or ally? Japan's role in American educational debates.* New York: Falmer.

Lewis, C., & Tsuchida, I. (1998). A lesson is like a swiftly flowing river: Research lessons and the improvement of Japanese education. *American Educator, 22*(4), 12–17, 50–52.

National Commission on Excellence in Education. (1983). *A nation at risk: The imperative for educational reform.* Washington, DC: U.S. Department of Education.

Schmidt, W. H., McKnight, C. C., & Raizen, S. A. (1997). *A splintered vision: An investigation of U.S. science and mathematics education.* Boston: Kluwer.

Stigler, J., & Hiebert, J. (1999). *The teaching gap: Best ideas from the world's teachers for improving education in the classroom.* New York: Free Press.

Thurston, D. (1973). *Teachers and politics in Japan*. Princeton, NJ: Princeton University Press.

Yoneyama, S. (1999). *The Japanese high school: Silence and resistance*. New York: Routledge.

Yoshida, M. (1999). *Lesson study: An ethnographic investigation of school-based teacher development in Japan*. Unpublished doctoral dissertation, University of Chicago.

PART I

The Creation of National Standards: Influences from Above and Below

AMERICANS FROM BOTH SIDES of the political spectrum take pride in our decentralized educational system and are skeptical of federal initiatives, especially those dealing with curriculum. This preference for local control makes it difficult to view Japan's centralized system as anything but a "top-down," "command-and-control" system that allows little local input. In fact, educational reform in Japan involves substantial give-and-take in the creation of national standards, the writing of textbooks, and the implementation of reform proposals.

The authors of this part describe the political context of Japanese educational reform, pointing out that policymakers move slowly as they test public support for their proposals. As national reform initiatives filter through the educational bureaucracy and into the schools, teachers and administrators alter them in response to classroom experience, parental desire, and societal context. The U.S. tendency to view Japanese education as an "efficient" system makes it difficult to see the important give-and-take among the Japanese education and policymaking communities, and the competition between the public and private sectors that strive to make adjustments in a rapidly changing educational environment.

Despite the dynamism of Japan's educational system, it still appears far more stable than the U.S. system. The Ministry of Education's attempts at reform, as they move through the system, might best be measured in decades. In the United States, reforms vary from state to state, even district to district, and results are expected in a few years if not in months. Given that most students take a dozen or so years to pass through the educational system, the U.S. approach seems somewhat myopic. In the current environment of rapid societal and technological change, however, the desire for immediate results seems appropriate, perhaps crucial, and the public in both countries perceives the educational system as failing to keep pace with the changing times.

In Chapter 1, Hiroshi Azuma, who served as a member of Ministry of Education advisory councils during his career as a developmental psychologist at the University of Tokyo, describes the process of curriculum development. Beginning with the creation of the *Course of Study* at the Ministry of Education, he outlines the resulting development of textbooks in the private sector, the ministry approval process, and finally the use of the textbooks at the classroom level. He concludes that while the system may limit the range of teacher creativity, it ensures a focus on important content. Ironically, as the ministry attempts to loosen its control over the curriculum, parents are beginning to exert more pressure on teachers to carefully follow the *Course of Study* as represented in textbooks. In the second half of the chapter, Azuma explores the political struggles revolving around competing visions of educational reform and concludes that the current diffusion of power has created a stability that will steady the pace of the ministry's attempts toward liberalization.

Gerald LeTendre, in Chapter 2, views the reform process from the level of teachers and administrators who are adjusting to changes not limited to those emanating from ministry reforms. At the local level, top-down reform proposals meet private-sector initiatives, demographic and social changes, and the entrance examination system. Teachers, in turn, make adjustments in response to changing conditions. Although Americans might expect to learn something about efficiency from Japan's centralized approach to national standards and educational reform, LeTendre concludes, the most valuable lesson might be in Japan's collaborative approach. The elaborate networks that link teachers by subject matter, grade levels, districts, and prefectures allow innovative approaches to spread rapidly throughout classrooms.

In the United States, by contrast, state policymakers and district administrators bring many educational reforms to schools without leaving room for significant teacher involvement, creating the impression among many teachers that reforms are capricious, political, and often harmful. Teaching in the United States is largely an individual profession, and when teachers close their classroom doors, they tend to follow familiar patterns rather than the innovations of reformers. Recent research shows that while American teachers support efforts to set education standards and improve rigor in the nation's schools, and also think that these efforts have indeed raised achievement levels, they are critical of achievement tests developed by outside agencies with little teacher input. Many U.S. teachers even argue that the tests hinder rather than promote good teaching.

The following chapters point out that rather than precluding teacher involvement, the Japanese centralized system in fact may create more avenues for teacher collaboration. The mechanisms that allow for this involvement, however, seem missing in the United States, where local control and teacher involvement, especially in the area of the curriculum, has eroded due to state and national reform initiatives that focus on proficiency tests and narrowly defined standards.

CHAPTER 1

The Development of the *Course of Study* and the Structure of Educational Reform in Japan

Hiroshi Azuma

IN HER PERCEPTIVE VOLUME on Japanese education, Merry White (1987) summarized the direction of Japanese educational reform as of 1985. Her analysis identified three agents that influenced the course of educational reform. They were the Liberal Democratic Party (LDP) and the Ministry of Education (MOE), on the one hand, and the Japan Teachers' Union (JTU) and educational academics, on the other, with the majority of parents standing in the middle. The policies of the Liberal Democratic Party's Education Committee and the ministry emphasized a strained combination of training human resources for global competition and restoring prewar morality. The policy of the Japan Teachers' Union was to defend the postwar reforms—introduced under the American Occupation—that stressed democracy, human rights, and decentralization. Between them stood the practically oriented majority of parents. While they may cherish the idealism of Rousseau and Dewey that briefly flourished in Japan in the 1920s and early 1930s, most parents focus their attention on helping their children adjust to the existing system and survive competition for the entrance to prestigious schools.

The picture seems to stand more than 15 years later, but time has brought about some changes in power distribution and ideology. After the end of the Cold War, the influence of the socialist-oriented Japan Teachers' Union rapidly declined, as has its membership. The majority of teachers have left the union, although it still carries influence in a few prefectures. On the other hand, the industrial and economic decline due to chronic deflation in 1990s made industrial leaders aware of the need to foster creativity and an experimental spirit that presupposes a focus on the individual in education. Still another important pressure for educational reform is the drastic increase in educational and psychological problems among youngsters. School absenteeism, bullying, and eating disorders are now commonplace at every level of school. And rare cases of teenagers killing friends, parents, or strangers also have received wide media attention. While there is no consensus as to what should be done, there is a strong public feeling that Japan needs warm and humane schools that better attend to the psychological and interpersonal problems of individual students. On the other hand, industry worries that making the schools "tender" may compromise academic excellence.

The governance of Japanese education extends through three tiers—national, prefectural, and municipal. Although all levels of government develop educational policy, the national Ministry of Education serves as the supervising body. Among its many responsibilities is the curriculum, including the development of the *Course of Study* and the approval of privately produced textbooks. I will begin with a brief sketch of the process of curriculum policymaking at the national level, followed by a description of recent reform efforts in this area. I am basing my comments on my experiences as a member of various councils and committees, including the Central Council for Education from 1967 to 1975, the Curriculum Council from 1984 to 1987, and an editorial board for an elementary science textbook in the 1980s.

NATIONAL ADMINISTRATIVE STRUCTURE OF JAPANESE EDUCATION

The Ministry of Education relies on the advice and recommendations of 13 advisory councils, directly accountable to the Minister of Education. Two of these councils are important in making curriculum decisions—the Central Council for Education (CCE) and the Curriculum Council (CC)—and their members, appointed by the Minister of Education, include academics, writers and other opinion leaders, industry leaders, education specialists, politicians, and retired high officials of the ministry. In addition, ministry officials also attend as resource persons. These two councils, organized as needed, typically last 3 years from the appointment of members to the final submission of a formal report. (In January 2001, 7 of the 13 councils, including the former CCE and CC, were consolidated into 5 divisions under a reorganized CCE.)

The Central Council for Education generates statements of general policies. The council begins its work in response to a ministry mandate in the form of a topic or question. The Minister of Education's inquiry may be as general as "What sort of educational reform is needed to meet the needs of the 21st century?" or as specific as "What educational measures should be taken in order to cope with the increasing violence and bullying in schools?" Council members often begin their discussion of the topics by inviting experts in the field and by visiting educational sites. During their deliberations, a writing team consisting of the chairperson, department heads of the ministry, and a few of the council members work toward the creation of a consensus document summarizing the discussion. The final report evolves from the work of the writing committee and receives the approval of the council members. Since its creation in 1952, the CCE has completed 17 sessions. The 16th session, begun in 1996, produced three interim reports before concluding its work with the final report in June 1998 titled *Measures for Cultivating the Mind That Opens the New Era.* They inherited this theme from the 15th session. The 17th session, completed in 1999, however, focused on a different, rather technical theme and produced the report titled *Improving the Connection between Elementary-secondary Education and Higher Education.*

The Curriculum Council, first established in 1949, conducts its deliberations during a period of about 3 years approximately each decade. Its primary purpose is to prepare a report with recommendations about the framework of the national curriculum. The Ministry of Education in turn uses the report as a guideline for its revision of the *Course of Study.* Curriculum Council reports typically include general sections on the purposes and goals of each level of schooling. Following these are specific details on each subject area, including what should be taught at which age level to what degree; what should be compulsory and what can be elective; and how many weekly class hours should be devoted to each subject. The report also covers school structure and informal activities, that is, the maximum number of students in an elementary class and the number of class hours to be allotted to extracurricular activities.

The Curriculum Council membership is similar to that of the Central Council, but somewhat more weight is given to subject-matter specialists and school administrators. Subject-matter research officers and textbook research officers, both appointed from among academics and teachers who have become curriculum specialists, sit in the room as resource persons and observers during some of the council's meetings. The most recent CC report of 1998 became the basis of the *Course of Study* to be implemented in elementary and junior high schools in 2002 and in high schools in 2003.

The *Course of Study* and Textbooks

After the Curriculum Council submits its final report, the Ministry of Education appoints a writing committee for each subject area. These committees—consisting of university subject-matter specialists, school curriculum specialists, department heads, administrators, and former teachers employed by the ministry—draft the new *Course of Study*, detailing the goals and content for each subject area at each grade level. On release of a new *Course of Study*, the ministry provides briefing sessions for representatives of textbook publishing companies. These sessions include general discussions of the revisions in the new *Course of Study* and specific sessions held for each subject area.

Textbook publishers then start to write and edit their new textbooks following the framework of the *Course of Study*. Although there is still some ambiguity about the ministry's ability to enforce this framework, most publishers very carefully work to ensure that their textbooks include all required content and nothing more. The competition among publishers thus takes place around the distribution of emphasis on different content items. In other words, rather than focusing on which content to include, the publishers concentrate on how neatly, attractively, and age-appropriately the content is presented. Usually, the publisher's editorial committee consists of one or two academic leaders in the field, teachers, principals, and education curriculum specialists. At the elementary level, teachers probably have more influence; at the secondary level, content specialists become more important.

About 2 years before the implementation of a new *Course of Study*, the publishers submit their new textbooks to the ministry for inspection (see Figure 1.1). Ministry inspectors, usually full-time employees of the ministry who have subject-matter expertise and teaching experience, working with the Ministry-appointed Textbook Authorization and Research Council, made up of university professors and teachers, judge whether the textbook follows the framework presented in the *Course of Study*. In addition, they evaluate the empirical validity of statements made in the textbook. The lead inspectors then write requests for changes, specifying whether a requested change is mandatory or encouraged. Schools must use textbooks approved by the ministry so the publishers take these comments very seriously and make revisions accordingly (see Lewis, Tsuchida, & Coleman, Chapter 4, this volume).

In the past, differences of opinion between inspectors and textbook editors often became public. In recent years, however, the ministry has softened its approach in an attempt to encourage creativity and originality in teaching. This change, together with depoliticization of educators in general and the teachers' union in particular, has made public controversy less frequent. When the subsequent revisions are made to the inspectors' satisfaction, the textbooks are approved. Finally, a year before the new *Course of Study* becomes effective, publishers present their approved text-

Figure 1.1. The Process of Textbook Development

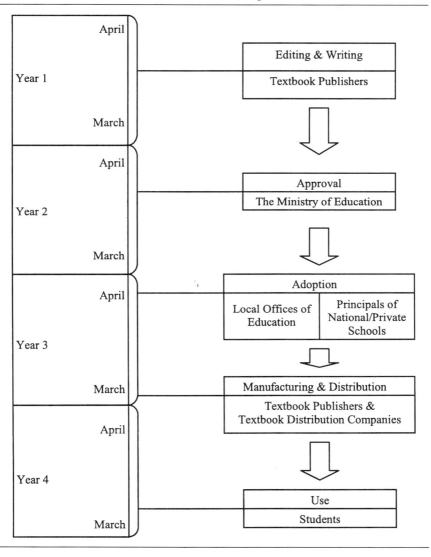

books to the schools in exhibitions held in prefectural capitals. Prefectural and municipal boards of education send teachers and education board administrators to the exhibitions to make recommendations regarding their choice of textbooks.

Based on the reports from those who attended, particularly from teachers regarded as experts in the subject matter, the local school boards choose textbooks for their schools. Although the involvement of teachers in this process differs in degree from place to place, most districts follow similar procedures. In the 1950s each school selected textbooks on its own. The selection system later changed to regionwide decision-making, however, for a number of reasons, including the convenience of students who change schools and the need to protect principals from union-organized teachers.

Since the Ministry of Education requires that all students receive a new textbook in each area of the curriculum at the beginning of the school year, publishers stand to profit considerably from the adoption of their textbooks. In an attempt to keep the selection process unbiased, sheets of white paper conceal the sample textbook covers and title pages so that the selection will not be made based on the names of publishers and editors. Thus in theory exhibition attendants do not know the identity of the publishing companies. In reality, however, the experience of these master teachers makes it impossible to completely conceal each textbook's identity. Strict regulations also prohibit companies from offering inducements in the form of supplemental teaching materials or gifts to teachers.

TEXTBOOKS AND TEACHING

The ministry's involvement in the publishing process makes the textbooks a concrete representation of the *Course of Study*. Even though many teachers have not carefully read this document, except perhaps during their university teacher education program, they study and teach with the approved textbooks. For this reason, the ministry's control of the curriculum is realized by its control of textbooks. Textbook publishers further the influence of textbooks through teachers' editions that include detailed teaching lessons based specifically on the textbook and *Course of Study* objectives. Some publishers provide even more suggestions through "red books" consisting of the student text with various statements and questions that direct almost all the teacher's utterances (Lee & Zusho, Chapter 5, this volume). As a result, most of Japan's classes revolve around the textbooks and thus are controlled by the *Course of Study*.

Educators and the public often debate the role of textbooks in teaching. In recent years, the Ministry of Education has begun to encourage teachers to exercise more latitude in their approach by recommending that they "not teach the textbook, but teach using the textbook." Ironically, after many years of complaining about ministry control, the public does not always respond favorably to this freedom. Parents, thinking ahead to their children's entrance examinations, often pressure the teachers to "teach the textbook." Recent ministry regulations requiring high schools to base their entrance examinations on the *Course of Study* increase this pressure. The ministry requirement that the National Center Test, the phase-one university entrance examination, be based on the *Course of Study* has the same effect (DeCoker, Chapter 9, this volume).

The entire process represents strong top-down control by the ministry, and, if abused, it could suffocate teachers. Nevertheless, teachers have room for creativity, especially at the elementary level where entrance examination pressure is minimal. Through workshops and seminars—organized by teacher groups, local and prefectural school districts, and universities— teachers participate in lesson study (Shimahara, Chapter 7, this volume). They may discuss approaches to each unit, develop model lessons, visit each other's classes to offer comments and advice, or invite outside speakers. A number of award programs recognize noteworthy work by teacher groups. Many of these lessons focus on textbook content and, in turn, on the *Course of Study*.

Whether ministry control promotes or thwarts teacher creativity is a difficult question to answer. The recent focus on deregulation among Japan's politicians and government bureaucrats has led the ministry to loosen its control. Nevertheless, teachers still are constrained by the intertwined network of the *Course of Study*, textbooks, and entrance examinations. In the end, the system seems to encourage teacher creativity that results in deeper exploration of the content, but it also limits the range of creativity. A good balance is hard to attain. How well it works depends on the policy of local boards, the pressure of parents, and the morale of the teachers.

MINISTRY INFLUENCE AND THE SPEED OF REFORM

When the U.S. Occupation developed the Council System, it sought to create a forum for public involvement and civil control. But in reality ministry bureaucrats guide the process. To begin with, council members are appointed by the Minister of Education based on the recommendation of high officials in the ministry. These officials also introduce and explain the inquiry items to the council. Although the outside members appoint the chairperson, the ministry bureaucrats have already written the script. Because many council members are not informed about current school problems, they depend on the briefings by bureaucrats. In addition, the meetings usually take place during weekday working hours, thereby limiting the participation of council members, many of whom work full-time elsewhere. As a result the ministry bureaucrats, as information sources and regular attendees, may easily take control.

Given that bureaucrats are supposed to follow the direction of the current government, intervention of the party line is sometimes inevitable. Nevertheless, national elections alter only the top levels of the Japanese government bureaucracy. Beneath the Minister of Education and a few of his appointees, the bulk of the ministry workforce continues its work without the direct influence of the newly formed government. This stable organizational makeup helps give the bureaucracy in general, and the Ministry of Education in particular, a reputation for slowness and resistance to change. In 1984, Prime Minister Nakasone attempted to circumvent the bureaucracy by appointing the Ad Hoc Council on Education (also called the National Council on Educational Reform or NCER), a supracabinet advisory council under the prime minister's office. NCER, in existence from 1984 to 1987, released four reports outlining its proposals for reforming the Japanese educational system.

Leonard Schoppa's *Education Reform in Japan* (1991) describes in detail the way the initial hope of significant reform gradually succumbed to the divisions in the governing political party and the weight of ministry control. Shoppa's book, published only a few years after the final NCER report, concludes that the Ad Hoc Council failed to reform Japanese education. One might similarly conclude that the councils of the Ministry of Education fail to make a significant impact on the current state of the educational system. Indeed, many proposals in earlier council statements and the four NCER reports seem to recycle through the decades. Some gradually work their way toward implementation; others fade away; still others linger in a perpetual state of anticipation. To conclude that such a slow pace indicates the Council System's failure, however, is to misunderstand the role of the councils in Japan's educational system.

In many ways, the statements on education made by the councils provide a format for discussion of important issues facing Japanese society and its educational system and serve to ready the public for future reforms. When a proposal finds a receptive public, the ministry moves to implement the reform. In contrast, when the public seems resistant to a proposal, the ministry moves more slowly, and the proposal might find its way into future council documents or be dropped altogether. In a rapidly changing social environment, the slow pace of change often is seen as a detriment. Yet in education, where the results of reform are embedded in the development of young minds and may not be revealed for a decade or more, caution can have its advantages.

EXAMINING RECENT REFORM EFFORTS

The end of the 20th century was not the first time that Central Council for Education and Ministry of Education documents had explicitly pointed out the need for large-scale reform. In 1971 the CCE also compiled significant recommendations concerning the need for educational reform. It called for reform in all phases of education in order to respond to the globalization of various aspects of life.

Origins in the 1971 Reforms

The recommendations by the CCE (1971) suggested a variety of coping measures, including flexible curricula, teacher exchange, and emphasis on international understanding. Additional recommendations focused on the ministry's policies, for example, limiting the size of the elementary school class to 40 students and experimenting with individualized instruction. In addition, world history became a compulsory subject in high school, and high schools received permission to increase the number of English classes. International efforts included teachers' receiving leaves to participate in overseas tour groups, national and local budget increases for the hiring of assistant English teachers from abroad, and special classes and college entrance examinations for Japanese students returning from overseas.

These early attempts, though meaningful, did not succeed in significantly addressing the problem of how Japanese education should cope with the challenge of globalization. Because of political pressure against quick liberalization within the ministry, the reforms did not go far beyond the technical periphery. However, the young bureaucrats who worked for the CCE in early 1970s are now leading the current reform plans. In April 1998, the CCE issued the final revision of a document titled *The Program for Educational Reform*, the guideline for educational reform in the coming years. In June of the same year, the CCE elaborated similar points under the title *Measures for Cultivating the Mind that Opens the New Era* (CCE, 1998a). Although I see little novelty over the 1971 recommendations, as a government policy statement rather than a mere recommendation, these documents will have more impact on government decision-making and school practice.

The 1998 Reforms

The ministry program includes a response to bullying, absenteeism, violence, and the overheated competition for college entrance, and it attributes these problems to the dysfunction of education, stating:

> So far, Japanese education inclined to be one-way teaching of knowledge and tended to downplay the ability for independent learning and thinking. Also, having been preoccupied with equality in education, sufficient attention has not been given to the variety of student personalities and abilities. The educational potential of families and local communities declined. Problems like school bullying, school absenteeism, and misconduct and violence of youngsters are related to this basic problem. (CCE, 1998b)

Following this analysis, the ministry identifies four major directions of the reform:

Priority I. "Education of mind" implies fostering respect for such things as social rules, a sense of justice, ethics, and empathy. On the other hand, in order to help Japan survive in an era of global competition, the ministry adds the need for respect of Japanese history and traditions, creativity, and "international sensitivity."

Priority II. "Individualization of education" aims at creating a school system in which individuality is valued and various alternatives are available. This proposal is based on the criticism that Japanese schools are too centrally controlled and excessively egalitarian.

Priority III. "School and local government initiatives in educational reform" are proposed to correct top-down, overly uniform education for which the Ministry of Education is responsible.

Priority IV. "University reform and promotion of research" suggests reinforcing graduate education and research, encouraging university-industry cooperation in research and development, and accelerating the dissemination and transfer of research results to the general public.

Within this context, specific recommendations include better socialization at home, utilization of the educational potential of local communities, less examination-oriented schools where students can take time for self-initiated activities, and teacher training to promote better communication with children, counseling, and internationalization.

Those points repeatedly have been raised since the Central Council for Education recommendations of 1971. In response, the government took a number of actual steps (e.g., sending teachers on tours abroad), but the reforms were piecemeal and lacked a coherent structure. This time, some 30 years later, the ministry seems more intent on beginning a viable, widespread reform.

Although the new *Course of Study* will officially go into effect in 2002–2003, the reforms have already started at various school levels. For example, schools already have begun implementing the 5-day-week system, which prohibits formal classes on Saturdays and Sundays, and the period of integrated study that provides teachers and schools the freedom to determine content. The goal of the 5-day-week system was to give students the opportunity to pursue their own interests and to draw on the educative potential of local communities. Unfortunately, it required a substantial cut in the hours used for subject-matter instruction. To compensate for that loss, integrated study was included in the *Course of Study* as the period to encourage students to learn about current topics that would cut across various subject areas (LeTendre, Chapter 2, this volume).

The Ministry of Education encouraged schools to begin integrated study prior to 2002, and also nominated 500 schools to develop experimental programs. Although many teachers are eager to develop these programs, some of them are afraid that the basic subjects will be compromised. One teacher told me that she will use the period for arithmetic drills. Her approach is possible because the Ministry of Education does not prescribe activities for integrated study. The majority of teachers, however, seem to look forward to the possibility of creative, child-centered teaching and are taking it as a challenge. Some are producing reports of their pilot studies. In summary, the short-term effect of these reforms is positive. The 5-day-week system, for instance, gave rise to community programs for students to do volunteer work and other forms of self-improvement. However, many students have chosen to defy the ministry's intentions and attend *juku* on the weekends.

The most obvious merit of the introduction of the period of integrated study is that it encourages teachers to think creatively about teaching. In the past, teachers in the upper-grade levels have tended to focus on the prescribed content of the *Course of Study*. Now teachers must think about and discuss teaching that is not subordinate to academic disciplines. This reform, however, requires good and continually encouraging leadership. In addition, if recent history is a guide, the ministry may not be consistent in following through with the reform. In 1971 the Central Council for Education made a similar recommendation for educational reform. The ministry, in turn, recruited pilot experimental schools, allowing them to go beyond the *Course of Study*, and many schools focused on integrated curricula and integrated classes. Within a few years, however, the ministry, taking a conservative turn, closed the ministry office that offered support for experimental schools and decided that only those schools working within a narrow ministry framework would receive support. Soon the more ambitious pilot studies disappeared. The present reform could easily suffer the same fate.

There is not much new in the 1998 CCE report compared with the 1971 version. The stress, however, is more on academic excellence, individuation, tracking, and moral education than on the humanization of education. This gives the impression of a move away from the progressivism of postwar education.

Reforms for the New Century

In March 2000, Prime Minister Obuchi announced the formation of a new National Council for Educational Reform, similar in structure to the NCER under Premier Nakasone. Leona Esaki, a Nobel Laureate physicist, was named chairperson. Although Obuchi suddenly passed away soon after the start of this NCER, his successor, Prime Minister Mori, decided to keep it as his private advisory committee. Coincidentally, there is a good deal of overlap in membership of the NCER and the CCE. The NCER's final report, issued December 22, 2000, included 17 recommendations under four major goals:

1. Foster within the Japanese people a rich sense of humanity: the family as the basis of a child's education and well-being; the need for moral education, student participation in community service activities, clear responses to troublesome schoolchildren, and protection of children from information pollution.
2. Develop the talent of individuals and foster individuals who are rich in creativity: an educational system that focuses on individuality instead of uniform progress through a standard curriculum; a shift in college entrance examinations from memory-centered tests to multiple routes with various screening methods; and promoting the connection between education and career.
3. Create new schools for the new age: the improvement of evaluation systems for teachers accompanied by an incentive system; construction of closer ties with the community; improved management of schools and boards of education; improvement of instructional techniques that guarantee better understanding from the child's perspective; and exploration of new types of schools.
4. Revise the Fundamental Law of Education (1947) to meet the needs of a new era and promote educational policies.

The NCER report was transferred to the 18th CCE in the spring of 2001. Although both the NCER and the Ministry of Education list similar priorities, the prime minister's council seems more concerned with the academic standards and traditional morality reflecting the attitude of industry and academia, while the ministry seems more concerned with well-being and psychological health in line with recent CCE reports. At this time, the ministry does not seem very enthusiastic about the nostalgic tendency of the NCER report, especially the tendency to frame issues in terms of prewar ideology, and is making efforts to consolidate the ministry reforms of 1998.

In April 2000, the ministry published a booklet for elementary and junior high school teachers as a preview of the changes that might occur in response to the new *Course of Study* that will become effective in 2002. Through various graphs, the ministry presented survey results showing that only 19.9% of elementary school students and fewer secondary school students say that they understand the instruction well, and that only about 50% of elementary, 15% of junior high, and 7.7% of senior high school students answer that school life is enjoyable. Through these data, the ministry hopes to keep the focus on the need to make schools more pleasant and instruction more understandable. In order for teachers to accomplish this goal, they argue, the new *Course of Study* reduces the number of weekly class hours by 2 (from 29 to 27 in elementary and 30 to 28 in junior high school), thereby allowing students more free activities. In addition, the content of the curriculum will be reduced on average by 30%. This reduction will make it possible to master the basics through individualized instruction, small-group learning, and team teaching. A wider range of elective subjects will allow for a multiplicity of aptitudes and interests. The ministry also emphasizes a shift from knowledge-centered teaching to the development of independent thinking and effective expression; moral education, including basic habits, a sense of justice, and social rules; volunteer social services; and health education. These initiatives complement the introduction of the integrated studies period, about 3 hours a week at elementary and junior high schools.

Reflecting on Merry White's (1987) analysis that began this chapter, Japanese educational reform in the early 1980s was a tug-of-war between the Liberal Democratic Party and the Japan Teachers' Union. The former was trying to push education back to prewar traditions, and the latter was trying to keep postwar reforms intact. Most of the public fell in between, wishing for improvement in education without drastic change. Because the majority of teachers became less political after the fall of the Russian communist regime, White's bipolar model seems less applicable. Instead, there are a number of agents for reform such as the prime minister and the

NCER, the Ministry of Education and the Central Council for Education, industry, and academia. These separate spheres of influence agree in the major objectives of reform, but differ in their priorities, as the comparison of the NCER report and the ministry's recent publication suggests. The tide seems to be moving very slowly toward multitracked schools, school-based and individualized curricula, and a less demanding course of study (Tsuneyoshi, 2001). The current reforms, however, should not be viewed as another bipolar confrontation or tug-of-war. The present tension is multipolar, making unlikely a dramatic move in any direction.

The nostalgia of senior politicians for the prewar state seems highly influential at present, but control is shifting to a new generation. Whether there will be a further return to prewar educational ideals, as reflected in the recently instated mandatory singing of the national anthem, is difficult to predict. But I believe that, given the balanced sense of the Japanese public and the diffusion of power in a multipolar system, Japanese education will avoid the extremes.

REFERENCES

Central Council for Education. (1971). *Basic policy for the overall expansion and improvement of education in the future.* Tokyo: Ministry of Education.

Central Council for Education. (1998a). *Measures for cultivating the mind that opens the new era.* Tokyo: Ministry of Education.

Central Council for Education. (1998b). *The program for educational reform.* Tokyo: Ministry of Education.

Central Council for Education. (1999). *Improving the connection between elementary-secondary education and higher education.* Tokyo: Ministry of Education.

Central Council for Education. (2000). *The school changes under the new "Course of Study."* Tokyo: Ministry of Education.

National Commission on Educational Reform. (2000). *Report by the National Commission on Educational Reform: 17 proposals for changing education.* Tokyo: Author.

Schoppa, L. (1991). *Education reform in Japan: A case of immobilist policies.* New York: Routledge.

Tsuneyoshi, R. (2001). *The Japanese model of schooling: Comparisons with the United States.* New York: Routledge/Falmer.

White, M. (1987). *The Japanese educational challenge: A commitment to children.* New York: Free Press.

CHAPTER 2

Setting National Standards: Educational Reform, Social Change, and Political Conflict

Gerald K. LeTendre

IN 1994–1995 THE MINISTRY OF EDUCATION (MOE) implemented the first step in reducing the overall school year by beginning the gradual transition to a 5-day school week. Until this time, all Japanese elementary and secondary students attended school for a "half day" on Saturday, with classes in the morning and club activities most of the afternoon. The MOE, ostensibly responding to widespread social concern that Japanese citizens lacked free time, implemented this reduction in phases. In the first phase, schools closed on the second Saturday of each month. The next school year included two Saturdays off a month. As in previous attempts to reform the basic educational process, however, the MOE had not accurately foreseen the opposition that would arise to such a seemingly simple reform (LeTendre, 1994).

In 1995, while working on the Third International Mathematics and Science Study (TIMSS), I recorded the following debate by teachers at a public middle school in a major Japanese city. The topic of the meeting was how to adjust the curriculum in the face of the MOE reform of the school week. The discussion focused on where during the week to add the class time lost on Saturday.

Head of Curriculum: The biggest problem [for next year] is what to do about Saturday. At least we will have [academic] classes. I don't know about *seikatsu* (life-style guidance) time, but we'll have classes. The parents are concerned about academics, so we'll teach.
Teacher 1: Maybe we'll have to cut back on clubs or activities.

Teacher 2: Make sure to get the opinions of the women teachers.
Teacher 3: I guess we'll have little free time (*yutori no jikan*).

My field notes provide further details about their discussion.

> They discuss how to fit the hours in. Making extra hours into the
> open spots on Mon. and Wed. . . . . They are discussing extending
> school on Wed. maybe pushing out the club time. The head of stu-
> dent guidance suggests putting one extra hour on Monday to make
> up for missing time. . . . Heated discussion of where to put the extra
> hours lost by the upcoming reduction of Saturday.

Years before, the MOE had attempted to reduce academic pressure in
the middle schools by introducing *yutori jikan*—free periods that teachers
could use to facilitate more creative classroom environments for students.
Japanese educators have long recognized clubs and other extracurricular
activities as a vital part of the educational curriculum. The vast majority
of Japanese teachers view the activities as a counterbalance to the academic
demands of middle school (LeTendre, 1994). But the concerns voiced by
these teachers seemed to compromise their beliefs and MOE intentions.
Teachers noted, several times, that parents would still hold them responsible for student performance on the entrance exam, and they wondered how
to cover enough academic content to ensure student success on the entrance
exams.
    In the end, they decided to continue the same coverage of core aca-
demic areas represented on the entrance test by using the *yutori jikan* and
club periods and by reducing class hours in art and music. Despite the
MOE's stated goal of reducing time in school and promoting more leisure
and freedom of choice, the 5-day-week reform had the opposite effect in
this school. Why then did the MOE institute a reform that appears to make
the school week even more constricted and academically oriented? Did
MOE officials foresee the possible reactions that this reform would entail
as they implemented a new national standard for Japan's public schools?
These questions raise the broader question that guides this chapter: How
much control does Japan's centralized Ministry of Education actually have
over the educational system?

EDUCATIONAL REFORM IN A "CENTRALIZED SYSTEM"

Since the release of *A Nation at Risk* in 1983, American educators and
policymakers have been discussing national education standards. Com-

pared with nations that have a highly centralized educational bureaucracy and a national curriculum, the U.S. system seems like a picture from feudal Europe. Over 15,000 school districts make curricular decisions following the guidelines of their respective states. Impressed by Japan's performance in math and science, many Americans have begun to question the curricular diversity of their own system and to consider national standards as a means of improving U.S. education. Many U.S. education reformers, however, tend to misrepresent the Japanese system by overemphasizing its homogeneity and equating national curriculum guidelines with national standards (LeTendre, 1999). The vignette above illustrates the fallacy of assuming that a centralized system is easily guided and reformed.

The issue of national standards is intensely political in both the United States and Japan. In Japan, however, the highly centralized system creates conditions whereby issues such as curriculum, standards, and even day-to-day school policies are contested in ways that prevent a straightforward implementation. Rather than viewing Japanese education as a highly "rational" system, Americans could gain a better grasp of educational reform by studying Japan's system as a way to understand the dynamics of a centralized system. In this way, analysis of the Japanese system could help guide U.S. thinking about the ramifications of centralized educational policymaking.

Japanese society and the Japanese educational system have undergone remarkable transformations, and many of these changes have outpaced the ability of the central government to respond through policy initiatives. The question of national standards, therefore, cannot be considered merely a matter of politics or policy debates. Societal change in Japan has created conditions that often drive the policy debates and directly affect national standards.

An understanding of how educational reforms dealing with national standards occur in Japan requires an analysis of the way forces outside the MOE impact reform initiatives. Research on the MOE has already provided a high level of detail on the internal political structure affecting educational reform (Schoppa, 1991). This chapter will focus on three factors that affect policy and reform initiatives: the institutional structure of the educational system; the effect of political conflict on educational reform initiatives; and growth and changing demands of the school population.

INSTITUTIONAL STRUCTURE

The first feature that has affected the government's ability to implement national standards is the relative stability and strength of the federal bureaucracies. The MOE, like other Japanese ministries, has far more auton-omy and cohesiveness than similar institutions in other countries. Bradley Richardson (1997) has noted:

> The dependence of the government on the bureaucracy is induced in part by the limitations on the scope of party control over ministerial appointments. In each ministry only the positions of minister and parliamentary vice-minister are held by political appointees. In the United States, Britain, and France there is direct party control over a much greater range of bureaucratic appointments than in Japan. (p. 102)

As a result, contrary to the image of a "centralized" system, new prime ministers are not able to effect policy change through a "top-down" ap-proach. Indeed, if they are to effect any change, the prime minister and cabinet ministers in new governments are significantly dependent on the support and cooperation of mid-level bureaucrats whose tenure extends far longer than that of the elected officials and their appointees. Dramatic re-form efforts, such as major changes in national standards, are unlikely to occur in a top-down manner unless the ministers carefully recruit the sup-port of MOE officials.

This structure, however, does not make educational reform sluggish in all cases. Rather, it requires ministers to gain the support of rank-and-file bureaucrats when they make dramatic calls for reforms (LeTendre, 1994). This pattern has typified the postwar period and explains why many of the top-down reforms urged by the postwar U.S. educational mission failed to take effect (Miyagi, 1998; Wray, 1991). On the other hand, reforms sup-ported by rank-and-file ministry officials have been implemented with rela-tive speed. The re-institution of a moral/ethics curriculum in the years after the Occupation provides a good example.

The passage of reforms, from the initiation of a policy directive to a for-mal MOE proclamation or curriculum revision, is affected by political con-flict within and between ministries. Schoppa's (1991) well-known "immobi-list" formulation is the most detailed description of the reform process at this level, although more recent work suggests that immobilism is a more com-plex phenomenon than he depicted (Roesgaard, 1998). The passage of for-mal proclamations or curriculum revisions, however, represents only part of the process of educational change in Japan. The implementation of curricu-lum revisions occurs at the local and regional levels through institutionalized teacher research programs and groups. And this change is often formulated quite independently from politicking and MOE internal debates.

As Shimahara details in Chapter 7, all Japanese teachers are involved in instructional research at some point in their careers, and most teachers participate throughout their careers in various research meetings or demon-stration classes. Research organizations, such as teacher research teams or larger research groups sponsored by local or prefectural boards of educa-tion, create tremendous amounts of information each school year. Because professional development and the culture of teaching in Japan support par-ticipation in research groups, teaching innovations can spread quite rap-idly.

In a district that I observed in central Japan, for example, every year one school held a series of demonstration classes, attended by curriculum specialists from the local board of education and teachers from surround-ing schools (LeTendre, 1996). New and mid-career teachers from every grade and several subject areas created model lessons. Senior teachers, prin-cipals, vice-principals, curriculum specialists, and visitors observed selected teachers conducting demonstration classes based on their lesson plans. At the end of the day, these observers gave a summary of their impressions at a meeting of all teachers. Subsequently, at summer workshops sponsored by the local board of education and subject research groups organized by the local Japan Teachers' Union (JTU), teachers throughout the prefecture received booklets of lesson plans covering the exact material they taught.

The demonstration classes and teacher research groups result in a pool of high-quality, up-to-date lessons that are rapidly disseminated. Although there is some variation in the process, most local and prefectural school boards support research meetings, demonstration classes, and the dissemi-nation of model lesson plans. As a result, every year teachers across Japan have the opportunity to visit at least one class and gain access to the printed summaries of several meetings. Admittedly, the content of these classes is often formulaic. Still, the classes and meetings serve to give teachers clear examples of the basic standards of the subject at their grade level.

The organization of these meetings and classes has the effect of stan-dardizing instructional practice at the local *and* regional levels. Where varia-tion in standards exists, therefore, it is largely between regions. For instance, the quality of research and lessons plans might decline as you move from ur-ban areas to rural prefectures. The local/regional uniformity contrasts with the situation in the United States, where contiguous school districts may have radically different curricula, standards, and quality of instruction. Because in Japan most local and prefectural boards of education send selected teachers to demonstration classes or research meetings in other prefectures, there is less regional variation in Japan than in the United States.

The overall educational system, then, can be characterized as one of loose vertical linkages with strong lateral connections. Teachers in local districts know each other well through the district's meetings and demon-stration classes. Furthermore, most Japanese districts practice a system of teacher rotation whereby teachers change schools every few years. This means that teachers work with a number of other teachers in the area, watch many colleagues present demonstration classes, and accumulate a variety of model lesson plans.

School districts are reasonably integrated into local/regional networks of research and dissemination throughout the three levels of schooling. At the prefectural level, however, curriculum specialists focus on high schools. Thus, because elementary and middle schools are supervised by municipal or smaller districts and high schools by prefectural districts, there is some de-coupling between local and regional curriculum research. High school teachers are more likely to be supervised by and have contact with colleagues who have a strong sense of regional standards. National contact with regional boards of education exists but is highly formalized. For instance, prefectural representatives routinely report to, and occasionally travel to, the MOE in Tokyo, but this contact does not result in a great deal of lesson-plan dissemination at the local/regional level. Furthermore, the MOE is not strongly connected to these teacher research networks. Even though the MOE recruits local teachers to work on advisory boards, this participation is not extensive enough to capture the vast amounts of information generated on local levels. Textbook companies, anticipating curricular change and teacher needs, appear to do a far better job of accessing this information by paying teachers to act as advisors and work on revisions of textbooks, thereby offering an alternative route by which teacher-led curricular innovation flows "upward."

When a top-down reform occurs in Japan, implementation on the regional and local levels varies immensely. Popular curricular innovations developed at the local level spread rapidly to the regional level, but may not flow quickly to the national level. The institutional structure of curriculum research and teaching practice in Japan limits the ability of the MOE to assimilate ideas and to rapidly respond to change while it increases the ability of teachers to modify, reinterpret, and sometimes circumvent top-down curriculum. This institutional structure would appear to exacerbate historic tensions between the MOE and teachers, further inhibiting the possibility of effective national educational reform initiatives, and suggests that standards in Japan may be best implemented by interaction on local and regional levels rather than from the top down.

POLICY GENERATION AND POLITICAL CONFLICT

The intense political conflict between the MOE and the Japan Teachers' Union has created a policy myopia that has afflicted educational reform and the production of national standards in Japan for decades. For example, Thurston (1973) provides case studies of conflicts in which JTU opposition effectively thwarted MOE attempts to implement reforms that would have led to increased national standardization through teacher efficiency ratings and nationwide achievement tests. Although the JTU has been very ineffective in lobbying for change within the MOE, it has been very effective in blocking or significantly diminishing the effect of MOE policies "on the ground." Thurston argues that the JTU, utilizing the strong lateral connections of the Japanese system, moved from a strategy of "absolute opposition by force," characterized by nationwide strikes and massive demonstrations, to one of "noncooperation" (pp. 263–264).

The structure of policy generation in Japan has developed in this adversarial environment. With most of the policy-generation responsibility coming from the long-term ministry officials wary of teacher noncooperation, a "slow" style of policy has evolved. In the previous example, while the MOE was able to implement a system of nationwide teacher standards, systematic JTU efforts to alter and defuse the ratings made them meaningless. Similar noncooperation tactics are used by JTU and nonunion teachers when faced with MOE policy changes they find untenable (McConnell, Chapter 8, this volume).

As in the United States and other countries, sweeping policy changes can occur in Japan when the Diet passes basic laws regarding education. Unlike in the United States, however, new national government administrations have little ability to institute sweeping educational reforms. The kind of dramatic revision of the goals and even basic functioning of the U.S. Department of Education under the Reagan administration is simply not possible in Japan. But it is not accurate to simply label the MOE "reactive." Rather, as Schoppa (1991) has shown, the members of the MOE see themselves as the developers of long-term policies and plans that they actively pursue (Azuma, Chapter 1, this volume). Because of the time needed to attain consensus and carefully review these plans, however, the implementation phase often significantly lags behind social need, thus reducing the effectiveness of the MOE.

Roesgaard's (1998) discussion of the Women's Democratic Council on Educational Reform (WDCER) is a good example of the limits of the MOE's tradition of "slow policy" in the modern political context. Established in 1985, the WDCER was organized to better represent the views of Japanese women on education. The group was remarkably heterogeneous in composition and took a socially admirable, but politically weak, stand that alienated it from socialist groups, mainstream bureaucrats in the MOE, and party affiliates from the dominant Liberal Democratic Party (LDP). But the blame cannot be laid entirely on the WDCER. As Roesgaard notes, "there was no tradition for taking much heed of opposition interest groups" among reformers tied to the ruling party (p. 130).

The content of the WDCER proposals, and the fact that they managed to get some attention in the press, demonstrates the rapid change in the views and expectations of ordinary Japanese citizens regarding such key issues as individual rights and social injustice (Women's Democratic Council on Educational Reform [WDCER], 1987). The areas of reform identified by the WDCER include calls for reforms that date back to the Occupation—for example, local bodies to settle conflicts and more mobility between high schools. They also include statements that sound like the report of the California Commission on Self-Esteem, such as to "increase the confidence and joy of learning" of children (Roesgaard, 1998, pp. 121–131). This apparent mixture of recurrent issues of contention along with apparently new conceptions of the basic role of learning pose considerable challenges for the MOE. Not only has the MOE been unable to meet long-term demands for educational reform, but it also appears to have little sense of current changes in the way the general populace views the educational system.

Because of the policy myopia, the MOE has often had difficulty creating policy that is informed by broader national and international concerns. The involvement of several ministries in one of Japan's most innovative educational reforms, the foreign English teachers program, suggests that the historical MOE/JTU conflict continues to have an effect on MOE policy generation. As McConnell (Chapter 8, this volume) notes, one of the most wide-ranging and effective educational reforms in the postwar era was largely organized with the MOE as a reluctant participant. Here again the MOE seemed unable to see policy around national standards in a broad perspective.

The historical conflicts around education have created a climate of mistrust and caution in MOE policy generation similar to the "immobilist" politics described by Schoppa (1991). The continued resentment toward the MOE with regard to control of curricular content on the part of many teachers predisposes them to "second guess" new MOE curriculum guidelines or any policy reform. Thus, the MOE, the JTU, and local nonunion teachers have become highly involved in conflict over policy implementation. The MOE has systematically pursued, usually successfully, long-term policy changes with regard to national standards only to find these policies made ineffective "on the ground" (e.g., the teacher rating system, nationwide achievement tests, the elimination of practice entrance examinations during school hours).

Even with the dramatic decline in JTU strength in the last 15 years, the specter of conflict has undermined the ability of the MOE to implement effective educational reform. The "slow" style of policy generation has been particularly limiting given the recent rapid changes in Japan's educational system, causing both the government and other groups interested in educational reform to misinterpret how parents view the educational system and how they exert direct pressure on teachers. Their influence in turn affects how teachers implement educational reform.

Powerful institutions like the top-ranking universities, private high schools, and cram schools have thus been able to pursue agendas with far more success than would be expected in a centralized system. These groups have been highly effective in organizing opposition to changes in the entrance exams, one of the major routes to a revision of standards in Japan. The growth and expansion of the overall private educational sector has proceeded with little or no guiding direction from the MOE.

GROWTH AND CHANGE

Over the last 40 years, the growth of secondary and postsecondary education has significantly reordered the configuration of Japanese education. Between 1955 and 1995 whole categories of educational institutions changed: Elite Tokyo public high schools dropped dramatically in status; a number of new colleges and universities appeared; national cram school chains grew with stunning speed. Overall, the expansion of the educational system appears to have promoted broad upward social mobility as the overall level of education of the population rose. A by-product of this expansion, however, is the extensive elaboration of status hierarchies within the various levels of the system, and an increasing segmentation of the educational system into specific "tracks." In other words, as the system has grown larger in terms of numbers of entrants, it has also become more differentiated, with certain institutions catering to relatively specific groups of students.

Viewed overall, the Japanese system is organized into patterns by grade level, source of control (local, prefectural, national), and curriculum. The elementary and junior high schools are largely unified under the rubric of compulsory public education (which ends with the equivalent of the U.S. ninth grade). They are characterized by a common instructional orientation that appears highly egalitarian. Penetration of private schooling at this level has been small, although participation in *juku* and private lessons has increased to nearly two-thirds for ninth-grade students. At the junior high school level high-status private schools have begun to appear in many urban areas and are attracting students who wish to prepare for prestigious high schools. At the postcompulsory high school level, private schools enroll about 24% of the students, and participation in *juku* remains high. Differences in social status among high schools reflect the ability of these schools to send students to specific universities. These status differences are so refined that high school teachers interviewed in the TIMSS study spoke of "slices" of homogenous-ability students that each school admits.

The expansion of educational enrollment in the postwar period amplified the elaboration of school hierarchies. Enrollments in high school rose so dramatically (from 2.5 million in 1955 to over 5 million in 1980) that prefectural governments throughout the country found it impossible to meet the rising demand for secondary education. As a result, enrollment in private high schools climbed, comprised mostly of those students who were turned away from public high schools. High school enrollment increased from 55% of males and 47% of females in 1955 to the 1980 rate of 93.1% for men and 95.4% for women. From 1980 to the present, the rates of attendance and graduation have remained at the level of nearly universal attendance through Grade 12. Attendance at the postsecondary level also has shown dramatic increases to nearly 50%.

Setting national standards for high school education in Japan in this period was thus "locked" into the parameters of increased growth in enrollment. The expansion of educational opportunity, in the form of movement to universal participation in high school, was a politically popular event. And the government was effectively prevented from creating national standards that would have limited or blocked this enrollment growth. As a result, the MOE pursued a policy of bi-level tracks within secondary education: academic and specialty schools. Nonetheless, within both tracks, the secondary system continued to evolve into a more hierarchical pattern.

A high school degree, once the mark of educated status, has become nearly universal among young Japanese regardless of gender or family background. As a status marker, therefore, a high school diploma per se is of diminished importance. On the other hand, other, more nuanced distinctions exist. Most notable among these are (1) the relative status of the high school, (2) advancement to higher education, and (3) the status of the college or university.

The status of national universities in Japan provides an example of the two processes of expansion and diversification. Within the national university category, for example, exist both the oldest, elite universities and also some of the newest, geographically peripheral universities. The latter are of relatively low status when ranked according to measures of difficulty of access, especially in comparison with the highest-ranked elite institutions like the University of Tokyo and Kyoto University. In order to better understand the workings of the educational status system and its role in allocating social status, the category "national university" must be broken down into its separate constituencies. Because national universities charge relatively low tuition compared with private university rates, the recent creation of new national universities represents a notable extension of low-cost higher education to a segment of the population that might otherwise be economically and geographically marginalized. These universities enroll primarily students from adjacent rural areas, many of whom are from families of below-average incomes. In Japan income correlates very strongly with urban-rural differences although the cost of living is significantly lower in rural areas.

The sudden tracking or streaming of virtually the entire school population at the end of 9 years of compulsory schooling raises significant questions about the ability of the national government to control education. From a comparative perspective, U.S. perceptions of Japanese education come largely from media reports of either primary or secondary systems. As a result, the general understanding of the overall school system has tended to be bipolar: benign, child-centered classrooms contrasted with exam pressures, cramming, and bullying (Cummings, 1989). Each level of schooling (primary, secondary, and tertiary), however, is characterized by distinct patterns of instruction, allocation of students into classes, and institutional connections with subsequent levels of education and employment.

The hierarchical structure of Japanese education constrains national standards in significant ways. Because of the entrance examination system, curricular decisions proceed essentially from the top down. But rather than following the direction of the MOE, each level of schooling looks to the next: high schools to colleges, middle schools to high schools, and to a lesser extent elementary schools to middle schools. The MOE, therefore, remains constrained in its ability to significantly alter national standards. Of course, the MOE has a great deal of control over the pre-university curriculum. For instance, it can add or delete courses from the required curriculum and drastically change the curricular emphasis in a given subject area. The effect of these changes on classroom practice, however, is determined by the way they affect student success on the entrance examinations.

Attempts to influence the high school curriculum by reforming college entrance examinations provide another example of the political constraints faced by the government in attempting to alter national standards (De-Coker, Chapter 9, this volume). Because of their central role in educational selection, the entrance exams significantly warp any reforms that would alter the basic core curriculum at the junior and senior high school level. The large, dynamic, and highly mercantile system of shadow education in combination with a powerful set of universities linked to Japan's status elite has left the MOE with little room to implement effective reform (see

Stevenson & Baker, 1992). Without significant reform of the entrance exam, most educators agree that substantial reform of national standards is a moot point.

CONCLUSIONS

The creation of national standards, over time, reflects an often highly contested political process. We cannot conclude that because of Japan's "cultural homogeneity" or its "centralized school system" the implementation of national standards is any less fractious and subject to the vagaries of the political process than in any other nation. The "Japan, Inc." view—a popular U.S. depiction of Japanese government ministries ordering companies to do their bidding in a scheme for world economic domination—is simply wrong. At best, the MOE has enacted substantial reform only after long years of planning and in the face of political controversy. And, in some cases, these hard-won reforms have been effectively nullified at the local level by teacher and administrator efforts.

The structure of Japanese bureaucracy creates the conditions for these stalemates, but the MOE as an individual ministry has exacerbated them. Attempts by MOE to exert control over the educational system have resulted in resistance by the Japan Teachers' Union, other groups, and individuals who object to centralized control over educational content. This opposition often results in noncompliance with MOE directives, thereby strengthening the lateral linkages among school districts even as the national teachers' organization weakens. But most significantly, it has diverted MOE attention and given the MOE a rather myopic policy focus in terms of setting national standards.

This myopic focus has meant that institutions, particularly elite institutions like the highest-ranking national universities and private high schools, have been able to protect the basic educational structures that insulate national standards from reform efforts. The imperviousness of the exam system to reform in Japan continues to influence any attempts to impose new national standards. Moreover, the continuing reorganization of secondary and tertiary education into a more hierarchically differentiated system—a process not controlled, and perhaps not well understood, by MOE bureaucrats—is likely to have a more significant effect on national standards than do MOE policy initiatives. Furthermore, given that the MOE has no power to regulate the cram school industry, national standards (in the core subjects) are more likely to be determined by competition on entrance exams than by government policy.

The increasing stratification of the educational system and the increasing influence of cram schools on the process of preparing students for exams and forecasting placement possibilities have also eroded local control of placement and, in turn, over the curriculum, particularly in the middle grades. In areas where middle-school teachers can regulate access to high school through recommendations, teachers retain greater control over interpreting and implementing MOE curricular guidelines (LeTendre, 1996). At present these teachers essentially face a situation where the MOE determines the curriculum guidelines, and the entrance exams drive how they implement these guidelines. Such a situation will continue to provide impetus for teachers to ignore or diffuse MOE reforms that are perceived to have negative consequences for student performance.

The most significant driving force in setting national standards lies in the complex forces generated by the entrance exams, the hierarchy of high schools and colleges, and the cram school industry. The MOE is thus unable to control external pressure on teachers, and its attempts to "jump start" the system and regain control over the policy generation process seem futile.

National standards in Japan are not created by a central agency that exists and operates in isolation from the political process. The desire of many American policymakers to "imitate Japan" by further centralizing curriculum decisions in the United States and instituting national standards is not based on empirical evidence. References to Japan's "efficient" system of education appear rooted in American tendencies to idealize the Japanese educational process (LeTendre, 1999). The most promising aspect of Japan's "standard" setting is not its centralization, but rather the extensive lateral networks at the district and regional levels that allow the rapid transmission of curriculum adaptation and implementation. In a search for effective models of educational reform and implementation, this aspect of the Japanese system is worthy of further study.

REFERENCES

Cummings, W. (1989). The American perception of Japanese education. *Comparative Education, 25*(3), 293–307.

LeTendre, G. (1994). Distribution tables and private tests: The failure of middle school reform in Japan. *International Journal of Educational Reform, 3*(2), 126–136.

LeTendre, G. (1996). Constructed aspirations: Decision-making processes in Japanese educational selection. *Sociology of Education, 69*(3), 193–216.

LeTendre, G. (Ed.). (1999). *Competitor or ally: Japan's role in American educational debates.* New York: Falmer.

Miyagi, K. (1998, March). The high school selection process in middle schools. *Issues in Modern Japanese Sociology,* pp. 29–47.

National Commission on Excellence in Education. (1983). *A nation at risk: The imperative for educational reform.* Washington, DC: U.S. Department of Education.

Richardson, B. (1997). *Japanese democracy: Power, coordination and performance.* New Haven, CT: Yale University Press.

Roesgaard, M. H. (1998). *Moving mountains: Japanese educational reform.* Aarhus, Denmark: Aarhus University Press.

Schoppa, L. (1991). *Education reform in Japan: A case of immobilist policies.* New York: Routledge.

Stevenson, D., & Baker, D. (1992). Shadow education and allocation in formal schooling: Transition to university in Japan. *American Journal of Sociology, 97*(6), 1639–1657.

Thurston, D. (1973). *Teachers and politics in Japan.* Princeton, NJ: Princeton University Press.

Women's Democratic Council on Educational Reform. (1987). *Oya no kyôiku sekinin wa jûhassai made* [A mother's responsibility for education extends to 18 years of age]. Tokyo: Author.

Wray, H. (1991). Change and continuity in modern Japanese educational history: Allied occupational reforms forty years later. *Comparative Education Review, 35*(3), 447–475.

PART II

Textbooks and Teachers' Editions: The Starting Point for Classroom Instruction

EVEN MANY U.S. EDUCATORS who react with suspicion to claims of the superiority of Japanese education are willing to concede that Japanese textbooks surpass the U.S. versions. Comparisons of mathematics and science textbooks in the two countries show that those in Japan are more focused, organized, and challenging. Japanese textbooks are also more uniform across publishing companies compared with the United States, where the same concept may appear in a third-grade book in one publisher's series and a fifth-grade book in another series.

The differences in the two countries' textbooks arise, at the most fundamental level, from the organizational structure of the two educational systems. Japan's centralized system leads to a certain level of uniformity; the decentralized U.S. system results in diversity. Japanese publishers look to a single set of national standards, while their counterparts in the United States must attempt to synthesize hundreds of curricular models developed by state agencies, local schools, professional organizations, and interest groups.

This structural difference, however, does not entirely explain the divergence of U.S. and Japanese textbooks. In the following three chapters, the authors point out other differences that affect textbook design in the elementary mathematics and science textbooks they compare. In Chapter 3, Ineko Tsuchida and Catherine Lewis point out that Japanese elementary school science textbooks, in comparison with those in the United States, include more tightly focused problem-solving activities, better visuals, and a more sequential introduction of concepts. U.S. textbooks rely heavily on written explanations and include more interdisciplinary connections. In a pithy statement, the authors capture a fundamental difference between the approaches in the two countries: U.S. students *read about* science and Japanese students *do* science.

In Chapter 4, the same authors along with Samuel Coleman explore the origins of the differences outlined in Chapter 3 through a description of the process of writing and revising science textbooks. In Japan, teacher collaboration and involvement is a crucial component of a publishing company's efforts throughout the process. A national course of study and agreements among publishers keep textbook content and length similar, allowing the authors and consultants to focus on the approach to and presentation of the content.

Shin-ying Lee and Akane Zusho, in Chapter 5, examine teachers' editions that accompany elementary school mathematics textbooks. They point out an emphasis on subject matter and presentation of information that parallels the student textbooks. The Japanese manuals, in the context of a sophisticated discussion of mathematics content and student learning, present detailed lesson plans to enhance teachers' knowledge of mathematics and mathematics pedagogy and to guide their use of the textbook. The U.S. manuals, in contrast, seem to focus more on frills geared to marketing and contain less meaningful discussion of content and approach.

In summary, the three chapters in this part point out that the Japanese textbooks emphasize visual images, depth of coverage, focused experimentation, precise connections to daily life, and carefully sequenced curricula. In contrast, the American approach emphasizes reading, breadth of coverage, parental involvement, interdisciplinary connections, individualized instruction, and repetition of content in a spiral curriculum. Although comparisons of textbooks in other subject areas and those at the secondary school level would raise additional issues, many of the fundamental differences described in these chapters would still hold true.

For the past three decades, the use of textbooks by American teachers, especially at the elementary school level, has been declining. Followers of the "progressive" movement in the 1960s and 1970s abandoned textbooks for a more child-centered and hands-on approach. In recent years, as U.S. politicians have placed increasing emphasis on state proficiency testing, some districts have encouraged their teachers to use materials geared specifically to the state's tests. Textbook companies, in turn, have responded with a plethora of new textbook series, supplementary books, and Internet sites focused on test preparation. Japanese textbooks, although often revised, have changed far less over the same years. All students receive them, and most teachers consistently use them. At first glance, the U.S. system appears more dynamic. Another interpretation, however, points to the continuity of the Japanese curriculum and textbooks as the source of a stable dynamism that helps Japanese teachers understand and teach the subject matter.

CHAPTER 3

How Do Japanese and U.S. Elementary Science Textbooks Differ? Depth, Breadth, and Organization of Selected Physical Science Units

Ineko Tsuchida and Catherine C. Lewis

THE THIRD INTERNATIONAL MATHEMATICS AND SCIENCE STUDY (TIMSS) reveals a U.S. curriculum that is "a mile wide and an inch deep," compared with the mathematics and science curricula of most high-achieving countries, and textbooks that are correspondingly large (Schmidt, McKnight, & Raizen, 1997). As one TIMSS researcher quipped, the United States undoubtedly ranks first in the world in textbook weight. This chapter, using qualitative and quantitative analyses, compares the content, approach, and organization of Japanese and U.S. elementary science textbooks, focusing on two topics in physical science—levers and electricity—that are taught in both countries.

SELECTION OF TEXTBOOKS AND TOPICS FOR ANALYSIS

We reviewed all five major Japanese textbook series for elementary science and chose two for analysis, based on their relatively large market share of 25%–30% each and their distribution (Shuppan Rôren, 1996). One series is more heavily used in Western Japan and the other in Eastern Japan, reflecting the location of the publishers.

Selection of the U.S. textbooks was more difficult. We initially intended to analyze U.S. textbooks adopted by New York, Texas, and California, large states considered influential in other states' textbook adoption. New York, however, leaves textbook decisions to local education authorities, and many textbooks adopted for use in Texas are not available in California's textbook display libraries; therefore, we selected textbooks from two major publishers recommended for adoption in California. In the early 1990s, U.S. Publisher I had a fairly small market share of 3% for both Grades 1–4 and Grades 5–8. In 1993, U.S. Publisher II had a large share of the science textbook market—31% for Grades 1–4 and 13% for Grades 5–8 (Weiss, Matti, & Smith, 1994).

In comparing the textbooks, we decided to analyze physical science units, both because of their shared content across cultures, compared with biology units that often focus on local organisms, and because physical science is an area of relatively low achievement for U.S. students (Schmidt et al., 1998). Several factors complicated our effort to study the same content at the same grade levels. First, while Japanese textbooks assign each science topic to a specific grade level, U.S. textbooks often give only rough grade-level guidelines, such as "Primary Span" or "Intermediate Span." U.S. textbooks also vary in the grade level to which a particular topic is assigned. Because Japanese textbooks follow the national *Course of Study*, they do not vary in this regard.

Second, even when two U.S. textbooks cover the same topic, their coverage often varies greatly in sophistication and depth. In contrast, all the Japanese textbooks cover virtually the same content with only minor differences in layout, illustrations, student activities, and writing style. For example, levers are covered at fifth grade by all five Japanese textbooks, and the content is similar across all five. In contrast, one U.S. textbook series includes levers in a third-grade unit on simple machines called "Pushes and Pulls," and another U.S. textbook series places levers in a fifth-grade module called "Pedaling Uphill."

The U.S. unit "Pushes and Pulls" covers 68 pages and includes an introductory chapter, a summary chapter, and four additional chapters ("From Here to There," "Push and Pull," "Is It Moving?," and "Machines and Work"), followed by a unit-summary chapter. The Japanese textbooks cover levers in units of 10–12 pages entitled "Function of Levers" in all five textbook series. Since the U.S. units cover content in addition to levers, we selected for comparison only the chapter or section that focused on levers. Similarly, because one U.S. textbook covers electricity in a 94-page module entitled "Electricity and Magnetism," we reviewed all eight chapters and selected the section that covered content most equivalent to that covered in the unit "Function of Electricity" from the Japanese textbook series.

ANALYSIS OF THE SCIENCE UNITS

Unit Composition

Even at first glance, the Japanese and U.S. science textbooks differ in obvious ways. In contrast to the two U.S. textbooks in which the year's content is divided into five to six distinct units or modules (each a separate paperback volume of 68–123 pages for U.S. Publisher I and 48 pages for U.S. Publisher II), Japanese science texts are slim paperbacks with a single volume for third grade and two volumes each for fourth to sixth grades. The third-grade volume has 90–100 pages, and the fourth-to-sixth-grade volumes have 55–60 pages. A major reason for their compact size is that Japanese science textbooks cover a smaller number of topics per grade than U.S. science textbooks (Okamoto et al., 1992; Schmidt et al., 1997; Schmidt et al., 1998). TIMSS researchers described U.S. mathematics and science textbooks as "voluminous, unselective, and filled with redundant content over the grades" (Schmidt et al., 1998, p. 23). The two U.S. textbook series we analyzed, however, were modular, each focusing on a single theme such as levers or electricity. Each modular volume was comparable in size to the Japanese volumes, but one or two volumes covered the Japanese school year, compared with five or six in the United States.

Table 3.1 provides data on the selected physical science units in the two Japanese and two U.S. textbooks. The greater use of language in U.S. textbooks is striking. Even when the Japanese and U.S. units cover an equivalent number of pages (for example, the electricity units of Japanese Publisher I and U.S. Publisher I), the U.S. textbook devotes many more sentences to the explanation of electricity (165 in the U.S. text versus 18 in the Japanese text). Despite this difference in verbiage, Japanese and U.S. textbooks are roughly similar in the number of scientific terms defined in each unit, suggesting that U.S. texts do not necessarily introduce a greater number of ideas about a particular topic such as levers or the function of electricity. Similarly, the Japanese and U.S. units do not differ substantially in the number of photographs, illustrations, or experiments they provide. The Japanese units have some text spoken by "side characters," small cartoonlike characters such as "wise guy" that provide hints, ask questions, and model thinking. This pattern is not found in the U.S. texts. In the Japanese texts, a friendly sidebar character of a child or animal might say,

Table 3.1. Unit Layout in Japanese and U.S. Science Textbooks

Topic/Unit/Index	JPN Publisher I	JPN Publisher II	U.S. Publisher I	U.S. Publisher II
I. Levers (Unit title and grade level)	"Function of Levers" (Grade 5)	"Function of Levers" (Grade 5)	"Pushes & Pulls: Machines and Work" (Grade 3)	"Pedaling Uphill: Work and Play" (Grade 5)
• Size of the textbook	$7\frac{1}{8}$ x $10\frac{1}{8}$ in	$7\frac{1}{8}$ x $10\frac{1}{8}$ in	8 x 10 in	8 x $10\frac{3}{4}$ in
• Number of pages analyzed	12	10	12	22
• Number of definitions	3	4	12	4
• Number of sentences in the main text	26	18	62	199
• Number of sentences spoken by the side characters	7	13	0	0
• Number of experiments/activities	3	4	5	4
• Number of photographs	26	20	4	19
• Number of illustrations	25	25	19	20
II. Electricity (Unit title and grade level)	"Function of Electricity" (Grade 6)	"Function of Electricity" (Grade 6)	"Electricity and Magnetism: How are electricity and magnetism related?" (Grade 6)	"Electricity: Electric signals" (Grade 5)
• Size of the textbook	$7\frac{1}{8}$ x $10\frac{1}{8}$ in	$7\frac{1}{8}$ x $10\frac{1}{8}$ in	8 x 10 in	8 x $10\frac{3}{4}$ in
• Number of pages analyzed	12, plus one fold-out page, that is equivalent to two additional pages	14	12	25
• Number of definitions	2	0	4	5
• Number of sentences in the main text	18	16	165	245
• Number of sentences spoken by the side characters	12	5	0	0
• Number of experiments/activities	3	6	4	4
• Number of photographs	23	24	11	35
• Number of illustrations	21	19	3	11

Note: A self-contained expression is counted as one sentence as defined in the Merriam-Webster Dictionary. For example, a short phrase such as a one-word question "Why?" or a short exclamation, "But wait!" is counted as one sentence. In addition, only the sentences in the main text are counted. Therefore, the count does not include the experimental procedures, titles, subtitles, headings, subheadings, annotations in illustrations, the sections for chapter summary or the chapter reviews, the captions to illustrations or photographs, and the reference readings in boxed articles. However, the questions written in bold that often precede the experiments in the Japanese textbooks are included as sentences in the main text.

for example, "This balance looks like the balance we used in fourth grade, doesn't it?" or "How about comparing electrical power?"

We also observed a somewhat different allocation of space in the Japanese and U.S. textbook units. The illustrations and photographs of activities or experiments in the Japanese texts are usually large, making the details of the experiments visible. In contrast, the sidebar characters, although they appear frequently in Japanese textbooks, are small, perhaps an inch or so, and appear near the margin of the layout or next to a critical question. Thus the clear visual presentation of the experiments compensates for the brief one- to two-sentence explanations.

U.S. textbooks are similar to their Japanese counterparts in the amount of space occupied by visual images. In U.S. textbooks, however, sometimes the images include what might be considered extraneous or eye-catching illustrations or photographs. For example, a girl blowing her long hair with a hair dryer takes up 40 square inches of space, but three photographs showing how to construct an electric motor occupy only 4 square inches each. Thus the details of the step-by-step photographs of the motor-building process are hard to see. As if to compensate for the inadequacy of the photographs, the accompanying written explanation for building the motor is long, ranging from one to five sentences for each step. Although U.S. textbooks often showed the step-by-step procedures for experiments, the illustrations did not clearly show the details.

Unit Flow

Our analysis of the connections among the illustrations, experiments, and definitions revealed that all four Japanese units have a cohesive unit flow and no unrelated elements. For example, for the 11–12 periods generally allotted for levers, Japanese Publisher I provides the following sequence of material: introduction to tools as a way to ease work (2 sentences); definition of terms; and three experiments on levers, each preceded by a critical question and followed with a statement of finding. These three experiments ask students to (1) study what happens when the object to be lifted by a lever is moved closer to/farther away from the fulcrum; (2) study what happens when force is exerted closer to/farther away from the fulcrum; and (3) find out the relationship between weight and distance from the fulcrum when two objects balance the lever.

In contrast, U.S. textbooks typically have at least a few breaks in the unit flow, and the connection between the reading and science activities is often weak. For example, the unit on levers from U.S. Publisher II starts with the provocative question "How can you move a brick?" followed by two discussion questions: "What is the purpose of the rubber band?" and

"What is the easiest way to pull the brick?" But this activity, labeled "Discovery Activity," leads to a two-page textbook description of work and friction that makes minimal reference to the previous activity with a brick. Following this are sections on the difficulty of riding a bike uphill (49 sentences on force, work, and friction), and on how tools make work easier (79 sentences on seven simple machines). Finally, the unit describes the ancient Egyptians' use of simple machines to build pyramids (71 sentences over six pages, including several large illustrations and a photograph). While the description may provide students with interesting, detailed information on simple machines and the history of science, it is not closely connected with the content to be learned about levers.

FURTHER COMPARISONS

Our review of the eight units suggests several other potential differences between Japanese and U.S. textbooks. We mention them here with the caution that larger-scale quantitative research would be needed to establish the reliability of these conclusions.

Promoting or Constraining Problem Solving

The statements preceding experiments in Japanese texts often use a tone designed to *elicit* students' active problem solving; for example, "Let's find out the principles for making a balance scale balance horizontally, by rearranging the number and location of weights on both arms," or "Let's find out what happens when electric current runs through a coil." At the same time, these statements *constrain* problem solving by focusing students on particular kinds of investigation. In contrast, the activities and experiments suggested in the U.S. texts are often extremely broad. For example, the third-grade unit on levers by U.S. Publisher I asks students to figure out how to use simple machines to move a piano into a truck and to get a roll of tape from the floor to the top of a desk. The range of possible solutions is very broad, and some may not increase students' understanding of simple machines. Indeed, we wonder whether the breadth of these problems might lead students to propose creative but impractical solutions, rather than focus on the properties of simple machines.

Within their more focused experiments, the Japanese texts often provide a wider "window" for students to determine experimental methods. The U.S. texts give more specific directions. For example, the lever unit in Grade 5 of U.S. Publisher II explicitly instructs students to place a plastic cup containing marbles at points 20 cm, 40 cm, 60 cm, and 80 cm from the fulcrum of a balance scale. In contrast, the two Japanese units do not provide explicit instructions, but simply suggest with an arrow that the point of resistance be moved away from the fulcrum. Students must decide how much to move the point of resistance.

It is difficult to determine the optimal window of exploration in experiments. In the above example from the U.S. text, some students might recall a time when movers came to transport the family piano and tie that experience to the use of simple machines. Because they could relate the example to their actual life experience, these students might benefit. Other students, however, could be disadvantaged by the example simply because they have not had a similar experience. By the same token, the narrow Japanese approach could possibly disadvantage some students by pushing them to examine the formula relating the point of effort, the point of resistance, and fulcrum before they themselves grasp connections among the three elements of leverage.

Definitions

Even though the Japanese and U.S. textbooks provide a similar number of definitions, the U.S. textbooks appear to include more definitions of complex scientific phenomena, as in the following explanation of electricity from a fifth-grade textbook (U.S. Publisher II):

> Protons crowd together in the nucleus of an atom. Electrons spin around the protons because the electrons are attracted to the protons. It's this force of attraction that holds the electrons in the atom. The force of attraction between an electron and a proton is the result of their electric charges. An electron is negatively charged, but a proton is positively charged. Negative and positive charges attract each other, so the electron is attracted to the proton. (p. 6 of "Module E Electricity")

Although no words are highlighted as new vocabulary, the content of this reading is fairly complex, and it is followed by 44 additional sentences explaining how electricity works. Although the accompanying photographs are friendly—for example, a hand pushing the button on a TV remote control and a boy rubbing his hair with a balloon to cause static electricity—the text itself is complex and scientifically sophisticated, and requires considerable reading skill.

The Japanese texts did not include an explanation of electricity, so we examined the following definition of an electromagnet (Japanese Publisher I, Grade 6):

A coil becomes magnetic like magnets when electric current runs through it. When an iron core is inserted in the coil and the iron core becomes magnetic with the electric current, it is called an *electromagnet*.

A coil or an electromagnet has N and S poles. When the direction of the electric current is reversed, the poles will be reversed as well. (p. 32; emphasis in original)

Compared with the U.S. explanation of electricity, the Japanese explanation of an electromagnet requires relatively little reading skill. This approach might benefit poor readers; however, it might offer less material to pique the curiosity of advanced students.

Interdisciplinary Focus

Another noteworthy characteristic of the U.S. textbooks is their interdisciplinary content. For example, the lever unit from U.S. Publisher II encourages students to discuss whether public buildings should have ramps. Similarly, the sixth-grade unit from U.S. Publisher I asks students to write an essay on the pros and cons of electronic surveillance in a store. The textbooks use substantial space for discussion of societal issues, but students are not necessarily provided with sufficient information to make intelligent decisions about the use of ramps or electronic surveillance. As Okamoto and colleagues (1992) note, sufficient information and well-structured organization are needed if texts are to promote students' problem solving. Japanese educators, on the other hand, may see the interdisciplinary focus of U.S. textbooks as a strength, as such material may strengthen students' awareness of relationships between their classroom learning and social issues (Lee & Zusho, Chapter 5, this volume; Ministry of Education [MOE], 1999).

In conclusion, judging from the activities and experiments, the Japanese and U.S. textbooks may be designed to spark students' interest in science in different ways: the Japanese textbooks through "Let's find out . . . " statements and carefully illustrated activities, and the U.S. textbooks through connections to students' lives (see Linn & Muilenburg, 1996, regarding the qualities of science instruction that facilitate lifelong science learning). The connection, however, seems broad in the U.S. units in contrast to the narrow focus of the Japanese textbooks.

Layout of Text

Since we analyzed only two content areas in each of two textbook series in each country, our findings must be considered tentative. Nevertheless, we think several findings deserve attention and follow-up. The first is the difference in layout between the Japanese and U.S. units. Compared with the Japanese texts, the U.S. texts rely heavily on written explanation that is often weakly connected to suggested student activities or experiments. While the U.S. texts emphasize reading about science, the Japanese texts emphasize doing science, through a series of tightly connected activities or experiments, supported with spare, simple prose.

We can speculate that the much greater verbiage in U.S. science textbooks could have a ripple effect on many aspects of instruction; for example, low-achieving readers in the United States may have more difficulty learning science content. The Japanese textbooks, however, suggest intriguing ways to teach science that rely less on students' reading ability. A second effect of the heavy verbal content in U.S. textbooks may be that teachers have to omit some topics, increasing the likelihood that students will not be exposed to the same science content. In fact, TIMSS revealed that some physical science topics in the U.S. are taught less frequently than topics in earth science or biology. For example, only 50%–74% of U.S. fourth-grade teachers teach the textbook units on "Matter" and "Forces and Motion" (Schmidt et al., 1998). As Okamoto and colleagues (1992) have pointed out, weak unit flow in conjunction with a heavy load of written content may make it difficult for students to retain what they read. In contrast, the tight unit flow and spare writing of Japanese textbooks make it likely that students will focus on the experiments and illustrations and cover the entire unit.

Underlying Assumptions

What assumptions regarding science learning might underlie the differences between science textbooks in the two countries? The Japanese textbooks suggest that students should *do* science in well-focused experiments where they are given leeway to shape the experimental method. In contrast, the U.S. textbooks suggest that students should read about science, engage in carefully prescribed experiments, and have their thinking sparked by open-ended, interdisciplinary activities. The interesting examples of scientific phenomena, events, or facts embedded in the reading materials in the U.S. textbooks reflect this difference. Okamoto and her colleagues (1992) refer to this characteristic of U.S. science textbooks as "the accumulation of facts that someone else has actually gathered" (p. 26). U.S. science texts are like treasure boxes filled with exciting and possibly exotic information that cannot necessarily be observed or replicated by students themselves. But textbooks filled with so much information make it likely that students will read selectively and that teachers will assign only some sections. The voluminous U.S. texts, therefore, may create a gap in science content that parallels the reading gap.

FUTURE RESEARCH

Although our analyses are exploratory, they supplement related research on Japanese and U.S. textbooks (Okamoto, Calfee, Varghese, & Chambliss, 1992; Schmidt, McKnight, Cogan, Jakwerth, & Houang, 1988; Schmidt, McKnight, & Raizen, 1997). In future analyses, we hope researchers will give more attention to identifying the links and redundancies across grade levels in the textbook series. For instance, the U.S. textbooks provide scientific definitions of many different words, such as *machine*, *force*, and *work*, in levers units in both Grades 3 and 5. In Japanese textbooks they are not defined in Grade 5. Are those words not included in the fifth-grade textbook because they have been introduced and defined in earlier grades, or is it because Japanese textbooks have fewer definitions in general compared with U.S. textbooks? Are the same words defined differently at different grade levels in the U.S. textbooks, or repeatedly introduced similarly in different grades? In order to answer these questions, we must conduct a cross-grade and cross-topic analysis reviewing all physical science units in both the Japanese and U.S. elementary science textbook series.

Beyond the analyses of specific textbooks, it would also be beneficial to consider broader issues and trends in the textbook industries in both countries. As TIMSS states, U.S. textbooks are *inclusive*, trying to please every party involved in the purchasing of textbooks. In contrast, the Ministry of Education supervises *exclusion* of content (Lewis, Tsuchida, & Coleman, Chapter 4, this volume). Such seemingly opposite trends in the two countries warrant further study of the pros and cons of the two approaches in fostering students' scientific literacy and problem solving abilities. Although we have presented information on text length and inclusion/exclusion of science content, still unanswered are the important questions of whether the textbook design and structure help students think and act like scientists, and whether students spontaneously apply classroom science to their everyday lives.

Last, although textbooks provide valuable insight into the effect of the intended curriculum, they cannot be studied in isolation. The use of textbooks in the classroom also must be studied in order to understand their effect on student scientific learning. We hope that the issues we explored in this chapter will be considered for textbooks in other subject areas and for studies of implemented curriculum.

Acknowledgement. This chapter is based on research supported by the National Science Foundation under grants REC-9996360 and RED-9355857. Any opinions, findings, and conclusions or recommendations expressed in this publication are those of the authors and do not necessarily reflect the views of the National Science Foundation.

REFERENCES

Linn, M. C., & Muilenburg, L. (1996). Creating lifelong science learners: What models form a firm foundation? *Educational Researcher, 25*(5), 18–24.

Ministry of Education. (1999). *Japanese government policies in education, science, sports, and culture.* Tokyo: Author.

Okamoto, Y., Calfee, R., Varghese, S., & Chambliss, M. (1992, April). *A cross-cultural comparison of textbook designs.* Paper presented at the annual meeting of the American Educational Research Association, Washington, DC.

Schmidt, W. H., McKnight, C. C., Cogan, L. S., Jakwerth, P. M., & Houang, R. T. (1998). *Facing the consequences: Using TIMSS for a closer look at United States mathematics and science education.* Boston: Kluwer.

Schmidt, W. H., McKnight, C. C., & Raizen, S. A. (1997). *A splintered vision: An investigation of U.S. science and mathematics education.* Boston: Kluwer.

Shuppan Rôren. (1996). *Kyôkasho repôto* [Textbook report]. Tokyo: Author.

Weiss, I. R., Matti, M. C., & Smith, P. S. (1994). *Report of the 1993 national survey of science and mathematics education.* Chapel Hill, NC: Horizon Research.

CHAPTER 4

The Creation of Japanese and U.S. Elementary Science Textbooks: Different Processes, Different Outcomes

Catherine C. Lewis, Ineko Tsuchida, and Samuel Coleman

WHY IS IT THAT A CALIFORNIA SIXTH-GRADER'S textbooks weigh 21 pounds, while those of his counterpart in Tokyo weigh just 3 pounds? Why do Japan's elementary science textbooks lay out a spare, coherent program of student-centered activities, while U.S. texts are packed with hundreds of pages of reading, facts, and activities (Lee & Zusho, Chapter 5, this volume; Tsuchida & Lewis, Chapter 3, this volume)? Although many people point to textbooks as a crucial element in science achievement (Schmidt, McKnight, Cogan, Jakwerth, & Houang, 1998; Schmidt, McKnight, & Raizen, 1997), few researchers have studied the development of either U.S. or Japanese science textbooks. During 1998–1999 we conducted interviews with textbook authors from all five major Japanese science textbooks and from several major U.S. publishers. Drawing on comments from those we interviewed and referring to them with pseudonyms, we have developed an account of the forces that shape Japanese and U.S. elementary science textbooks. Given the small sample size and the fact that the U.S. sample did not cover every major publisher, however, findings should be regarded as tentative. We do not know whether our findings generalize to other academic subjects or levels of schooling.

The overall contours of the textbook system are quite similar in the United States and Japan. In both countries, independent commercial publishers develop textbooks, and local educational entities choose among competing textbook series. In both countries, textbooks are reviewed and approved by public agencies—the Ministry of Education in the case of Japan, and state or local education agencies in most U.S. states. As we will see, however, textbook development differs greatly in the two countries within these overall contours.

THE INFLUENCE OF PRIOR TEXTBOOKS

Both Japanese and American authors pointed out that each textbook inherits much material from its predecessor. Despite revisions every 3 to 5 years, textbooks tend to remain essentially the same. As Ms. Espar, a U.S. teacher and consulting author, said, "When they write a book, they use all their previous stuff and they just tweak it a little bit." A Japanese author echoed: "When you create a textbook, you rely very heavily on the past textbook as a base. You don't start from zero."

Mr. Motofuji, a classroom teacher who has written sections of an elementary science textbook for the past 13 years, explained the pressure to maintain textbooks as they are:

> If you change textbooks too much, then teachers are troubled. So we try to limit ourselves to small changes. For example, if teachers are used to observing a certain butterfly and then you change the textbook to observe another butterfly, that could be troubling to teachers.

Ms. Oshima, a principal who began writing textbooks as a young teacher 20 years ago, described the biggest change she made over that time:

> The biggest change I made was in the unit on the nature and function of liquids. Traditionally, that unit used hydrochloric acid and sodium hydroxide. I thought ammonia would be better, because something white is left over after the substances combine. The white substance left over might spark in children the idea that the substance had really changed, not just dissolved. I suggested ammonia to the publishing company, but adding new things to the textbook is difficult. There is resistance to giving up the traditional materials that have always been used; such changes can affect sales. For that reason, the publisher didn't want to drop the two substances that had traditionally been used. Instead they added the two that I suggested. I would've preferred that they'd just switched to the new substances.

Dr. Bennett, a university professor who had a contract to write an innovative science text, explained how a similar preference for the familiar has restricted his efforts:

> Even though this publisher knows what we are all about, and we were very clear to her what we were all about, they still want to see more and more content. Publishers are always driven to see more and more content. And sometimes more and more content doesn't necessarily mean that people learn more. . . . The editor I'm working with now really wants to create good materials, but they're driven by a market. She keeps coming back with, "But chemistry teachers are expecting to see it this way." And we keep coming back to say, "But that's not why you wanted us to write this textbook. You said you wanted something different." They go and look at the best-selling textbook and tell us it has certain features. But we say, "If that's the textbook you want, then why create another one like it?"

TEACHER PREFERENCES

In both Japan and the United States, the local educational entities that choose among competing textbooks typically base their decisions to some degree on teacher preference (Azuma, Chapter 1, this volume). Mr. Mishima, a retired principal, gave the following account of textbook adoption:

> Adoption is done in different ways by different prefectures. Within Tokyo, each school sends to the Board of Education the number of teachers who voted for each textbook series in each subject. So it's really like a vote. But other prefectures do it differently. Sometimes teachers just rank their top three preferences of texts, or sometimes it is a committee that makes the decision.
>
> Teachers use the textbooks, so it is right that teachers choose them. They are given time off from class to look at the textbooks. Sometimes they just choose the most colorful or the one with the most pictures, or the thinnest, or the one that has the most careful description of the experiments. Sometimes they don't really have a good basis for choosing. In Tokyo, the Board of Education doesn't specify the characteristics teachers should look for in textbooks, because that would be considered too much guidance. But in Tokyo the Board of Education does make a table that lists the length of each textbook, the number of pictures, etc. . . . Within each Tokyo ward,

everybody uses the same textbook, but across wards, there are different textbooks.

In Japan (but not in the United States) interviewees mentioned that industry guidelines also constrained textbook change. Mr. Shioda, an editor, explained:

> The industry association of textbook publishers agrees on a maximum and minimum page limit range for each textbook, on the proportion of pages that will be four colors, on the proportion of pages that will be two colors, etc. We can't set the price because that would create a monopoly; so instead we set the things that affect the price. There is something called "industry guidelines." It's like regulations that cover the textbooks.

By agreeing to limit the overall number of pages and the number of colored pages, Japanese textbook publishers eliminate the danger that competitors will offer a substantially larger or more colorful product as a "loss leader" to drive other companies out of the market. Competition thus shifts to other qualities such as the textbook's ease of use, clarity, visual appeal, and responsiveness to recent educational trends. Mr. Motofuji, however, noted that teachers tend to stick with their current series:

> The shares of textbooks don't change much. If teachers are used to one, they might be likely to maintain that, and also the sales representatives are always keeping relationships up with the people who use their textbook, so there often aren't great changes.

The adoption system may push Japanese textbooks to be usable and familiar to parents as well as to teachers. Mr. Mishima explained how parents influence teachers' textbook preferences:

> Parents want everything in the textbook taught, so teachers want textbook content limited so that they won't have to teach too much. Parents also want answers in the textbook, even though teachers might feel that it's better not to give some answers.
> Parents also like similarity. They like to know when they move that children will be doing the same things. There's a sense of comfort if the textbooks are more or less the same. Sometimes this results in ridiculous things, like children all over Japan studying crabs, even though some children have never seen a real crab in their local environment.

Several American interviewees also made the point that textbooks may fail to be adopted if they depart greatly from what the public is used to. Dr. Cary, who helped write a "lean, kid-centered, activity-based" science textbook for a major U.S. publisher, believed that it flopped because it was "ahead of its time":

> It flopped real bad. Like . . . "Oh boy, do I get my advance royalty?" . . . it was all printed, and out there in the market, and it would just keep losing out. The problem with textbooks is that there's no real number two. You don't come in second place. Most states that are buying them will buy one type of textbook, and if you just almost made it . . . you get zero percent of the bucks.

Researchers have described significant differences between U.S. and Japanese textbooks, and the pressure against change may help ensure that those differences remain.

APPROVAL

Both U.S. and Japanese elementary science textbooks are reviewed and approved by public agencies, but the process takes quite different forms in the two countries. In the United States, the approval process (even whether one exists) differs by state. According to Dr. Aller, a university professor, textbook publishers try to make sure their texts meet the requirements of the largest states:

> One of the things that controls the content that's put in elementary science books is the state guidelines. And so they have editors whose job is to go through all the states for state adoption states like California and Texas. They do some charts that say, "Well, they call for weather at third grade in Florida, and they call for weather at fourth grade in Texas," or whatever. They have to write these books to meet those guidelines. So essentially what happens is you have every topic every single year because some state calls for it.

Similarly, Mr. Cary observed:

> One problem is what the states want. Because the publishers, like any supply company, will meet the demand. . . . If New York State says that they want electricity in grade four, and Texas says they

want electricity in grade five, what do you do? It's a real trade-off, because which market do you sacrifice?

In Japan, textbook approval is conducted centrally by the Ministry of Education in conjunction with the Textbook Authorization and Research Council, a council of elementary, secondary, and university educators appointed by the Ministry of Education. Textbooks are submitted to the Ministry of Education for approval about 2 years prior to their use in the classroom. Without knowing the identity of these "blank cover" textbooks, the council evaluates each as "pass," "fail," or "needs revisions." After receiving the council's comments, compiled by the ministry's lead inspectors, textbook publishers may revise and resubmit their books, keeping in mind the overall adoption cycle described by Azuma in Chapter 1.

Table 4.1, given to us by a Japanese textbook author, provides counts and examples of the changes that the council requested in one elementary science series. Although many requested revisions were designed to improve textbook accuracy or to eliminate confusing or difficult activities and words, a substantial number of requested changes—about four per text—restrained textbooks from providing information beyond the content of the *Course of Study*, the document that defines the national curriculum and goals. Mr. Onishi and Mr. Motofuji provided examples of such requests to eliminate "excess content":

> At the textbook approval process we were told we couldn't write the word *liver* on a diagram of the human body. The unit was about the digestive tract and they said it was okay to draw the liver there because it's in the body but not to write *liver*, because if we wrote it people would feel they had to teach about its nature and function, and the unit was just about the digestive tract. The strong trend away from complexity began about 8 years ago, when we started getting forceful feedback not to go beyond the *Course of Study*. It's probably true of all subjects, not just science. We used to be able to write the word *liver* by its illustration. The request probably has to do with junior high entrance exams including very difficult, specialized problems and the Ministry of Education not wanting to play into that. . . . It's okay to name things and to do things beyond the *Course of Study* in your classroom lessons, but it's not okay in the textbooks. If a junior high school used an exam problem that went beyond what was in the *Course of Study*, there could well be complaints from local board of education members.
>
> There's a push against teaching too much. In the unit on birth we showed a picture of two chickens together so that we could show

Table 4.1. Items Designated [as Problematic] by the Textbook Authorization and Research Council—Selected Examples

	Number of Items Designated (as Problematic), by Grade of Text			
Approval Standard	Third	Fourth	Fifth	Sixth
I. <u>Scope and Extent</u>	5	4	4	4
(Selected Examples)				
• Digressed from the content of the Course of Study (because the Course of Study does not address the development of particular organs). (Grade 3)				
• Digressed from the content of the Course of Study because the statement "probably because the insects which are the food source increased" deals with the relationships between living things. (Grade 4)				
• Remove all content related to soil because soil is not addressed in the Course of Study. Formulate an alternative content. (Grade 5)				
II. <u>Selection, Treatment and Organization, Amount</u>	7	5	6	9
• It is difficult to observe in a mirror. (Grade 3)				
• Missing temperature recording on students' recording sheet. In addition, it is all right to have an approximate conclusion under some circumstances. (Grade 4)				
• The expression "to cool off gradually" is insufficient to describe production of the crystal shown. Either add a concrete time for gradual cooling or a plan to evaporate it naturally. (Grade 5)				
• Inappropriate questioning: The level of the question falls into third grade. Mention the sixth-grade content on the function of roots. (Grade 6)				
III. <u>Accuracy and Notation, Expression</u>	12	8	14	21
• Science now starts from third grade, so children don't have any prior experience with morning glories. (Grade 3)				
• Correct that snails are sitting in the sun because they usually stay in shade. (Grade 4)				
• It is unclear whether the pointers point at the pollen sack or the capital. Change the position of the pointers. (Grade 5)				
• The ratio between oxygen and carbon dioxide is strange (inadequate?). Needs further research. (Grade 6)				

Note: This table summarizes a table prepared by a textbook publisher in September 1994, which listed all items identified as problematic by the Ministry of Education's Textbook Authorization and Research Council for the elementary science series (which covers Grades 3-6, since science is not taught as a separate subject during Grades 1-2). The original table provided page and line numbers, and the original text, so that authors and editors could review and discuss each example. We provide selected examples.

what happens before the fertilized egg. The Ministry of Education said to cut out that picture, which was just two chickens sitting next to each other, and just start with the fertilized egg. When you think about it, that's ridiculous, because how does that fertilized egg start? ... I guess the idea is that teachers in the field would be confused if there were too much that they had to teach. The fact that it's not in the *Course of Study* is a common reason that's given that we shouldn't write something.

The approval system, then, works in sharply different ways, leading to proliferation of content in U.S. textbooks and paring down content in Japanese textbooks.

RECRUITMENT OF TEACHERS AS AUTHORS FOR TEXTBOOKS

In both the United States and Japan, publishing companies seek out distinguished teachers as authors for their textbooks. Ms. Espar explained how two major U.S. publishers sought her out because of her experience writing curricula, serving on committees, and conducting workshops:

The publishers' sales reps are out asking questions and trying to find teachers who are involved in curriculum, in different movements, teachers who are involved actively, who do presentations. The sales reps show up at things like the Science Teachers' Association. Through the grapevine, through their asking questions, my name came up. And it came up in several different arenas. I was involved in so many things in this state that to say I was on board might mean to them that it was credible.

Ms. Oshima similarly described the Japanese publishers' recruitment of authors:

Educators who are working hard at improving science education are noticed and the publishers try to recruit them. They are noticed at places like research lessons and research meetings. Also people already working for the publisher recommend colleagues. The textbook company gathers them together and has a research meeting that occurs about once a month. Within that, they identify the people with good ideas who do work on time, write well, etc. ... If you're called to the research meeting it doesn't necessarily mean that you'll become a textbook writer. ... There's a year of research meet-

ings during which they examine you . . . and only some people are selected to work on the textbooks.

In both countries, then, textbook publishers recruit respected, profession-
ally active educators to serve as textbook consultants.

INDIVIDUAL VERSUS COLLABORATIVE PARTICIPATION

Textbook authors in both countries discussed their efforts to improve textbooks by incorporating new content and pedagogy, and by drawing on
their own classroom experiences. The U.S. authors, however, tended to
contribute as individuals, while the Japanese teachers often worked in long-
term collaborative groups. For example, Ms. Espar received chapter drafts
by overnight mail, reviewed them, and put them back in the mail to the
publisher: "You're in isolation . . . you don't have the luxury of having a
discussion where a good idea will evolve, or three or four ideas." Mr. Cary
observed:

> Often you're writing in a vacuum. You don't know what the other
> writers are doing because you're working pretty much with your
> grade editor or the other editors within the series who are looking at
> other pieces.

The chance to work collaboratively with other science educators was
mentioned as a major benefit by several Japanese authors:

> The good thing about being involved in creating textbooks is that
> you can hear lots of other teachers' ideas. There are times when your
> ideas are listened to, and times when they're not. . . . I want to see
> how other people react to the unit flow I designed. I want to see my
> lessons used among other teachers. Something that went well in my
> class—I want to see how well it went elsewhere, more widely. I
> might change my own approach based on that. (Mr. Ono, a class-
> room teacher who has been a textbook author for 12 years)

> The textbook committee has about 40 members. When it was a busy
> time we sometimes met twice a week. For example, we met twice a
> week for 6 months when we were creating the textbook. When it
> wasn't so busy, we might meet just twice a month. We read each oth-
> er's drafts, discussed them with everyone in the group, and then if
> that group agreed, sent them to be reviewed by the higher group of

about 10 people. There were four groups of about 10 people each who did the particular subject areas within science, and then a higher group of about 10 people, university professors and others, who reviewed the work done by each group to check for mistakes, etc. In addition, every year the publishers used their network of personal relations to request comments from teachers all over the country. Writing textbooks contributes to your own training and study. You have not just your own evaluation of your lessons but how others see your lessons. Also you can see the strengths of others, not just your own strengths. People who are advisors to textbook companies often become curriculum specialists or principals. It's a place to study well, and to form strong human relationships. (Mr. Mishima)

Despite the relatively small amount of text in Japanese elementary science books, tremendous time and effort are expended on it (Tsuchida & Lewis, Chapter 3, this volume). When asked how much time it took to write one textbook unit (typically 10–14 pages of sparse text), Vice-principal Hajime said:

To write the manuscript for the unit? I can't even estimate the total time. I can only say it was immense! We shared drafts with the committee two or three times . . . in between there was time like a cooling-off period, in which I would think things over and then I would go back to the next meeting to be beaten up again. It was fine to be beaten up because we were arguing with each other in order to make a good product. Then, I returned with a revised version. I repeated that a number of times.

A staff member of a Japanese publisher estimated that each unit is reviewed by about 10 classroom teachers before the draft is final. Given this thorough review, mistakes are unlikely to slip through. When Mr. Ono devised an experiment comparing the weight of empty and air-filled plastic bags, his colleagues in the textbook-writing group for the publisher rejected the experiment, pointing out that the air-filled bag would have to be pressurized to be heavier than the empty plastic bag. While U.S. policymakers often talk about the need for greater science content knowledge among U.S. teachers, Mr. Ono's example points out that even Japan's leading science teachers do not have perfect science knowledge. They do, however, have a collaborative situation in which they can have their ideas critiqued and thereby improve their science knowledge.

The need for collaborative review and critique of lesson ideas seemed to transcend even the desire to keep lesson ideas secret from competing textbook companies. When asked whether new lesson ideas would be kept within the textbook company, Mr. Motofuji's answer was vehement: "No, if you have a really good idea you want it to be seen by as many people as possible because otherwise the upper echelons within the textbook company might not see it as good and they might refuse it." Similarly, Ms. Oshima tried the ammonium approach at a districtwide research lesson before writing it into the textbook. When asked if she was worried about other people taking the idea, she said, "No. In fact, just the opposite. The more people who have seen your idea and reacted to it the more data you have to argue that this might be a good change."

In their group meetings, Japanese authors discussed new educational approaches that the textbook would need to reflect and shared information from research lessons that used these approaches (see Lewis & Tsuchida, 1997). As Mr. Motofuji explained:

> The *Course of Study* and the *Instructional Guidelines for Science* are discussed at great length by the textbook-writing groups. If you're off the mark in what you think they mean, then it causes a lot of problems at the time of textbook approval. We talk about what is okay to keep . . . and what needs to be changed and what materials and lessons follow from that. For example we'll come to a consensus on what *ikiru chikara* ["zest for living," a recent *Course of Study* goal] means. . . . The same issues are being discussed at teachers' research meetings all over Japan, so I don't think there's a chance that we're likely to be off greatly.

In contrast with this group sense-making in Japan, U.S. teachers drew more heavily on their own interpretations of new approaches and on their own classroom experience. This difference no doubt reflects larger differences between the two educational systems: While many U.S. teachers plan and deliver lessons individually, Japanese teachers often plan collaboratively and work together on lesson improvement (Shimahara, Chapter 7, this volume; Yoshida, 1999). In addition, educational policy and its implementation are often separate processes in the United States: Policymakers make policy, and individual teachers figure out how to implement it in their classrooms. Japanese "research lessons" mix policy and implementation, as teachers collectively figure out how new educational approaches and content can be brought to life in the classroom; in some cases, the new approaches pioneered in these lessons also influence policy (Lewis &

Tsuchida, 1998). All of the Japanese authors had been continuously involved with a single publisher, working in collegial groups that remained the same except to accommodate retirements and occasional new members. In contrast, the U.S. authors had been involved as individuals, sporadically, and in some cases with more than one publisher.

THE CENTRAL ROLE OF CLASSROOM TEACHERS

The interviews also suggest a second major difference between the participation of Japanese and U.S. teachers in textbook writing: Japanese elementary teachers are the primary architects and writers of Japanese elementary science textbooks, whereas U.S. elementary teachers serve as consultants. Indeed, Ms. Espar distinguished the classroom teachers, called "consulting authors," from the "real" authors: "The real authors and their editors had a tremendous hand in the decisions. The consulting authors as classroom types were further down on the line." In contrast, Mr. Motofuji says:

> I think the voice of classroom teachers is decisive in the textbooks. No matter how much professors say "Let's do X" or "Let's do Y," it's the classroom teachers who are actually central. Whether it makes a good lesson or not is the deciding factor.

Vice-principal Hajime confirmed the central role of classroom teachers in conceiving and writing the units:

Mr. Hajime: For the units that you are assigned, you design the flow of the unit and write the text. Then, everyone discusses what you've written, and you listen to the various opinions, and revise and resubmit it. . . .

Interviewer: Are the people who actually write it more often classroom teachers or university professors?

Mr. Hajime: Classroom teachers. Unless you are a classroom teacher, you can't write it, can you? . . . University professors might be good at writing, and might be able to write textbooks for junior high or high school, but not textbooks for elementary school. That's why it is important that elementary teachers participate in the process.

Yet another Japanese author commented: "It's actual teachers who are central, and university professors who are secondary in the textbook writing." Although Japanese elementary teachers are forbidden from taking side jobs, an exception is made for textbook writing, because, in the words of one interviewee, "There is a recognition on the part of the national government that teachers are essential to the creation of textbooks. You can't make textbooks without teachers."

The fact that textbooks provide a wall-to-wall science curriculum for teachers all over Japan may also make textbook writing very compelling to Japanese teachers. When asked why they engaged in the exacting and time-consuming work of writing textbooks, Mr. Motofuji answered:

> If I were talking just about my own personal development as a teacher, I would've been happy just to do my own original thing, but the textbooks have a huge influence on Japanese teachers. Personally, I'm not someone who really uses a textbook, but when you think of the influence that textbooks have all over Japan, this is a huge influence on Japanese teachers. I'm not 100 percent satisfied with the textbooks, but I think they are 80 percent good and guarantee a certain level of education all over Japan from Hokkaido to Okinawa.

Former principal Mishima echoed this sentiment: "Of course we take textbook writing very seriously. The future of Japanese science education is in our hands."

The leading role taken by elementary teachers in Japan may stem from the fact that Japanese elementary science texts focus on *doing* science rather than on *reading about* science (Tsuchida & Lewis, Chapter 3, this volume). Mr. Ono described changes he made in the textbook, based on his own classroom experiences:

> Here's another change I made. I thought the unit on balances and weight was hard to start the way it was, which was with children making a mobile and trying to get it to balance. Realistically speaking, it's hard for children to get two balls of equal weight, suspend them from a stick that's suspended from another stick, and get it to balance. So I moved that activity to later in the unit and started instead with a two-sided balance scale. It's easy to use it to make two things balance. Much easier than using a mobile.

Mr. Ono described yet another change he made, in a textbook manuscript yet to be approved by the Ministry of Education at the time of the interview:

> I suggested this time that volume be investigated by submerging things in water. We used to teach about volume by giving the same

weight of sawdust, sand, and clay, but different volumes. But I thought maybe it would be better to do it by water, because things that are uneven can be measured by water and that's the way it's really done. When you're looking at sand versus sawdust you don't know whether it's the size or characteristics of it that are changing and so it's confusing—there is a qualitative difference, as well as a quantitative difference. But to show that something displaces a different amount of water with the same amount of weight is interesting. This is new. Still, it may be cut by the Ministry of Education during their approval of textbooks.

In contrast with the Japanese focus on doing science, U.S. publishers appeared to be seeking expertise related to *reading* and textual organization: "The publisher brought in a foremost expert on how children read, and how material can be written to help them get the most information out of it."

INVOLVEMENT OF RANK-AND-FILE TEACHERS

In addition to the exemplary teachers who write textbooks, a fairly large group of elementary school classroom teachers are consulted by Japanese publishers before they embark on revisions. A major job of the editorial staff at a textbook company is to keep in regular contact with teachers across Japan, in order to hear what is going on at local research meetings and to gain feedback on their products. One Japanese publisher convened groups of about 40 teachers in five areas of Japan to identify what they liked and disliked about the current textbook that the company was about to revise. Another Japanese publisher convened groups of five or six teachers in each of 40 locations across Japan. The textbook writers are influenced by these field data, as Mr. Motofuji explained:

When you write a textbook, you look at how the textbook has been used, study how it is actually used in practice, and you improve it and shave off parts. The textbook company has a sales force that is constantly in contact with science teachers. They hear from the teachers what is good and what isn't. They gather together the teachers and solicit their comments before the textbook revision. For example, teachers might say that a certain experiment can't be done easily, or suggest that, instead of A-B-C order, something be done in B-A-C order, or they might point out parts of the textbook that are hard to use. Teachers' comments are solicited all over the country and used as the basis to rewrite the textbooks. So it's not as if you're starting from zero.

Mr. Ono explained how one of the textbook sections he wrote was rejected by teachers in the field:

There are things of mine that have been not well received. For example, I designed one experiment where the air from a ball goes into a balloon and the ball shrinks and the balloon becomes larger than the ball. It became part of the textbook, but it was too difficult for most teachers to do. It was hard because when they attached the hose between the ball and the balloon, air leaked from somewhere. That was the feedback that the textbook company got on that section of the textbook. So, in the next textbook we changed the experiment to one in which you put something inside of water. The idea behind the ball and balloon was that air is not just air. A child has a hard time grasping the idea that air shrinks or expands. So the fact that the balloon would get bigger than the ball was interesting to them. But air leaked out and so it was too hard to do. The textbook company gathered feedback from around the country, and they identified that unit as being one that was hard to teach. Also I think the things needed to do that particular experiment—the pump and so forth—took some trouble to gather. The textbook companies regularly bring together teachers to get their impressions of the textbooks. So they hear what units are difficult to do or to understand and they tell us that. You might call it a kind of market research that we learn from. The textbook has to be something that anyone can use.

There's some split between our ideas as textbook writers and those of the teachers in the field. So the teachers writing textbooks are leading other teachers, to some extent. Teachers are conservative and do not want to change.

Both U.S. and Japanese publishers conducted field tests of the activities to be included in the science textbook. But U.S. authors did not see this as a source of information for their work. In some cases, they did not even know what the field testing found. As Dr. Aller said, "An editor could tell you that because they're the ones who get the copy." None of the U.S. interviewees mentioned systematic data-gathering on the current version of the textbook by publishers in order to determine which parts of the textbook were difficult to use. Japanese textbooks may lend themselves to this type of market research because the whole textbook is covered in class and it is used to guide lessons, not just as a reference or reading book.

PRESSURE FROM MANUFACTURERS

Japanese interviewees mentioned manufacturers of school supplies as another source of pressure on textbooks:

> Students don't use abacuses in daily life now. But the abacus manufacturing association is strong. And the members of the Diet [Japanese parliament] help them by contacting the Ministry of Education or the Ministry of International Trade and Industry. Diet members get votes from the abacus industry association, so they want to make sure abacuses remain in the curriculum. In fact, they don't care whether the abacus is taught more than one or two lessons, as long as they're bought.

According to the Japanese interviewees, such pressure results in some "ridiculous" decisions:

> The Ministry of International Trade and Industry exerted pressure so that eight-bit computers were put in the schools a number of years ago, but there was no software for them—not even game software. And if the computers are sitting around in sight and nobody's using them, it looks bad, so people put them in the storage rooms. The same kind of pressure operates for calligraphy, and music is probably the biggest issue—what instruments are used. It's hard to change that. Same with art. Same with whether bread or rice is eaten at school. Whenever there's a surplus of something, people try to make the schools use it!

No U.S. authors mentioned commercial pressure, perhaps because U.S. textbook companies themselves sell science kits and other curriculum materials. In Japan, by law, such ancillary curricular materials cannot be sold by textbook companies.

HOW DO JAPANESE TEXTBOOKS CHANGE?

Japanese teacher-authors provided several examples of the way they honed textbook lessons based on their own classroom experience. These examples recall the way that Japanese educators "polish the stone" of a classroom lesson through lesson study (Lewis & Tsuchida, 1998). Japanese authors also changed textbooks in response to new goals in the *Course of Study* such as student "initiative," "active desire to learn," and "pursuing problems . . . in their immediate environment with interest and concern" (Ministry of Education [MOE], 1998, p. 58; 1993, p. 3).

> Teachers are now looking for textbooks that support children's self-motivation to do experiments, so that might be a selling point for texts. We used to just begin the unit on plant growth by having children plant seeds. Now we begin by saying, "Let's go to the garden and see what's blooming," and have that be the starting point to talk about seed planting. There are also places in the textbooks now where the students make choices; they decide as a class whether to do experiment A, B, or C. That's new. (Mr. Motofuji)

> One thing we did is put more children in the pictures to make them interesting to the children, so that children would look at them and say, "Yes, I'd like to do that." . . . In the electricity unit, I also made some changes. Originally the unit started with trains and power plants. But our goal now is to start with electrical things that are familiar to children from their immediate environment, such as a bell or a motor, rather than with a compass, which is rather strange to them. (Mr. Ono)

Policymaking and policy implementation may be closely intertwined processes (Lewis & Tsuchida, 1997), as Mr. Motofuji noted:

> It's not just the ideas of our textbook group members that we talk about [when revising the textbook]. What's important is our knowledge of what's going on all over Japan, conversations with the Senior Science Specialist [of the Ministry of Education], research lessons, research groups, the Ministry of Education's new science plan, for which they've had designated research schools—all these shed information on the direction of science education. There are designated research schools at the ward level, the city level, the prefectural level, and the national level. The Senior Science Specialist sometimes goes to those schools and might make comments like "This is what I was hoping to see." The Senior Science Specialist also edited a volume called *The New Science Plan* . . . and I did lessons for that book and helped write it.

The Japanese authors did not see all changes in the *Course of Study* as improvements. When asked for an example of a change in textbooks caused by the *Course of Study*, Mr. Oshima, an ex-official of Ministry of Education, laughed and recalled:

Chicken eggs! At one point children all over Japan were hatching eggs at school. It was instituted in 1958, and then removed from the *Course of Study* 10 years later, at the time of the next revision. I think it was put in because someone, probably the Senior Science Specialist at the time, saw it happen in America and thought it would be good. But it created great havoc. What do you do with all the baby chicks? You can't kill them because they were created at school. And some children became unable to eat hard-boiled eggs for lunch because they felt they were eating babies!

Another change in textbooks prompted by the *Course of Study* is discussed by two educational researchers:

Researcher 1: Another change in textbooks was to combine the study of pendulums with collision of objects, probably just because someone saw them in a lesson in America or something. If it's in the *Course of Study*, then you have to put it in the textbook. That's a problem. You can't just skip over it.

Researcher 2: I was a textbook writer when that occurred and that particular section of the *Course of Study* was incredibly specific. It was really hard to write the textbook. It took us about 6 months just to figure out what it meant and how you could do it concretely. It's just a lesson that someone saw somewhere, liked, and decided to stick in. One of the committee members stuck it in.

Several Japanese interviewees expressed concern about cutting the already spare science curriculum in order to accommodate to the 5-day school week. Mr. Shioda said, "The current curriculum is just a skeleton—like the bones that are left over when you eat fish." Mr. Nagata added:

The attitude toward textbooks is like the attitude toward food rations during World War II. In principle, each person's ration was enough to keep healthy. Officials said: "This isn't enough food to keep you alive? Then chew it better." The current textbooks are like wartime rations. There's not much there, so we're supposed to chew it really well.

CONCLUSIONS

Although Japan's elementary science textbooks embody the focused, coherent approach that is often advocated by U.S. reformers, Japanese educators do find fault with their textbooks. Likening their textbooks to "wartime rations," Japanese educators argued that even simplicity can be taken too far—as when authors are cautioned not to label the liver in an illustration of the human digestive tract. Japanese authors also criticized industry pressure to include equipment such as the abacus and certain computers within the curriculum. Japanese science textbooks are, in the words of one Japanese teacher, "80% textbooks"—that is, 80% of the ideal.

Yet to many U.S. educators, even "80% textbooks" may be enviable. Less than two-thirds of the American teachers in Grades 1–4 considered their science textbooks good or excellent, according to the 1993 National Survey of Science and Mathematics Education (Weiss, Matti, & Smith, 1993). How might our findings be useful to U.S. educators who wish that their textbooks were more like Japan's? First, we might underline the Ministry of Education's crucial role in making Japanese elementary science texts lean and simple. Indeed, protecting textbooks against "extra" content appears to be a primary function of the approval system for science textbooks. Although many voices in the United States call for a focused, coherent curriculum, who will actually step forward to cut content? Ironically, the move toward increased standards and accountability in many U.S. states may further expand the content U.S. textbook publishers believe they must cover.

A second striking feature of the Japanese textbook-creation process is the leading role played by classroom teachers—both a select group of teacher-authors and a much larger group of "ordinary" teachers who critique textbooks based on their classroom use. Leading teachers work collaboratively to hone ever more sophisticated textbook lessons and ordinary teachers veto activities that are too difficult or time-consuming. Through these two processes, Japanese textbooks become the repository for lessons that continue to be refined by leading teachers. Yet they remain true to the principle that "the textbook needs to be something that anyone can use."

Third, the amount of time spent on creating Japan's thin paperback science texts is noteworthy. Although the successive editions of a textbook often look quite similar, writers report that they labor over the order, flow, examples, and experimental materials. Drafts are written, debated, rewritten several times, and critiqued by numerous individuals, including many classroom teachers, university-based researchers, and publishing company staff. One author described the writing process as "extraordinarily painstaking." Indeed, careful attention to the writing of each section of the textbook parallels the way they are later used—for example, students spend 12 to 14 lessons studying the function and nature of levers, a topic covered by just 30 sentences of text.

Although it might be tempting to think we could simply translate Japanese elementary science textbooks for use in U.S. schools, our findings also point out the strong interconnections between elementary science textbooks and many other features of Japan's educational system. Textbooks can focus on *doing* science (rather than reading about it) because the national Ministry of Education takes on the hard job of limiting content. And the limited content enables Japanese teachers to focus their attention on honing lessons—instead of reviewing voluminous texts and choosing what to teach, as American teachers must do. In addition, Japan's widespread practice of research lessons, where educators help define in concrete lessons the abstract goals of the national course of study (Lewis & Tsuchida, 1997), may provide the grass-roots support essential to ensure that the national course of study is not subverted at the local level, a fate suffered by some Ministry of Education reforms (see LeTendre, Chapter 2, this volume). Yet research lessons themselves probably could not exist without a national curriculum and an emphasis on *doing* science. These elements make it worthwhile for teachers to observe one another as they teach shared content. The Japanese elementary science textbook may be one puzzle piece of Japanese achievement. If we hope to study and adapt it to the U.S. system, however, we will have to reshape many of the surrounding pieces.

Acknowledgement. This material is based on research supported by the National Science Foundation under grants REC-9996360 and RED-9355857. Any opinions, findings, and conclusions or recommendations expressed in this publication are those of the authors and do not necessarily reflect the views of the National Science Foundation.

REFERENCES

Lewis, C., & Tsuchida, I. (1997). Planned educational change in Japan: The shift to student-centered elementary science. *Journal of Education Policy, 12*(5), 313–331.

Lewis, C., & Tsuchida, I. (1998). A lesson is like a swiftly flowing river: Research lessons and the improvement of Japanese education. *American Educator, 22*(4), 12–17, 50–52.

Ministry of Education. (1993). *Shogakkô rika shidôsho shiryô: Atarashii gakuryokukan ni tatsu rika no gakushû shidô no sôzô* [Elementary school teaching guidelines for science: Creating science instruction based upon new concept of academic ability]. Tokyo: Author.

Ministry of Education. (1998). *Shogakkô shidôsho* [Elementary school teaching guidelines]. Tokyo: Author.

Schmidt, W. H., McKnight, C. C., Cogan, L. S., Jakwerth, P. M., & Houang,

R. T. (1998). *Facing the consequences: Using TIMSS for a closer look at United States mathematics and science education.* Boston: Kluwer.

Schmidt, W. H., McKnight, C. C., & Raizen, S. A. (1997). *A splintered vision: An investigation of U.S. science and mathematics education.* Boston: Kluwer.

Weiss, I. R., Matti, M. C., & Smith, P. S. (1993). *Report of the 1993 national survey of science and mathematics education.* Chapel Hill, NC: Horizon Research.

Yoshida, M. (1999). *Lesson study: An ethnographic investigation of school-based teacher development in Japan.* Unpublished doctoral dissertation, University of Chicago.

CHAPTER 5

Comparing Japanese and U.S Teachers' Manuals: Implications for Mathematics Teaching and Learning

Shin-ying Lee and Akane Zusho

TEXTBOOK MATERIALS PLAY A SIGNIFICANT ROLE in shaping what students learn in school. Although education authorities define the curriculum framework and objectives, the textbook curriculum sets daily content, and teachers' manuals often play a significant part in determining a teacher's instructional agenda. At their best, teachers' manuals offer interconnections between curriculum standards, instructional guidance for students, and learning opportunities for teachers. When teaching is viewed as a cultural activity (Stigler & Hiebert, 1998), the information provided and approaches adopted in the teachers' manuals also suggest the cultural beliefs and assumptions for teaching and learning.

Japanese students have consistently shown high levels of mathematics achievement in international comparative studies, and researchers consider effective mathematics teaching significant in creating high-level mathematics competence. These effective teaching practices are observed regardless of region, rurality, or size of the schools. Many observers mention national curriculum as an instrumental factor leading to effective mathematics teaching and learning in Japan. National curriculum itself, however, does not lead to high student achievement, nor does it guarantee effective teaching practices in any country. The recent TIMSS (Third International Mathematics and Science Study) research showed that of the 41 countries participating in the study, 29 had a national curriculum. Countries with a national curriculum were found among the highest- and the lowest-performing countries (National Center for Education Statistics [NCES], 1996; Schmidt, McKnight, & Raizen, 1997). Academic success requires two additional conditions that complement a national curriculum: a common vision of effective pedagogical strategies and mechanisms to share the pedagogical approaches among the teachers. American scholars recently have observed that Japanese educators create these conditions through a very efficient system of teacher professional development (Kinney, 1997; Lewis & Tsuchida, 1998; Shimahara, Chapter 7, this volume). A second possibility, given less attention by researchers, is the role of teachers' manuals. Because teachers' manuals serve as a resource for obtaining instructional ideas and planning for daily lessons, they inevitably distribute knowledge about teaching.

In this chapter we analyze features of Japanese teachers' manuals for elementary school mathematics, focusing on how the manuals provide the mathematical knowledge necessary for teaching and how they suggest teaching strategies for the actual teaching of lessons. In particular we asked: What kinds of mathematics content knowledge and pedagogical suggestions are presented in the manuals? How are they related to the national curriculum standards? Is there any relationship between the instructional suggestions and Japanese classroom teaching? By comparing the characteristics of the Japanese teachers' manuals with those in the United States, we hope to highlight the different approaches in both countries and to uncover cultural views such as the role and expectation of teachers and the beliefs related to learning and teaching mathematics.

CURRICULUM AND TEXTBOOK DEVELOPMENT

Japan's Ministry of Education outlines the national curriculum in the *Course of Study* (see Azuma, Chapter 1, this volume). In addition, the ministry publishes instruction manuals based on the *Course of Study* for each subject area at each school level. The instruction manuals give a detailed explanation of the subject-matter knowledge and the principles of instruction for that subject. The ministry instruction manuals for elementary school mathematics, written mostly by university professors, school administrators, and ministry officials, outline the national vision of pedagogical approaches. Although the manuals focus on the mathematics content identified in the *Course of Study*, their approach is highly technical, often abstract, and lacks examples from classroom teaching materials. As a result, private publishing companies often publish books to help teachers and parents understand the manuals.

Textbook publishers follow the *Course of Study* and instruction manuals when developing their textbooks and teachers' manuals. The manuals, usually written by expert teachers in a user-friendly format, provide a coherent body of subject-matter knowledge and specific pedagogical suggestions for teaching the textbook content. These suggestions often involve activities from research lessons or regular classes that demonstrate their effectiveness in guiding students to meet the particular lesson goals.

In the United States, by contrast, the Department of Education does not determine what students should know and be able to do in any subject at any level of schooling. The *Goals 2000 Educate America Act*, however, has led nearly every state to design and implement curriculum frameworks and assessment instruments to monitor the state's progress toward certain standards, and the National Council of Teachers of Mathematics (NCTM) has made an effort to establish national mathematics curricular and teaching standards. Nevertheless, when setting the curriculum guidelines and selecting textbooks, local communities do not necessarily abide by national and state standards documents and instead refer to state-administered achievement tests (U.S. Department of Education, 1998). Teachers also vary greatly in their degree of reliance on textbooks for in-class instruction. School districts usually provide textbook materials for students, but the autonomy of teachers contributes to diverse teaching practices (Ball & Cohen, 1996).

Curriculum materials have played a less critical role in teaching practices in the United States for several other reasons. U.S. curriculum developers have few, if any, conversations with teachers, and they fail to appreciate the need for teachers to learn how to use new materials (Ben-Peretz, 1990; Sarason, 1982; Schwille et al., 1983). Although the curriculum designers aim to create particular kinds of learning experiences for students, U.S. educators often view textbook materials as an attempt to constrain and control both teacher knowledge and teaching (Ball & Feiman-Nemser, 1988). The ideal of professional autonomy leads American teachers to the opinion that good teachers do not follow the textbooks, but instead create their own curriculum, tailored to their students. The lessons often reflect the individual teacher's beliefs about what is important, when the material should be introduced, and the role of the student and teacher (Ball & Cohen, 1996).

CHARACTERISTICS OF TEACHERS' MANUALS

The cultural characteristics of the Japanese teachers' manuals for elementary mathematics become much clearer through comparison with resources available for American teachers. We examined the *Shinpan Sansu* series by Kyôiku Shuppan, Inc. (1993a) and two widely used American elementary mathematics series: *Everyday Mathematics* (Everyday Learning Corporation, 1998) and *Addison-Wesley Mathematics* (Scott Foresman–Addison Wesley Publishing Company, 1995a). *Everyday Mathematics*, developed by the University of Chicago School Mathematics Project, is one of the leading textbook series created specifically in response to the NCTM standards. To help teachers use the program successfully, the developers carefully integrated supplementary material for students and teachers. *Addison-Wesley Mathematics*, a mathematics textbook series popular for many years, claims to conform to NCTM standards, but the format and approach of the Addison-Wesley teachers' edition is fairly traditional. Teaching suggestions for every lesson revolve around student textbooks.

Compared with U.S. manuals, four dimensions characterize the Japanese teachers' manuals:

1. Japanese materials are concise and informative with clear adherence to the Ministry of Education curriculum guidelines.
2. The manuals provide systematic and solid mathematics content knowledge for teachers.
3. The lesson plans offer principles of conceptual organization and realistic suggestions for instruction.
4. The information in the manuals is highly mathematics-specific with little discussion of the broader learning context.

Appearance and Format

The Japanese teachers' manuals are plain and compact compared with American textbook series materials for teachers. Japanese teachers' manuals have two volumes per grade with the exception of one volume in first grade. Each volume measures 7 by 10 inches, with a thickness of approximately half an inch. Each 200- to 250-page volume weighs about one pound.

In contrast, both of the American series package the teachers' manuals in colorful and attractive boxes, with numerous books for each grade level. The *Everyday Mathematics Teacher's Resource Package* for one grade contains a total of seven books and a scope and sequence chart. They are: *Teachers' Manual and Lesson Guide* (two volumes), *Teacher's Reference Manual for Grades K–3* or . . . *for Grades 4–6* (definitions of mathematical terms and other curriculum-specific vocabulary), *Resource Book* (master copy of materials for student activities), *Balanced Assessment for K-3* or . . . *Grades 4–6*, *Creating Home-School Partnership Book* (a guide to help families understand the curriculum), and *Minute Math Booklet* (quick computational exercises for students). Each 300-page volume of *Teacher's*

Manual and Lesson Guide measures approximately 8½ by 11 inches, with a thickness of about three-quarters of an inch and a weight of about 2.5 pounds. The entire teacher's resource package for one grade weighs approximately 11.5 pounds. The *Addison-Wesley Mathematics Teacher Support Package* also comes with a one- or two-volume teachers' edition per grade, and many other supplementary materials such as student practice booklets, assessment tools, record-keeping booklets, and family math letters. The teachers' instructional edition measures 10¼ by 12 inches, with a thickness of three-quarters to one and a quarter inch per volume. Some volumes of the teachers' edition contain more than 500 pages weighing more than 5 pounds.

The differences between the appearance of American and Japanese teachers' manuals parallel the differences between the student textbooks in the two countries. Japanese textbooks are smaller, thinner, and paperback. Each student receives a personal copy and takes it home daily. They contain few, if any, illustrations and focus primarily on mathematically relevant pictures and problems. The materials present the essence of the mathematics content and are used as the main source for the lessons (Stevenson & Stigler, 1992). The thick hardback American textbooks are loaned to students for the year. In the attempt to enliven the materials, American textbooks include colorful illustrations and stories that often are related but not central to the mathematics content. Some teachers make the textbooks central to their lessons; others do not. And the size of the books makes it difficult for students to take them home.

A simple comparison of the overview section of the teachers' manuals illustrates the differences between the Japanese and American approaches. The introduction in the Japanese manuals is a succinct five-page overview that includes a discussion of the main objectives of the student textbook, a table that outlines the content topics and instructional plan for the year, and a brief summary of the kinds of information provided in the four main sections of the manual. In the American manuals, the overview is 20 pages in *Everyday Mathematics* (Everyday Learning Corporation, 1998) and 35 pages in *Addison-Wesley Mathematics* (Scott Foresman, 1995a). American manuals also include pages describing the "key features" of the series in the form of "program highlights" or "the advantage," clear attempts at marketing without regard for the usefulness of the information.

While American publishers provide materials in separate books and resource packages, Japanese manuals include all the necessary information in one compact volume with four distinct sections. In addition to the brief overview of the instructional manual, there is the red-book section, the research section, and the resource and reference section. The red-book section comprises the bulk of the Japanese teachers' manual, containing an exact duplication of the student textbook pages, surrounded by key instructional notes in the margins. All of the instructional information, as well as the answers to any math problems presented in the student textbooks, is printed in red ink, a format probably taken from traditional American teachers' manuals.

The research section consists of two main parts. The first volume of each grade contains an explanation of the mathematics concepts by strand across the 6 years of elementary school followed by more detailed grade-specific mathematics content knowledge for each unit in the book. Within each unit, teachers receive general guidance in hour-by-hour lesson plans that include mathematics goals, instructional activities, and specific points to consider during instruction. Each unit ends with a traditional paper-and-pencil form of assessment.

The last section, resource and reference, provides general pedagogical information related to the principles of developing lesson plans and the assessment of student mathematical understanding. This section also contains a complete scope and sequence chart for the entire elementary school mathematics curriculum, a materials list, and a glossary of mathematical terms introduced during that year.

Although the Japanese teachers' manuals look very plain and thin compared with the American packages, they present information in a systematic way that addresses the in-depth elementary mathematics knowledge necessary for teachers. They also provide the conceptual organization to help teachers understand and interpret the structure of the entire elementary curriculum. In other words, they include the essential elements of effective teaching. The American materials, by contrast, present a "cluttered exposure" approach. The packaging and appearance of the materials suggest that the main concern of the publishers is to make the materials appealing to a wide range of school districts and teachers. Given the variation in educational philosophy and emphasis in mathematics education across the United States, this approach to marketing seems inevitable. U.S. teachers expect materials that meet their unique needs, and publishers attempt to address these needs while creating mass-market books.

Presentation of Mathematics Content

Effective teaching develops from a teacher's understanding of the content, the scope and sequence, and the teaching method. Teachers must begin with an in-depth, substantial, and comprehensive understanding of the concepts. Add to this understanding a concern for the teaching process and the students' learning, and teachers can then proceed through a series of activities that provide students with specific instruction and opportunity for learning. Mathematics courses alone do not provide teachers with the knowledge they need to teach. It is the teachers' version of subject matter knowledge that has the most direct effect on their teaching (Ma, 1999).

The most significant difference between Japanese and American teachers' manuals is the content orientation and systematic presentation of the Japanese manuals. They present content knowledge in multiple facets, each providing slightly different information that together contributes to a coherent body of sophisticated knowledge of elementary mathematics that is highly relevant to the concepts taught. American teachers' manuals, on the other hand, function like a dictionary that defines mathematical terms in the curriculum with little attention to the structure and sequential nature of mathematics knowledge. The manuals also fail to provide substantive information to bridge teachers' understanding of the essence of the standards promoted in the textbook series and how the standards can be translated to everyday teaching.

Scope and Sequence. The Japanese *Course of Study* identifies four mathematics content areas: numbers and operations, quantities and measurement, geometrical figures, and quantitative relations. The scope and sequence charts included at the back of every teachers' manual clearly lay out the sequence of all the mathematics content knowledge students will learn in those four areas over the 6 years of elementary school. The mathematics content strands are structured in accordance with the *Course of Study* content areas except that the area of numbers and operations is further separated into two strands: one on number sense, and the other on operations. Each strand is presented on a one-page systematic chart. A flowchart represents the sequence of mathematics concepts by the units within each year and their relation to the subsequent years (see Figure 5.1). The chart lays out the structure of mathematics knowledge in a longitudinal and coherent fashion throughout the elementary school years. By examining the chart, teachers can orient themselves to the systematic and hierarchical nature of elementary mathematics as well as the developmental nature of the mathematics learning process of the students. They also can grasp the focus and expectation of student proficiency at each grade level.

Although scope and sequence charts are available in the American teachers' manuals, they contain less information on the structure of mathematics. The *Everyday Mathematics* (1998) series includes only one poster-size scope and sequence chart for each grade. The charts are organized by content strands and by monthly division from September through May, but not all of the strands relate to mathematics content, and the cells contain a mixed list of mathematics content, processes, and activities (see Figure 5.2). For example, the first-grade scope and sequence chart contains the strands

Figure 5.1. Examples from the Systematic Chart for Numbers and Operations—Operations in the Japanese Teachers' Manuals (Grades 1–3)

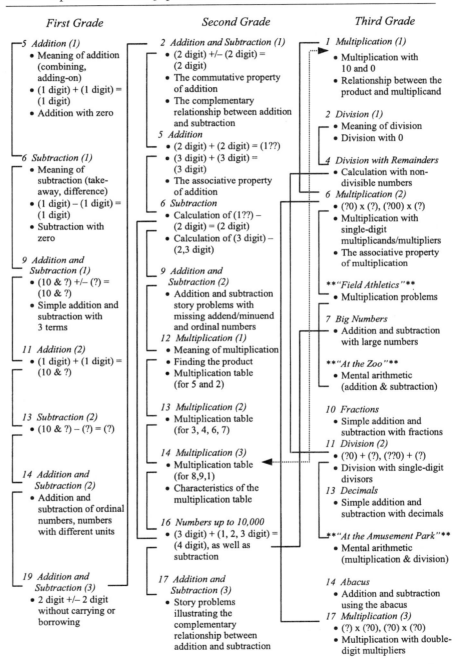

First Grade	*Second Grade*	*Third Grade*
5 *Addition (1)* • Meaning of addition (combining, adding-on) • (1 digit) + (1 digit) = (1 digit) • Addition with zero	**2** *Addition and Subtraction (1)* • (2 digit) +/− (2 digit) = (2 digit) • The commutative property of addition • The complementary relationship between addition and subtraction **5** *Addition* • (2 digit) + (2 digit) = (1??)	**1** *Multiplication (1)* • Multiplication with 10 and 0 • Relationship between the product and multiplicand **2** *Division (1)* • Meaning of division • Division with 0
6 *Subtraction (1)* • Meaning of subtraction (take-away, difference) • (1 digit) − (1 digit) = (1 digit) • Subtraction with zero	• (3 digit) + (3 digit) = (3 digit) • The associative property of addition **6** *Subtraction* • Calculation of (1??) − (2 digit) = (2 digit) • Calculation of (3 digit) − (2,3 digit)	**4** *Division with Remainders* • Calculation with non-divisible numbers **6** *Multiplication (2)* • (?0) x (?), (?00) x (?) • Multiplication with single-digit multiplicands/multipliers • The associative property of multiplication
9 *Addition and Subtraction (1)* • (10 & ?) +/− (?) = (10 & ?) • Simple addition and subtraction with 3 terms	**9** *Addition and Subtraction (2)* • Addition and subtraction story problems with missing addend/minuend and ordinal numbers **12** *Multiplication (1)* • Meaning of multiplication	****"Field Athletics"**** • Multiplication problems **7** *Big Numbers* • Addition and subtraction with large numbers
11 *Addition (2)* • (1 digit) + (1 digit) = (10 & ?)	• Finding the product • Multiplication table (for 5 and 2) **13** *Multiplication (2)* • Multiplication table (for 3, 4, 6, 7)	****"At the Zoo"**** • Mental arithmetic (addition & subtraction) **10** *Fractions* • Simple addition and subtraction with fractions
13 *Subtraction (2)* • (10 & ?) − (?) = (?)	**14** *Multiplication (3)* • Multiplication table (for 8,9,1) • Characteristics of the multiplication table	**11** *Division (2)* • (?0) + (?), (??0) + (?) • Division with single-digit divisors **13** *Decimals* • Simple addition and subtraction with decimals
14 *Addition and Subtraction (2)* • Addition and subtraction of ordinal numbers, numbers with different units	**16** *Numbers up to 10,000* • (3 digit) + (1, 2, 3 digit) = (4 digit), as well as subtraction	****"At the Amusement Park"**** • Mental arithmetic (multiplication & division)
19 *Addition and Subtraction (3)* • 2 digit +/− 2 digit without carrying or borrowing	**17** *Addition and Subtraction (3)* • Story problems illustrating the complementary relationship between addition and subtraction	**14** *Abacus* • Addition and subtraction using the abacus **17** *Multiplication (3)* • (?) x (?0), (?0) x (?0) • Multiplication with double-digit multipliers

Figure 5.2. Examples from the First-grade Scope and Sequence Chart, from *Everyday Mathematics,* © 1998 by SRA/McGraw-Hill, Chicago, Illinois. Used with permission.

	Operations (+, −, x) and Relations (<, >, =)	
	Games and exercises for skills in arithmetic. Memorized number facts. Many ways to get the same result. Operation families. Informal work with properties.	Problem solving and number models: Mental and written arithmetic in problem contexts.
September (approx. Lesson 1–18)	• Two-Fisted Penny game for equivalences	• Number stories: addition and subtraction with pennies and animal contexts • Penny Dice game for probability • Dice Throw tally count
October (approx. Lesson 19–33)	• Top It card game for <, >, and = • One or two more or less dice game • *Review:* Two-Fisted Penny game	• Number Stories: specified numbers • Number Stories: verbal, concrete, pictorial, and number-model representations
November (approx. Lesson 34–49)	• Top It game with total dots on dominoes for <, >, = • Fact Drills with sums of parts of dominoes • Sort dominoes for equivalent sums • Beat the Calculator game for simple sums • *Review:* relation words and symbols (<, >, =) • Top It card game with relation symbol cards • Secret Number Calculator game for relations	• Number stories: comparison subtraction with pennies context • Number stories: comparison and ordinal numbers with animal poster • Number stories : addition and subtraction using weights on animal poster • Number stories: contexts and labels • Mental arithmetic: routines • *Numbers About Me* books

Figure 5.2. (*Continued*)

December (approx. Lesson 50–56)	• Domino Top It game with relation symbol cards • Top It card game for subtraction • Penny Grab game with written number models • Addition/subtraction number families with parts and totals on dominoes • What's my Rule? game for addition and subtraction facts practice • Number models from Penny Grab game	• Use of context box (measurement unit or other reference) for all number work including drills • *Review*: various meanings of addition and subtraction • Number stories: number models • Mental arithmetic: continue sharing strategies using numbers from animal weights poster
January (approx. Lesson 57–79)	• Pan-balance and relation-symbol games • Sorting dominoes by sums 1-10 • Extension of single-digit addition facts to sums of 10's	• Number stories: comparison with School Store poster • Number stories: with children's weights and calculators • Mental arithmetic: extend strategies with adding and subtracting 10's
February (approx. Lesson 80–96)	• Tric-Trac game for addition facts • Sums on the number line • Differences as distances on the number line • Mental arithmetic: adding 10's to any number • Mental arithmetic: subtracting 10's from any number	• Mental arithmetic: continue solution strategies • Number stories and mental arithmetic: coin-value and animal posters

of numeration and counting, operations and relations, data collection and analysis, geometry, measures and reference frames, rules and patterns, and money—all in the domain of formal mathematics. Other strands such as problem solving and mental arithmetic are processes rather than content. In the monthly charts, none of the strand cells is empty, implying that learning of mathematics concepts in all strands should take place in every month. Some of the mathematics concepts are ambiguous, and there is little indication of the connection between strands within the year or across grade levels. In other words, they do not provide coherence through horizontal nor vertical connections.

Addison-Wesley Mathematics teachers' editions do provide the longitudinal scope and sequence information from kindergarten through eighth grade. But it, too, is cumbersome: a 13-page scope and sequence chart with 18 strands. The strands identified in the curriculum include broad non-mathematics content that seems to characterize the American approach to mathematics education. Specific mathematics content strands include algebra, concepts and computation, data collection and analysis, geometry, graphs and graphing, measurement, time and money, pattern relations and functions, ratio proportion and percentage, and statistics and probability. Others are related to mathematics processes; for example, estimation, problem solving, mental math, and critical thinking and logic. In addition, the strands touch on topics related to technical aspects of mathematics such as calculator skills, computer technology, and consumer math. Cooperative learning skills also make up a strand. Within each strand, there is a list of the subcategories that are coded Teach and Reinforce across the span from kindergarten through eighth grade. For each subcategory the time span to teach and later to reinforce usually lasts for several years. The sequence of learning the subcategories within the strand, however, is not indicated, implying that mathematics concepts take several years to introduce, develop, and learn.

Although both *Everyday Mathematics* (Everyday Learning Corporation, 1998) and *Addison-Wesley Mathematics* (Scott Foresman, 1995a) claim that their curricula were developed based on National Council of Teachers of Mathematics (NCTM) standards, they do not make clear how the curricula specifically relate to the standards. Japanese manuals, in contrast, provide teachers with clear cognitive maps to understand the structure and connectedness of the entire elementary mathematics curriculum through the information presented in the scope and sequence charts.

Content Knowledge. The mathematics content information presented in the Japanese and American manuals reflects significantly different approaches to the structure of the curriculum. Because Japanese view learning mathematics as sequential tasks based on the structure of mathematics knowledge, the manuals organize the information according to the fundamental elements of elementary mathematics. In the United States, following the spiral exposure approach to mathematics teaching and learning, the manuals tend to offer generic and definitional information relevant to mathematics concepts.

The research section of the Japanese teachers' manuals presents an overview of the four mathematics content areas, again according to the Japanese *Course of Study*. These 20 pages give a big-picture overview of the mathematics knowledge students need to learn in elementary school and a quick and coherent overall orientation to the mathematics concepts students learn within each content area. It provides the set of relationships between mathematics concepts, significance, and procedures. For example, in three pages, the explanation for the content area of quantities and measurement includes the following:

1. The definition of "quantities" in this series of textbooks and how measurement is related to quantity. It describes the domains of quantities covered, the instructional goals, and the significance of measurement when one tries to measure or compare quantities.
2. The general approaches used for comparison and measurement of the quantities. The approaches include direct comparison of two quantities; indirect comparison of two quantities with the help of a third object using an arbitrary unit and using a standard unit; and indirect measurement for quantities that cannot be measured directly.
3. The mathematics formulas introduced in the textbook series and the advantage of using formulas. It lists all the formulas used in the curriculum in the domains of area, volume, and speed and presents a justification of the merits of these formulas related to their usefulness for the analysis of the indirect measurements. It then presents examples of how to derive the formula for measuring the area of a rectangle and a circle. Finally, it offers suggestions of ways to present the topic to students in order to convince them of the merit of the formula.

In this matter the manuals present the general orientation and the significant key elements embedded in each of the mathematics strands.

The research section also goes beyond the overview of the mathematics content for the entire elementary curriculum to present more detailed, grade-specific content knowledge. For every unit in every grade, it indicates the overview of the mathematics content and goals, the mathematics instructional system, the overall instructional plan, and the key points for instruction. The focus then shifts to pedagogically relevant content knowledge. Mathematics information is explained in the context of the critical pedagogical issues that are important for teaching students at that particular grade. For example, in the overview of teaching "Area" in fourth grade:

> As far as the concept of the "extent"(size) is concerned, students had experiences in the first grade when they (1) compared two pieces of paper figures that overlap, (2) compared the space of the bulletin board by counting the number of pictures pinned onto it, and (3) counted the number of squares on a graph paper while they were crossing out the checkers. In the second grade, they had the experience of paving a flat floor with a number of congruent squares, or with isosceles right triangles. Thus, students have acquired, to some degree, the understanding of the concept of the "size."
>
> Those experiences, however, provided only a vague concept of "area," and it is merely intuitive, based on manipulative experiences. For example, when we talk about "extent of a room," we do not know if it means two-dimensional or three-dimensional or whether "extent of a room" would be judged by the narrowness of the room. This is because we are not strictly distinguishing two different concepts: "Length is a one-dimensional quantity" and "extent is a two-dimensional quantity."
>
> In addition, we have practiced the measurement of quantities such as length, volume, weight, etc., in the following four steps: (1) Direct comparison, (2) Indirect comparison, (3) Measurement in units of an arbitrary unit, and (4) Measurement in units of the international standard unit.
>
> In this unit, we will again follow these four steps for students to learn the concept of area. Thus, we can tell students that once we choose an appropriate unit, the area can be numerically expressed as the amount of unit area within the concerned area. It is important to make sure students understand the concept of area and the meaning of the measurement (*Kyôiku Shuppan, Inc.*, 1993b, p. 132).

The explanation gives teachers a better understanding of the typical level of mathematics knowledge at this particular grade by presenting the relationships that connect the mathematical concepts over time. The discussion includes how the particular concepts learned in this unit are related to what the students have learned in previous years; where the concepts of this unit will lead in the future; the critical aspects of instruction; and the interconnected knowledge of the field of elementary mathematics and mathematics learning. In other words, it outlines the linear sequence in the topics for every content area, thereby providing the vertical continuity of the horizontally arranged curriculum.

Both of the American teachers' resource packages adopt the mathematics dictionary approach. Teachers receive reference manuals with several hundred pages of information, grouped according to the mathematical content strands. But the orientation often focuses on the explanation of individual mathematics terms and only implicitly provides the structure of mathematics knowledge, without discussing issues relevant to the teaching of those mathematics concepts.

The *Everyday Mathematics Teacher's Reference Manual, Grades 4–6* (Everyday Learning Corporation, 1999b) discusses eight mathematics topics in 121 pages. The topics identified do not match the topics from the NCTM standards or the strands in their own scope and sequence chart. Although teachers are supplied with rich resources to review and gain mathematics knowledge, the knowledge is not structured in a way that can directly benefit teachers in their teaching. This lack of the orientation and focus on elementary mathematics is illustrated in the overview for "Topics" by the teachers' reference manual:

> In some ways these strands are similar to the branches of mathematics in secondary and college curricula. Much of the familiar arithmetic content of the elementary curriculum is found in the topics Numeration and Order, Operations, Measures and Measurement, and Reference Frames. However, many applications of arithmetic are found in the topics Algebra and Uses of Variables, Data and Chance, and Geometry and Spatial Sense, and activities based in these topics are often used to motivate more traditional arithmetic. (p. 1)

Using the content topic of Measures and Measurement in *Everyday Mathematics Teacher's Reference Manual, Grades 4–6* (Everyday Learning Corporation, 1999b) as an example, there are 15 pages of explanations organized by different types of measures including personal, U.S. customary and metric, other measures, and measures in geography. Within each type are additional definitions. The terms have a clear definition, but they are isolated. The authors make few attempts to integrate the mathematics framework or the process of mathematics teaching and learning. In their attempt to relate mathematics to children's everyday life experience, they explain only the superficial and procedural. For example, the overview statement states:

> Measurement is one of the most common uses of mathematics in daily life. Children need to know how to measure and how to interpret other people's measure. Because all measures are estimates, knowing how to measure means knowing how to approximate and deal with error. Measures may provide the most common context for which we need to know arithmetic. Measures along with their units, tell "how much" of something there is. You can perform arithmetic operations with measure numbers and obtain results that make sense. (p. 46)

These types of orientation differ greatly from the Japanese approach, which offers specific mathematics and pedagogical information. After wading through pages and pages of information, American teachers may find the definition of the concept, but not the elements necessary for their teaching.

As for the grade-specific information that goes along with the lessons, *Everyday Mathematics* (Everyday Learning Corporation, 1998) presents significantly more math content information than does *Addison-Wesley Mathematics* (Scott Foresman, 1995a). The information, however, is again presented at a superficial level without specific mathematical background and approaches to teaching. The explanation of "What is Area?" in the *Everyday Mathematics Fourth Grade Teacher's Manual and Lesson Guide, Volume B* (Everyday Learning Corporation, 1999a) content highlights offered this example:

> Just as *length* and *perimeter* (or *circumference*) are measures of distance along a linear path, *area* is a measure of a finite amount of surface. This surface may lie in a single plane (for example, the interior of a rectangle), or it may exist in 3-dimensional space (for example, the curved surface of a cylinder or cone).
>
> It is important to note that, like other numerical measures, a measure of area always includes both a number and a unit. Units of area are typically *square units* based on some linear unit (for example, square yard, square meter, square mile). Note that there are also some traditional units of area that are not square units; for example, an *acre* of land is said to have been based, a long time ago, on the amount of land a farmer could plow in one day. (pp. 494–495)

The focus on the fundamental mathematics concepts also extends to the glossary. Here again, the Japanese manuals provide a clear and thorough explanation of the mathematical meaning of the terms. Table 5.1 lists the glossary definitions for "fraction" in the three sets of teachers' manuals. The Japanese definition provides a thorough explanation of the meanings of fraction throughout elementary mathematics. Both the American manuals provided a simple definition unlikely to help teachers extend their understanding of the concept.

The multifaceted presentations of the mathematics knowledge in the Japanese manuals offer teachers a systematic mathematics knowledge base for the content defined by the *Course of Study*. With those understandings, teachers have the foundation to teach mathematics with depth and thoroughness.

Orientation Toward Teaching and Suggestions for Instruction

The actual lesson plans in the Japanese and American teachers' manuals reflect the differences in mathematics teaching observed in the classrooms

Table 5.1. Glossary Definitions for "Fraction" in Different Teacher Manuals

Shinpan Sansu	*Everyday Mathematics*	*Addison-Wesley Mathematics*
In *Teacher's Edition*, all grades	In *Teacher's Reference Manual, Grades K–3* (p. 244)	In *First Grade Teachers' Edition* (p. T4)
	Fraction	**Fractions**
There are several situations in which fractions are used. One can think of these situations as representing the meaning of fractions. The fraction $\frac{a}{b}$:	A way of naming a number of the equal parts of some unit.	one half one third one fourth
1. Can represent "a" pieces of an amount divided into "b" equal pieces.	In *Teacher's Reference Manual, Grades 4–6* (p. 327)	In *Fourth Grade Teachers' Edition* (p. 530)
2. Can represent a certain measure	**Fraction**	**Fraction**
3. Is the ratio between "a" and "b"	A number in the form $\frac{a}{b}$ or a / b,	A number that expresses parts of a whole or a set.
4. Is the quotient of $a \div b$	where a and b are whole numbers and	
5. Can represent "a" times the simple fraction $\frac{1}{b}$	b is not 0. Fractions are used to name part of a whole object or part of a	
6. Can represent the action of dividing an amount into "b" equal pieces, and gathering "a" parts of "b"	whole collection of objects, or to compare two quantities. A fraction can represent division; for example	Example: $\frac{3}{4}$
Sometimes, is referred to	$\frac{a}{b}$ can be thought of as a divided by b.	
1. as "partition fractions"		
2. as "measurement fractions"		
3. as "proportional fractions" or ratios		
4. as quotients		

by researchers. Japanese manuals present a conceptual approach whereas the American ones approach teaching as a procedural task. As Japanese and American teachers use the manuals, they are guided to different views of what mathematics teaching entails.

Conceptual versus Procedural Approaches to Teaching. Researchers report that Japanese teachers teach mathematics lessons in a coherent fashion. Stevenson and Stigler (1992) use the analogy of a good story to describe Japanese lessons that engage the students' interest in a series of interconnected events. The lesson has an introduction, a conclusion, and a consistent theme. The suggestions for teachers in the resource and reference section reveal the Japanese view of the "lesson." When teachers plan their lessons, the first critical elements to consider are the mathematical goals and learning sequences for the "unit." Each unit contains a coherent body of mathematics knowledge components and clear mathematical goals. With these in mind, the content goals for each lesson are set, and activities are planned to meet the lesson goals. The approach focuses on attaining the mathematics goals through successively building an understanding of the components of a given mathematics concept. The concepts and skills students learn in one lesson become the foundation for the activities in the next lesson. By meeting the specific instructional goals for each lesson, teachers will eventually accomplish the mathematics objective for that unit.

A lesson plan from the teachers' manual for the unit of "Area" in fourth grade provides an example of the Japanese approach. The unit goals are:

1. To understand the concept of area and the meaning of measurement in the context of area
2. To learn the methods used to figure out the area of rectangles and squares, and then derive the formula for calculating the area
3. To understand the different units for measuring area including cm^2, m^2, acre, hectare, and km^2.

With those goals identified, 10 hours of lessons are set. The lessons begin by introducing the concept of area and the unit of area, exploring the concept of the area of squares and rectangles, and developing the concept into mathematical formulas. It then moves to understanding bigger units of area, relationships between the different units, and finding the area of complicated shapes consisting of a combination of squares and rectangles. Finally, it introduces the understanding of bigger units of area that are relevant in real-life settings. This kind of orientation to lesson plans relies heavily on the teacher's thorough understanding of the components of elementary mathematics.

Because the unit guides students to develop mathematics concepts in a sequential order, the learning activities within each lesson and among the lessons over time must be connected. Each lesson builds on the next. This interconnectedness of the lessons is one of the main differences between the Japanese and American approaches to teaching mathematics (Tsuchida & Lewis, Chapter 3, this volume). Understanding of a mathematical concept takes in-depth discussion of the topic over several lessons. Coherence in learning not only happens within a lesson, but also takes place over several lessons. In addition to these general principles for constructing individual lesson plans, Japanese teachers' manuals also suggest the instructional plans for every unit in the curriculum.

Setting clear mathematics goals for the unit and for each lesson in the unit, however, does not necessarily lead to effective lessons. In addition to the mathematics concept, when planning a lesson teachers must consider the motivation of students, the use of materials, the control of time, and the specific focus for instruction. The Japanese materials prepare teachers to think about "teaching" in broad and specific lesson contexts: From clearly understanding the mathematics unit goal to engaging students in a particular activity in a lesson. The manuals treat teachers as professionals who need to have content and pedagogical knowledge in order to prepare their lessons.

American teachers' resource manuals suggest a different approach to teaching. The information in the manuals presents the view that teachers are "managers" of the classroom. The teaching section in the *Everyday Mathematics Teacher's Reference Manual, Grades 4–6* (Everyday Learning Corporation, 1999b) includes classroom management, curriculum management, and a literature list. Information on managing classroom displays, activity materials, and the students themselves are presented as rules for teachers to follow. Mathematical ideas receive no mention. Teaching is oriented to procedures, materials, and activities, but not mathematics itself. A typical example from the management strategies for "built-in" mathematics stated:

> When disputes that could be settled either way arise, have each disputant choose a number between 1 and 100. Pick a number yourself and tell it to a third party or write it down secretly. Explain that the one whose guess is closest to your number will be the "winner." After settling the issue, ask questions such as "Is this fair? What makes it fair?" You can extend the range of numbers as appropriate for the situation or the grade level. Whenever the opportunity to choose an option arises, have students vote. Tell them to vote

for what they want, and that they can vote one time. Be sure that they understand that the option receiving the most votes is the one by which all must abide. Students can then tally, count, and compare totals. In case of ties, ask the students about a fair way to proceed. (p. 203)

Examples such as this suggest that the teacher's responsibility in the lessons is to focus on setting up the activities and making the rules clear. The mathematics understanding presumably will derive from the process of the activities. In this sense, teaching is a collection of procedural management tasks rather than development of specific mathematics knowledge.

Guided Instruction. Teachers' manuals in both countries provide lesson plans that use an inductive approach to sequencing lessons, usually requiring a blending of content and pedagogy information. The manuals differ, however, in the conceptual and procedural guidance given to teachers. The Japanese manuals provide the basic structure of the lesson plans for each unit, hour-by-hour in most cases, both in the research and red-book sections. In the research section, the lesson plans are based on the principles of mathematics teaching. For each hour of the lesson, mathematical aims, instructional activities, and particular key points are presented in a synchronized chart. The information goes one step beyond the instructional plan for the unit by outlining the particular features of the mathematics, the developing nature of the mathematical thinking of the students, and the critical mathematical ideas. It also presents the conceptual outline for the lesson script.

In the red-book section, the actual lesson scripts are presented in a brief and succinct form following the students' textbook pages. The mathematical goal of each lesson is again highlighted and here the lesson flow is structured mainly through leading questions that engage students to think about, discuss, or debate the mathematics content. This type of question contrasts with questions that ask for a specific answer. Because Japanese teachers use the whole-class approach to teaching, motivating all students to engage in the mathematics learning activities is a prerequisite to a successful lesson. Since there is no immediate correct answer, leading questions play the significant role by inviting all students to engage in the problem-solving process. Japanese education promotes the idea that students learn best by struggling to solve the problem, either individually or through a disagreement with other students. By inviting students to think through problems, teachers can engage all students in discussions and debates about methods to solve the problem, pros and cons of different methods, and the relationships between the different approaches. Therefore, leading questions begin most lessons. For example, in the first lesson of the area unit, the lesson plan suggests that teachers present two pieces of paper, one 3 × 5 cm rectangle and one 4 cm square. The two leading questions are: "Which one is bigger?" and "How can we figure out which one is bigger?" Mathematics activities and discussions focus on responses to these questions. And all students can participate in the learning process.

Scaffolding students through the thinking processes is the central art of mathematical teaching. Japanese manuals give teachers the means to engage students in in-depth discussions. Each lesson plan usually contains two or three leading questions, including examples of common student responses and suggestions for handling student misconceptions. This information constitutes a rough script of the lesson. Teachers can anticipate the nature of the discussion that is likely to occur and therefore better lead the discussion.

The American teachers' lesson guides adopted the "cluttered exposure" approach to teaching and learning. The materials include ideas and pictures that may or may not be relevant to the actual mathematics ideas being presented to the students. Virtually every unit includes information not related to mathematics, such as vocabulary or the application of current educational theories and approaches (cooperative learning, connecting mathematics learning to literature and reading, connecting to community, technology in the classroom, and multiple intelligences). The American concern for different student populations results in information on meeting the needs of specific populations of students such as gifted, at-risk, English-as-a-second-language (ESL), and those with different learning styles. In addition, there are also a number of recommendations for supplemental activities (i.e., math center activity, project activity, backpack activity, one-minute activity, math log, math journal, math messages, math boxes). All of the above information is presented in a seemingly endless mish-mash of boxes and sidebars. Viewed positively, teachers could use this plethora of information as a source to meet their needs. But the information also makes it difficult for teachers to differentiate what is important and what is peripheral, a problem that is exacerbated for teachers who do not have a solid understanding of the content.

The actual lesson plans offered in the American manuals resemble modules of activities. The objectives of the lessons, when presented, often are procedural and lack delineation of the essence of the mathematical concept. For example, objectives such as "To measure area in square centimeters and to multiply to find area" or "To solve problems by finding related problems" basically describe the activities of the lessons rather than address the mathematics content goals. The lessons follow a consistent format within each series. In *Everyday Mathematics Fourth Grade Teacher's Manual and Lesson Guide* (Everyday Learning Corporation, 1999a), the sequence is "Getting Started," "Instruction and Activities," and "Practice and Extension." In *Addison-Wesley Mathematics Teacher's Edition* (Scott Foresman, 1995b) it is "Motivate and Teach," "Check Understanding," and "Practice and Apply."

The suggestions almost always follow a step-by-step series of activities for teachers or students. The lessons often start with rote memorization of certain mathematics facts, review of the definition of certain mathematical concepts, or checking the answers for a previously completed worksheet. Sometimes the beginning relates to the day's math concept; sometimes it does not. As a result, it does not always create a motivating atmosphere. The main instructional activities for the lessons include steps and procedures. In many cases specific procedures are clearly stated. For example, in the lesson on area in *Everyday Mathematics Fourth Grade Teacher's Manual and Lesson Guide, Volume B* (Everyday Learning Corporation, 1999a), students are to estimate the area of polygons by counting squares from a page in the journal book. The manual states: "For Problems 2–4, students should count whole squares and half squares to find the total area of each polygon. In problems 5–7, a good strategy is to count whole squares first, and then combine partial squares to form whole squares" (p. 513). If teachers follow the lesson script, they will inevitably teach in a procedural fashion. Although the layouts of the lesson plans are different in the two American series, both take a procedural approach to instructional activities.

Teaching Schedule. An important factor allowing the Japanese to successfully implement the national curriculum is the cultural idea and practice of "keeping up with the teaching schedule." The Japanese *Course of Study* sets up the mastery expectation level for students, and the instructional manuals to the *Course of Study* include suggested amounts of time for each unit. The textbook companies follow these guidelines in their textbook materials and lesson plans, setting up lessons that teachers can usually finish in an hour. Teachers, in turn, try hard to keep up with the suggested teaching schedule. Even if they do not follow the textbook lesson plan, they are aware of the expectation to meet the unit goal on schedule. In this way the national standards are reinforced.

In the United States, there is no expectation to finish the curriculum at any grade level. Teachers often pick and choose what content they include and which lessons they teach. In the *Everyday Mathematics Fourth Grade Teacher's Manual and Lesson Guide, Volume B* (Everyday Learning Corporation, 1999a), this approach is explicitly stated:

> Covering all the lessons in the unit should take about three weeks. . . . If there are fewer than three weeks left, consider doing Lessons 129, 134, 135 first so

that you can use the results of the assessments to help you identify which topics your students need to review. You need not worry if students do not complete all the lessons in the fourth grade program—all important topics will be revisited in Grades 5 and 6 in new contexts. (p. 592)

The statement reflects the American belief in the spiral curriculum approach to math education, that is, that students learn when provided with repeated exposure to concepts, skills, and procedures in a variety of different contexts over time. There is no clear standard or time frame to expect students to master the specific mathematics content and, therefore, no clear standard and expectation of what to teach within any school year. The idea of meeting the needs of individual students further complicates the matter. Every student is considered an individual learner with his or her own learning characteristics, perhaps a different competency level or a different learning style. Teachers believe they must provide different instruction for students at varying levels, and the teachers' manuals reflect these beliefs. Because Japanese teachers believe that all students should and can learn the same material, they attempt to help all students learn and to keep the class on the teaching schedule. Although the manual states that "some students may have difficulty learning this concept at this time," it does not suggest using different learning materials or giving different assessments to students.

Specific Focus on Mathematics versus the Broader Learning Context

Compared with the American manuals, Japanese manuals contain only information specific to mathematics teaching and learning in the classroom, probably indicating that the most important role for a Japanese teacher is to guide student learning and that mathematics lessons are the main setting where serious mathematics learning takes place. In the American view, learning experiences outside of school mathematics lessons affect student competency. Because lack of parental involvement is often considered a cause of low achievement, schools and teachers work hard to introduce activities that involve parents in their children's mathematics learning. For that reason, communicating with parents and encouraging them to help their children at home becomes an important role of American teachers. In turn, American manuals include family activities, family math, home links, home messages, and sample letters for teachers to send home. By contrast, the Japanese teachers' manuals contain absolutely no mention of the role of the parents or the home environment as it relates to student learning of mathematics. Perhaps it is the norm that Japanese parents support their children's academic endeavors either at home or through supplementary private education so there is no need for this discussion in the manuals. In any case, the manuals' emphasis on the classroom as the main learning site and teachers as the main knowledge source seems to reflect and reinforce the cultural expectation of the role of teachers in Japan. When it comes to mathematics teaching and learning, ability and family background differences among the students are not important.

The American manuals also make suggestions relating mathematics lessons to the learning of other subjects—for example, to topics relevant to science, health, social studies, language arts, or fine arts. Additional non-mathematics content information includes the life of certain mathematicians, the history of mathematics, and world geography. This information reflects the effort to encourage mathematics learning in broader educational contexts and to make learning mathematics more relevant to the real world and to students' everyday life experience. In Japan, the goal of mathematics education in elementary school is to introduce the "formal" mathematics in an interesting and relevant way. Japanese manuals, therefore, approach the teaching of elementary mathematics from a highly defined, subject-specific dimension.

CONCLUSION

Research indicates that effective mathematics instruction is a norm in Japanese classrooms. Japanese teachers are able to deliver effective lessons because they have a solid understanding of the topics taught and are knowledgeable of the elements of good mathematics instruction. Japanese teachers' manuals contribute to professional practice by creating and sharing the knowledge base for mathematics teaching. The manuals interpret the Ministry of Education *Course of Study* and instructional guidelines in a clear, systematic, coherent, and sequential fashion that guides teachers in their everyday teaching. The focus of the manuals is on formal elementary mathematics knowledge and how to help students acquire that specific knowledge. For every lesson in the curriculum, the manuals illustrate the conceptual structure and the actual sequence that would lead to a good lesson. The hierarchical and developmental approach to mathematical concepts helps teachers to analyze the learning stages of the students and to orient their teaching. The implementation of the national curriculum is achieved through the cultural expectation that all teachers teach and all students learn the mathematics concepts laid out in the curriculum.

The National Commission on Teaching and America's Future (1996) claimed that in the United States there is no system in place to ensure that teachers get access to the knowledge they need. "Most schools and teachers cannot achieve the goals set forth in new educational standards not because they are unwilling, but because they do not know how, and the systems they work in do not support them in doing so" (p. 1). The search for effective teaching in the United States has focused on generic relationships across subject areas and has ignored the content-specific character of teaching. As American mathematics educators struggle to translate research findings related to the development of mathematics knowledge and mathematical thinking and to implement the NCTM standards, it is important and necessary to consider the quality of teachers' manuals and their use in creating a common vision of mathematics teaching and sharing successful pedagogical approaches.

REFERENCES

Ball, D. L., & Cohen, D. K. (1996). Reform by the book: What is—or might be—the role of curriculum materials in teacher learning and instructional reform? *Educational Researcher, 25*(9), 6–8, 14.

Ball, D. L., & Feiman-Nemser, S. (1988). Using textbooks and teachers' guides: A dilemma for beginning teachers and teacher educators. *Curriculum Inquiry, 18*(4), 401–423.

Ben-Peretz, M. 1990. *The teacher-curriculum encounter: Freeing teachers from the tyranny of texts.* Albany: State University of New York Press.

Everyday Learning Corporation. (1998). *Everyday mathematics.* [The University of Chicago School Mathematics Project.] Chicago: Author.

Everyday Learning Corporation. (1999a). *Everyday mathematics fourth grade teacher's manual and lesson guide, Volume B.* [The University of Chicago School Mathematics Project.] Chicago: Author.

Everyday Learning Corporation. (1999b). *Everyday mathematics teacher's reference manual, grades 4–6.* [The University of Chicago School Mathematics Project.] Chicago: Author.

Kinney, C. (1997). Building an excellent teacher corps: How Japan does it. *American Educator, 21*(4), 16–23.

Kyôiku Shuppan, Inc. (1993a). *Shinpan sansû* [New Mathematics]. Tokyo: Author.

Kyôiku Shuppan, Inc. (1993b). *Shinpan sansû kyôshiyô shidôsho, grade 4 second semester* [New Mathematics Teacher's Edition]. Tokyo: Author.

Lewis, C., & Tsuchida, I. (1998). A lesson is like a swiftly flowing river: Research lessons and the improvement of Japanese education. *American Educator, 22*(4), 12–17, 50–52.

Ma, L. (1999). *Knowing and teaching elementary mathematics: Teachers' understanding of fundamental mathematics in China and the United States.* Mahwah, NJ: Erlbaum.

National Center for Education Statistics. (1996). *Pursuing excellence: A study of U.S. eighth-grade mathematics and science achievement in international context.* Washington, DC: U.S. Government Printing Office.

National Commission on Teaching and America's Future. (1996). *What matters most: Teaching for America's future.* New York: Author.

Sarason, S. B. (1982). *The culture of the school and the problem of change.* Boston: Allyn and Bacon.

Schmidt, W. H., McKnight, C. C., & Raizen, S. A. (1997). *A splintered vision: An investigation of U.S. science and mathematics education.* Boston: Kluwer.

Schwille, J., Porter, A., Floden, R., Freeman, D., Knapp, L., Kuhs, T., & Schmidt, W. (1983). Teachers as policy brokers in the content of elementary school mathematics. In L. Shulman & G. Sykes (Eds.), *Handbook of teaching and policy* (pp. 370–391). New York: Longman.

Scott Foresman–Addison Wesley Publishing Company. (1995a). *Addison-Wesley mathematics.* Menlo Park, CA: Author.

Scott Foresman–Addison Wesley Publishing Company. (1995b). *Addison-Wesley mathematics teacher's edition.* Menlo Park, CA: Author.

Stevenson, H. W., & Stigler, J. W. (1992). *The learning gap.* New York: Summit Books.

Stigler, J. W., & Hiebert, J. (1998). Teaching is a cultural activity. *American Educator, 22*(4), 4–11.

U.S. Department of Education. (1998). *The educational system in the United States: Case study findings.* Washington, DC: Author.

PART III

Teaching and Professional Development: Working to Improve the Standards

E VEN THOUGH MOST STATES have standards documents and most school districts have created corresponding courses of study in each subject area, U.S. teachers have a great deal of latitude in choosing the content of their lessons. If pressure to conform to an external standard exists, it comes from the need to prepare students for the proficiency tests that have been employed by most states over the last 2 decades. A second constraint on a teacher's ability to decide content comes from various prepackaged programs that are adopted at the local level—for example, Math Their Way at the elementary school and History Alive at the high school.

Because Japanese teachers, in contrast, must follow a national curriculum, their freedom would seem to be restricted. The authors in this section, however, point out many ways that Japanese teachers exercise freedom within the context of a centralized system of education—as individuals in their own classrooms and as members of professional teams. In some cases, the Ministry of Education has taken the lead by supporting professional development activities and by encouraging teachers to exercise more pedagogical creativity and innovation in order to respond to the diversity of their students. In other cases, teachers have taken the initiative in groups and as individuals.

In Chapter 6, Harold Stevenson points out that although the Ministry of Education creates a national curriculum and requires schools to distribute approved textbooks to their students, it does not have a mechanism to ensure that Japanese teachers are indeed following the curriculum and using the textbooks. The greatest pressure to conform to the national curriculum comes from the high school and university entrance examinations that include content from the national curriculum. Within the heterogeneous classrooms of the compulsory grades (1–9), however, teachers must respond to the intellectual and social diversity among students while following a uniform curriculum. Stevenson outlines ways in which teachers, using many strategies also found in U.S. classrooms, respond to the individual differences among their students. At the high school level, where tracking exists between and within schools, the national curriculum allows for curricular differentiation within each of the major subject areas, and some publishers have responded by creating various levels of textbooks for the same course.

Nobuo Shimahara, in Chapter 7, describes a way in which the national curriculum affects Japanese in-service programs. Because Japanese teachers of the same grade or subject area follow the standard curriculum, they are able to collaborate across local, prefectural, and national levels, making it possible for in-service programs to focus on specific approaches to teaching the subject matter. Compared with U.S. graduate and professional development programs that often neglect content and focus on generic teaching strategies and other broader information, the Japanese in-service system has a far greater focus on pedagogical content knowledge—that is, ways of teaching specific content.

At the level of daily classroom practice, the institutional structure and culture of the U.S. educational system provide teachers few opportunities to collaborate. Graduate programs dominate teacher professional development in the United States, and for most teachers an advanced degree is an individual pursuit that takes them away from their colleagues. One place collaboration occurs, however, is in the writing of educational standards, and many of the best teachers sit on standards committees at the local, state, or national level. In this highly creative process teachers may influence educational reform, but the way their efforts actually affect classroom instruction is less clear because the majority of teachers do not view these standards documents as useful in the preparation of their daily lessons. Most U.S. teachers, instead, consider their classrooms of students as distinct entities that require unique preparation tailored to the group and to individual students. In this context, standards that might increase uniformity may seem counterproductive. Yet, as Stevenson points out, Japanese teachers, in a collaborative context, adjust the national curriculum to fit their particular classrooms of students.

CHAPTER 6

Individual Differences and Japan's *Course of Study*

Harold W. Stevenson

JAPANESE CHILDREN AND YOUTH are among the world's most successful students. Again and again, they have been among the top-scoring groups in cross-national studies of academic achievement in mathematics and science. In addition to Japan's top performers, average Japanese children also perform at a high level compared with their foreign counterparts on tests of these and other subjects (Stevenson, Chen, & Lee, 1993).

In searching for explanations for the remarkable performance of Japanese students, it is necessary to examine the structure and operation of the Japanese educational system. As pointed out in previous chapters, one feature that has been constant throughout the decades is the supremacy of the Ministry of Education in directing education. Public schools are mandated by law to follow the Ministry's *Course of Study*, the required curriculum for all grade levels in all academic subjects.

How can a common curriculum be applied to all students when some learn easily and others struggle to understand their daily lessons? How can teachers be expected to handle the wide variety of students at every grade level when a national curriculum must be followed? How can the boredom of faster learners and frustration of slower learners be reduced?

My purpose in this chapter is to describe the mechanisms and practices that have been adopted by the Japanese in their efforts to accommodate children of all levels of ability and skill. I discuss specific ways in which Japanese educators have established and adopted practices to ensure that students receive an education that will continue to produce academic success.

Relying primarily on the results of the case studies and other research that we have conducted during the past decade (Hofer, 1998; LeTendre, 1998; Stevenson & Lee, 1990), I have tried in this chapter to describe some of the reasons why the Japanese top-down, centrally controlled education system has flourished despite wide individual differences among students in interests, willingness to work, cognitive ability, prior experience, and other characteristics potentially related to academic achievement. The examples that I use are vivid but representative of the responses we obtained.

The Case Study Project, a component of the Third International Mathematics and Science Study (TIMSS), was conducted by a group at the University of Michigan in the mid-1990s. In the course of conducting this project, the researchers interviewed a large number of teachers, parents, students, and academic administrators in the United States, Japan, and Germany. The interviews, along with conversations and observations, dealt with students' daily life at school and home. Rather than attempting to review the methods employed, however, I refer the reader to a description of our research procedures and results in Stevenson and Nerison-Low (2000).

A CHANGING CURRICULUM

Practices and policies in education that were barely considered a decade ago are now being presented by the Ministry of Education in the most recent *Course of Study*. A major change places more emphasis on motivating children, rather than on refining methods for evaluating them—the goal of the prior set of guidelines. A related change is the emphasis placed on the effort to increase the independence of students by allowing them to decide what and when they would learn.

This effort to provide greater freedom for students, by increasing the number of hours available to them for electives, has not been a uniform success. Some parents of high school students, eager to have their children admitted to good universities, urge the schools to cover only the aspects of the curriculum that will appear on the entrance examination. Some parents even express the desire to have this done in 2 years so that the 3rd year can focus on preparation for the university entrance examinations. Students at less prestigious high schools, on the other hand, have gained more freedom from the easing of ministry requirements. A further problem of increasing the number of electives is that some students cease to enroll in the more difficult subjects, such as physics and mathematics, and opt for courses tailored to their own preparation for college entrance examinations (De-Coker, Chapter 9, this volume).

The emphasis on individualized education has resulted in a paradox for teachers. On the one hand, they are being asked to bring all students up to the level described in the guidelines; on the other hand, they are being instructed to provide more individualized education for their students. Students, in turn, are challenged to discover topics in which they have a special interest, and to look for problems and solve them on their own.

At the elementary school level, where examination pressure is minimal, the emphasis on student initiative has changed the role of the teacher. In the past, teachers were likely to demonstrate or direct attention to phenomena that would engage the students' interest. Now, teachers are expected to follow the child's lead and not interfere or attempt to direct their students' activities or observations. These practices differ markedly from those that existed when teachers were taught to function as well-informed guides who led students to attempt to discover different solutions to problems that they, the teacher, had devised.

Many teachers are having difficulty adjusting to the change in emphasis from guidance and instruction to motivating students to work on problems they discover themselves. One high school teacher, for example, expressed his sentiments about the new *Course of Study* in this way: "You are free now; think on your own." Accompanying his brief description of the new approach was his prediction that achievement scores will decline and the possibility of constructing tests applicable to all graduating students will vanish. Moreover, he predicted that experiments in physics or chemistry conducted to interest students may attract their attention, but the value of the whole process would decline unless the experiments were accompanied by clear explanations of the concepts being studied.

CLASSROOM INSTRUCTION

Despite the stereotype of rigidly controlled curriculum and teaching practices, a visitor to a Japanese school quickly realizes that individual differences among students are as pervasive in Japan as in other countries. Japanese teachers, therefore, must provide special opportunities in order to compensate for what some of their students might have missed in their regular school classes. They do this through a variety of practices and procedures.

Whole-group Orientation

Japanese classrooms, from the early grades through high school, are organized for whole-class instruction. This fact immediately raises the question of how all students can be brought to appropriate levels of understanding.

The answer is that they are not. None of the teachers we interviewed said they believed that all children could be brought to the level of the average child, but many expressed an optimistic view, suggesting that all "will improve accordingly."

As an alternative to whole-class instruction, teachers assign seat work, where the student works on assignments in the textbook, practice book, or a handout provided by the teacher. The teachers do not consider this to be a time to go to their own desks or to engage in other tasks, such as preparing for the next lesson or grading students' papers. Instead, they use the opportunity to provide individualized instruction and make suggestions to individual students. This form of in-class instruction may be quite systematic. For example, teachers may prepare sheets on which they list the problems students have encountered in the past. Alerted to these problems, the teacher is in a good position to anticipate errors the child might make, and on the basis of this, to guide the child to the correct response. Thus, rather than being forced to provide assistance only in an impromptu fashion, the teacher is prepared, both with information about the individual child and about ways in which the child's understanding might be improved. One teacher described her activities in the following manner:

> I go around the class, and if I find someone who's having trouble, I give him or her a hint. I give able students smaller hints and less able students bigger hints. Either way, I would like them to think about the problem for themselves.

Peer Instruction

Another form of supplementary in-class instruction comes from fellow students. Rapid learners can help those who are slower, and students who do not understand the lesson can ask questions of the fast learners. The fast learners, in turn, benefit from being placed in the position of clarifying their understanding as they explain and expand the discussion along the lines of the questions raised by the slower students.

Handouts

Handouts are often viewed as a second textbook. In fact, some teachers use handouts as the primary source of information and rely on the textbooks for examples and illustrations that supplement the handouts. Many of the most effective handouts, passed from teacher to teacher during study lessons and demonstration classes, represent interesting, challenging, well-designed sets of questions for children to think about and resolve.

Because handouts typically have been tried out with previous classes, they may be more readily understood than some of the exercises contained in the students' textbooks. A high school chemistry teacher described his use of handouts:

> During the first half of the term, well, that is rather theoretical and it is called theoretical chemistry. There aren't many handouts for that part and I write on the board. After that I talk about it. Say it in words and when there aren't enough pictures or things in the text, I use handouts and thus teach in that way. During the second half of the second year we have inorganic chemistry and in third year we have organic chemistry. Well, the area is quite difficult to write on the board and I use handouts every time.

Homework

Homework as defined in the West is not commonly assigned in Japan. Instead, students are expected to study on their own or to solve practice problems. Rather than follow teacher-assigned sets of problems or tasks, it is assumed that students will review the day's lesson and anticipate the lesson that will be studied during the next meeting of the class.

Although Japanese students are expected to engage in study after school, many teachers assume that homework is not an especially effective means for improving students' academic achievement. Some teachers assign homework; others never do. One teacher described practices involving homework as follows:

> Well, it depends on the teacher, I think. For example, when one unit is finished, there are problems that are not covered, problems that are difficult. Here, teachers might give students who do well extra problems. Also, teachers might give problems to determine students' levels of understanding and/or to establish mastery of the materials.
>
> There are teachers who may give a few problems every day. They might say, "Try to do these seven or eight problems by tomorrow." Students who do well might solve all of the problems and those who do not do well might do only a few.

Answers of teachers to our inquiry about homework revealed a variety of ways in which they use homework. Teachers may assign problems in the practice books, provide children with handouts, or provide practice problems that reinforce the central concepts in the day's lesson. Whatever the teacher's attitude about homework, major dependence is placed on the child's self-motivated review of the day's lesson and anticipation of what will be covered in subsequent class periods.

SUPPLEMENTAL EDUCATION

The Japanese have instituted a variety of supplemental forms of education to accommodate students who possess different goals, interests, and other characteristics. These include *juku*, *rônin*, *hoshû*, and practice tests.

Juku

There is great ambivalence among parents and teachers concerning the role and value of *juku* in primary and secondary education. These private after-school academies have gained an increasingly important role in Japanese society as students compete for entrance into prestigious high schools and leading universities (see Russell, Chapter 10, this volume). Some dismiss *juku* as being a harmless, if expensive, means of providing students with opportunities for social interaction with their peers. These advocates argue that attending *juku* adds to students' social life by providing a facility outside the confines of the school where students can get together for social interaction. Others who hold positive attitudes about *juku* regard the after-school classes as an important adjunct to schooling in that they increase students' preparedness for entrance examinations. Some argue that students attending the nonacademically oriented *juku* gain opportunities to acquire skills and knowledge not available in their regular schools. A teacher explained the value of *juku* as follows:

> In Japan, we teachers have to teach many students at once. When we do that, we have to direct our lectures to those who are average. Then, those who are advanced feel dissatisfied. But if they go to *juku* they can tackle more difficult questions. Those who are slow, on the other hand, will benefit if they are taught individually by tutors or taught over and over again at *juku*. Including those who are average, every student could have some benefit from training outside of school.

Countering these arguments are those of teachers who condemn *juku* as an unnecessary and even potentially harmful supplement to regular education. Teachers fear that all but slow learners may become bored if they attend classes during both the day and evening and hear similar material covered in both sets of lessons.

Rônin: An Additional Year or More of Study

After graduation, some high school graduates assume student status (*rônin*) once again and enroll in private academies (*yobikô*) devoted to preparing students for the college entrance examinations. During the year or two that they function as *rônin*, they devote themselves primarily to studying for the college entrance examinations. Because the examination is a primary criterion for admission to most high-ranking schools, a student who makes the required score is admitted, regardless of the number of previous attempts. Through study as *rônin*, students who have left high school without mastering the high school curriculum may gain the requisite knowledge and skills for passing the entrance examination.

Hoshû: Special Help Sessions

In addition to *juku* and *yobikô*, a third form of assistance is available to students having problems in their academic lives. *Hoshû*, or special help sessions, are conducted by teachers, primarily at the high school level, during summer and other vacations, before and after school, and during other free times in the students' lives. Students often pay a nominal fee for materials, and teachers sometimes receive a small stipend for their efforts. Although the content of these special help sessions focuses primarily on examination preparation, some schools offer remedial sessions. *Hoshû* sessions are especially helpful as a substitute for *juku* in small towns where insufficient numbers of students limit the development of *juku*.

Practice Tests

Another technique used to improve students' scores on the entrance examinations is to make copies of earlier university entrance examinations available to all students. Students can review the content of practice tests given during previous years, and copies of the tests are available at schools, *juku*, *yobikô*, and most bookstores. The National Center Test, used by all public and some private universities, is based on topics included in the students' textbooks; material outside the high school *Course of Study* is not included (DeCoker, Chapter 9, this volume). High school teachers, therefore, make strong efforts to give as close attention as possible to the topics that might be included on the test.

The close relation between the content of the textbooks and the entrance examination leads to concerns about the Ministry of Education's recent reduction of the number of school days each week to five. Parents and teachers are worried about this reduction because there has been no corresponding decrease in the topics included in the *Course of Study* and hence in the content of the entrance tests. They fear that the level of student achievement will decline with the shortened number of hours available to cover the curriculum.

EFFORT AND ABILITY

Beliefs among educational authorities on the relative roles of effort and ability in children's academic achievement in Japanese and American societies have significant implications for educational programs and learning. Americans are more likely than the Japanese to emphasize innate ability over effort as an influence on achievement. They are also more prone than their Japanese counterparts to categorize children as having "high ability" or "low ability" and expose them accordingly to different levels of academic challenge. As American teachers reduce the level of academic expectation for children who they perceive as having "low ability," so too do they reduce their expectation that these students will apply the extra effort needed to function alongside their "high-ability" peers. Japanese educators, in contrast, offer no excuses for lack of progress in school; regardless of a student's current level of performance, opportunities for advancement are always believed to be possible through heightened effort. These differences in orientation have profound implications for the skills children are expected to obtain throughout their education and their abilities to function competitively in contemporary society.

One of the most effective motivators for Japanese students has been the Confucian emphasis on the value of hard work and the minimal emphasis on the importance of innate characteristics in learning and intelligence. One respondent characterized Americans as people who believe that some children were born as a sports car, some were born as a motorcycle, some as a bicycle, and so on. He continued with his metaphor:

> They [Americans] think it is impossible to expect them to run as though they were all the same types of vehicle. The Japanese, on the other hand, have been teaching students as though all children were born as a car and that everyone can run at 40 kilometers an hour. So now what the new guidelines are trying to do is to accept that every car is different and a car which runs slowly is good as it is.

Comments about the relative functions of effort and ability pervaded a high percentage of the interviews, and in these interviews Japanese respondents rejected the assumption of innate differences in ability. One of the more thoughtful statements was the following:

Although I haven't done research on this subject myself, I don't think there is much difference in terms of what a person is born with. What makes a difference is what one acquires after birth. Preschool and elementary education in particular make the big difference. I must say that there are times when I wonder if inborn differences might exist, but in terms of my most honest feelings, I tend to believe that differences are created after birth. The environment in which you were born and grew up—you can call it the environment or culture in which you were born or you can just call it the family. But whatever it is this is where one acquires differences in ability.

Students, as well as teachers and parents, expressed firm convictions about the importance of effort. Two high school boys described their opinions:

Student I: I don't think there are people who are extremely smart biologically. The differences that come to exist are the result of how much effort each person makes after being born.

Student II: I don't think there are any differences. Everyone is studying the same thing and starting from the same level. But there are differences in the amount of time each student puts into studying.

Whether the question is framed in terms of ability or intelligence, there is a common belief among Japanese students, parents, and teachers that improvement is possible if the student is attentive and diligent, and has an encouraging and supportive home environment. Because of this belief, parents and teachers focus on changes that might foster better performance, rather than attributing the child's lack of improvement to any type of innate differences.

When asked what is done for top students, the response was consistent: Special programs for bright students do not exist and whatever additional work they are assigned is done in the few moments when the teacher is not attending to the remainder of the class. Lack of time rather than lack of interest was the most common explanation of the teachers' inability to provide special programs for the top students. In order to maintain the interest of these students, teachers often assign them the more difficult problems, and teachers may attempt to strengthen the abilities of these rapid learners by offering special after-school or summer sessions.

TRACKING

Tracking involves the placement of students in different classes, groups, or schools on the basis of their intellectual ability or other characteristics such as personality or social skills. In Japan, the segregation of children by "tracks" is viewed as potentially elitist and unacceptable in a modern democratic society. As a result, there has been a consistent effort to avoid tracking, especially during the early years of elementary school. The prevailing belief among Japanese parents and teachers is that all students can improve their performance despite individual differences in cognitive ability. Furthermore, determining the appropriate track in which to place young children is apt to be error-prone inasmuch as the set of skills and aptitudes they possess is still developing.

Japanese parents and teachers are more accepting of tracking during secondary school years. They believe that by then a student's motivation, interest in academic courses, and willingness to study hard can be more reliably evaluated, and tracking can be helpful in preparing them for future professional and vocational opportunities.

Tracking exists at the high school level in several ways. First, high schools are organized hierarchically. They are ranked from the most demanding and prestigious schools that provide the majority of students with the knowledge and skills that will help them pass the entrance examination to schools that are designed to meet the needs of slow learners or students seeking vocational training. A second type of tracking occurs during high school in the student's choice of a curriculum. Most schools offer two academic tracks, science or humanities; some include vocational or other tracks (see also DeCoker, Chapter 9, this volume).

Tracking also takes place when high school students are divided within a class into groups based on the students' ability and their college aspirations. A secondary school teacher explained this in the following way:

> After all, there is a range of ability within the classroom. Right now we are doing proofs, and proofs are difficult for children in the lower ability range. And some just can't even do it. I break up students into three groups based on the students' abilities. For those who can do everything, I ask them to do all the problems. I ask students who can do less to do only the problems that they want to. And for the student who can do even less, I ask them to just draw diagrams. So, I break everyone into three groups and have them do what they can.

Teachers complained that there were social costs to tracking:

> Education is not about efficiency! There are all kinds of people in this world. Does a smart person live only among other smart people? No. All kinds of people live together, and that is our society. To di-

vide students when they are still in elementary schools . . . yes, it may be efficient in the classroom, but what does that teach about our world? From the point of teachers, I think if the students were divided it would be easy to teach them. However, from the point of students, I don't think dividing them is good.

Finally, the emotional costs of tracking were also pointed out:

> Dividing students in such a way disturbs them emotionally. Those who are in the slow group will not do any work because they would be discouraged by the fact that they were placed there. They feel their teachers gave up on them. I think it is unbearable for students to be labeled like that.

Moreover, tracking is rejected by the Japanese as a violation of the democratic ideal and a reversion to an earlier emphasis on education as elitist. Teachers often explained that differences in environments and experiences, not innate ability, provided some of the most important contrasts in the explanations for the high-achieving students in Japan and the United States.

CONCLUSION

What emerges from a consideration of Japan's *Course of Study* is a picture of a dynamic system that seeks to adapt to individual differences in academic achievement, to changing demands of educators, and to various needs of the country. Although the system of education in Japan continues to be directed by a central ministry, schools and teachers are able to interpret the ministry's directives in a surprisingly varied and relaxed manner. Guided by the goal of developing a responsive educational system, the ministry allows local schools the autonomy to foster practices and develop mechanisms that meet students' needs. This movement toward individualization has resulted in modifications to the curriculum that are increasingly similar to many of the goals and practices existing in the United States.

In addition to allowing for increased local autonomy, Japanese schools also are experimenting with several organizational plans typical of those used by many contemporary American school systems, including instituting special classes for students encountering academic problems both within and outside of school, having faster learners help slower learners, and not requiring all students to master the entire curriculum. Underlying these modifications in the Japanese curriculum, however, is the continued belief in the power and effectiveness of study and hard work. Buoyed by a belief in the positive outcomes of such efforts, students and their parents are willing to devote large amounts of time and resources to the student's education, and teachers are willing to expend the time necessary to present lessons in the most effective manner.

The Ministry of Education's current interest in motivating students and reducing school hours counters the criticism that the curriculum was too abstract and too difficult for below-average students. How successful the new approaches will be is of interest to all who are concerned about improving schools. Although changes that take place in Japan do not necessarily transfer to other countries, some of the alternative approaches being tried in Japan will be a potentially fertile source of ideas and practices for foreign observers.

REFERENCES

Hofer, B. (Ed.). (1998). *The education system in the United States: Case study findings*. Washington, DC: U.S. Department of Education, National Center for Education statistics.
　　Available online at *http://www.ed.gov/pubs/USCaseStudy/*.

LeTendre, G. (Ed.). (1998). *The education system in Japan: Case study findings*. Washington, DC: U.S. Department of Education, National Center for Education statistics.
　　Available online at *http://www.ed.gov/pubs/JapanCaseStudy/*.

Stevenson, H. W., Chen, C., & Lee, S. Y. (1993). Mathematics achievement of Chinese, Japanese and American children: Ten years later. *Science, 259*, 53–58.

Stevenson, H. W., & Lee, S. Y. (1990). Contexts of achievement: A study of American, Chinese, and Japanese children. *Monographs of the Society for Research in Child Development, 221*, 1–2.

Stevenson, H. W., & Nerison-Low, R. (2000). *To sum it up*. Philadelphia: Mid-Atlantic Eisenhower Consortium for Mathematics and Science Education.

CHAPTER 7

Teacher Professional Development in Japan

Nobuo K. Shimahara

STRATEGIES TO ENHANCE PROFESSIONAL DEVELOPMENT vary among industrialized nations, reflecting the availability of resources, the historical and political context of teaching, and the culture in which teaching is embedded (Organization for Economic Cooperation and Development [OECD], 1998). In all countries, however, professional development is a key to creating effective teachers.

In Japan teacher development is commonly known as *kenshû* ("mastery through study)" or *genshoku kyôiku* (in-service education). In this chapter, I will use these terms interchangeably to designate teachers' efforts to achieve mastery through study. The Japanese *kenshû* system has four structurally different types. The first is a top-down arrangement governing in-service education throughout the country, and it reflects the centralized, hierarchical system of Japanese education. In this type of *kenshû* the Ministry of Education presents a policy framework for teacher development that the prefectural boards of education follow. This structure, extensively developed since the early 1960s, includes the National Education Center in Tokyo with in-service education facilities in both Tokyo and Tsukuba. The center's activities focus on leadership development for teachers and administrators. The second type of *kenshû* is long-term training sponsored by prefectural boards of education for selected full-time teachers who enroll in master's programs at national universities on government scholarships. The third type of *kenshû* is a school-based structure in which teachers take responsibility through peer collaboration and management. The fourth and last type of *kenshû* represents large numbers of national teacher networks, completely independent of government control and subsidies. Data for this chapter were collected in three ethnographic studies I conducted in 1989, 1994–1995, and 1998 in Japanese schools and education centers (for further information, see Shimahara, 1997; Shimahara & Sakai, 1995).

GOVERNMENT-SPONSORED IN-SERVICE EDUCATION

Most of the government-sponsored in-service education is provided at the national and prefectural education centers, the latter established and operated by each of the 47 prefectural boards of education. Full-time personnel, including many experienced teachers on leave from their schools, staff each prefectural education center. Likewise, large cities, including Yokohama, Osaka, Kyoto, Kobe, Nagoya, Hiroshima, Fukuoka, and each of Tokyo's 23 wards, run education centers with full-time staff under the direction of their boards of education.

Kenshû at the Prefectural Education Center

The basic structure of *kenshû* programs is largely the same across the country. The education centers vary in size and facilities, but generally are housed in well-equipped modern buildings. Tokushima Prefectural Education Center, financed by a small rural prefecture, for example, is staffed by 55 full- and part-time professional employees and offers over 70 courses a year; Hiroshima Municipal Education Center, staffed by 28 full-time professional employees, offers nearly 150 courses each year.

Two *kenshû* categories, obligatory and voluntary, enhance teacher development at different career stages. The obligatory category, supported by the Ministry of Education, consists of several mandatory programs designed to enhance the career objectives of designated cohorts of teachers through a career development model. The first obligatory program includes 30 days of internship sessions for all first-year public school teachers. The second obligatory program, 5 days a year, targets fifth- and tenth-year teachers. In addition, some centers, such as the Nara Prefectural Education Center, offer an obligatory program for teachers with 11 to 20 years of experience who are moving toward leadership positions in schools. To develop leadership and managerial skills in this same cohort of teachers, several centers offer intensive *kenshû* courses for selected personnel ranging from 12 days (73 hours) at Hiroshima to 51 days (328 hours) at Gunma. The third program consists of short seminars for administrators, including beginning curriculum specialists and principals, to brief them about changing administrative functions and issues.

In addition, each prefectural education center offers a number of voluntary or elective *kenshû* courses for teachers, which last from 3 to 8 days and focus on special topics such as minority education, environmental education, mathematics, science, counseling, curriculum development, and English education. Further, each center provides a long-term professional development program, lasting from 3 to 12 months. The Tokushima Education Center, for example, recruits 28 teachers for full-year *kenshû* every year, and grants them a paid leave from school to launch research projects at the center.

The last category of *kenshû* at the prefectural education centers is teacher development through "social participation," that is, prolonged work experience in workplaces outside the formal educational institution, including service and manufacturing industries, welfare and medical institutions, and social education facilities. (Social education encompasses a variety of educational programs for youth and adults offered outside the school system.) This type of *kenshû* targets experienced teachers for career enrichment in order to

- Provide opportunity for self-actualization as a teacher by broadening the professional perspective through an exposure to workplaces other than schools.
- Provide opportunity to reflect on teaching through social participation, thereby developing one's sense of mission in education.
- Promote sensitivity to students and parents through social participation in other workplaces where teacher participants must deal with clients, customers, and colleagues. (Ministry of Education, 1998)

Kenshû through social participation started around 1990 and are gaining popularity at a time when the Japanese public views teachers as parochial and unfamiliar with the social world outside the school. Thirty-six prefectural and municipal boards of education offer social participation programs involving over 700 teacher participants.

Incidentally, the Japanese Employers' Association (*Keidanren*) also offers an in-service program of work experience to over 500 teachers (OECD, 1998). The program, jointly administered with the Japan Teachers' Union (until recently an anticapitalist union), provides a 3-day experience in one of over 60 participating companies during the summer vacation. *Keidanren* offered a one-day course to 1,400 teachers in Tokyo in 1998.

Kenshû at the National Education Center

The National Education Center, established in 1964 to contribute to the promotion of professional development, operates under the direct purview of the Ministry of Education. It has a large conference facility for short-term courses in Tokyo, a small campus for social education in the suburbs of Tokyo, and a large, modern campus in Tsukuba. The Tsukuba campus is equipped with a multipurpose lecture hall, several conference rooms, seminar rooms, a computer laboratory with advanced facilities for 50 participants, a library, and computer study rooms. It accommodates over 300 participants for residential courses from a few days to 3 months in duration.

The Tsukuba campus concentrates on leadership development, and the major features include residential courses for 200 principals and head teachers for 22 days and 200–300 experienced teachers for 36 days. These courses are repeated four times a year. Other, less-intensive residential courses focus on information technology, bullying, and student "school refusal" (the recent phenomenon of increasing numbers of otherwise healthy students refusing to attend school). The Tsukuba center also offers leadership development courses for social education staff. The Tokyo center offers 2-day courses for beginning principals, board of education staff (including former teachers who are serving in administrative positions), school superintendents, and directors of prefectural and municipal education centers, each enrolling 1,000 participants. The suburban social education campus specializes in *kenshû* courses for social education employees, lasting from 3 to 38 days and designed to enhance their skills in developing programs for youth and adults.

Internships for Beginning Teachers

Mandatory internships for beginning public school teachers, a recent government initiative begun in 1989, enroll all beginning teachers at the elementary and secondary levels for 1 year. The ministry set up and funded the internship program through a 2-year pilot project designed to provide a model to local school systems. Prefectural boards of education are responsible for the construction and implementation of the internship program.

In essence, an internship comprises two components: an in-house induction program of about 5 hours a week designed by a mentor; and a program developed by the prefectural education center. A mentor is an experienced teacher chosen by the principal. If there is more than one beginning teacher at the school, mentoring is a full-time assignment. The in-house induction program focuses on both teaching and noninstructional roles. To develop teaching skills, interns observe senior teachers' classes; present lessons for critique by the mentor; and consult the mentor about lesson plans, teaching materials, and student evaluation. Interns also offer "study lessons" (discussed below) before their senior colleagues for observation and critique. To become familiar with noninstructional roles, under the guidance of the mentor, interns learn about school-community relations and the broad range of intra- and extramural responsibilities related to school programs.

The internship component designed by the education center, on the other hand, includes formal lectures on the legal framework and ethical foundations of teaching, human rights and minority education, moral education, classroom management, student behavior, and so forth; the opportunity to broaden the perspective of interns through special arrangements to teach at schools other than their own and to visit various types of social institutions; information technology workshops; and a 3-day retreat that allows interns to reflect on critical issues in teaching and to share their own experiences as first-year teachers. The Ministry of Education offers an alternative 10-day retreat for beginning teachers each year, for which a large ship is rented for accommodation, activities, and visits to several sites. A total of 30 days is devoted to the center-based program, during which interns are relieved of their teaching responsibility. They also receive a reduced teaching load to participate in their induction program.

Teacher Development Through Graduate Study

Teacher development through graduate study is a recent innovation in Japan, but it has been gaining popularity. In response to Ministry of Education pressure in the mid-1970s, the national legislature approved its initiative to establish three universities of education where full-time teachers could pursue 2 years of graduate study leading to a master's degree. In the early 1980s, Hyogo, Joetsu, and Naruto Universities of Education, established by this legislation, began enrolling students. Prefectural boards of education, the employers of most public high school teachers, are authorized to grant selected teachers a 2-year paid leave. Currently about 450 teachers across the country participate in full-time graduate study through this arrangement. Following their studies, they are expected to return to their schools.

At other public institutions, full-time teachers receive a 1-year paid leave from the prefectural board of education to pursue a graduate program. These teacher-students complete the program requirements in the second year while back on the job. Reforms of certification standards in 1988 stimulated a significant increase in graduate programs for full-time teachers (Miwa, 1992). Consequently, nearly 70 institutions now offer such programs. The total number of teachers enrolled in this type of graduate education now exceeds 550.

The cost to prefectural boards of education, especially for teacher salaries, has significantly constrained the enrollment of teachers at all participating universities and resulted in their failure to meet their enrollment goals. Limited access to part-time study also restricts the number of teachers enrolled in graduate studies. In 1997 the percentages of elementary, middle-school, and high school teachers with a master's degree were only 4.4, 8.2, and 15.3, respectively.

In response to the demand for graduate studies, the Teacher Education Council, an advisory committee to the Minister of Education, recommended expanding access through part-time and off-campus graduate programs (Teacher Education Council, 1998). The council recommends that 15%–25% of the teaching force in Japan have access to graduate education by 2010.

SCHOOL-BASED TEACHER DEVELOPMENT

In contrast to top-down, government-initiated *kenshû* programs, school-based professional development is initiated by teachers. As a result, teacher participation in school-based *kenshû* varies significantly depending on the level of schooling and the leadership of the teachers and subject-area associations. In general, school-based *kenshû* is more active at the elementary level and, by comparison, it tends to be formalistic and inactive at the secondary level.

The "intensification" of teaching at the secondary level limits school-based teacher development. A dominant source of constraint is the high school and university entrance examinations, which drive classroom teachers to concentrate on a traditional noninteractive and unreflective transmission of knowledge. Moreover, secondary teachers must perform a number of duties outside the classroom, including student placement in high schools and colleges, student club activities, noninstructional work specified in the faculty handbook, and student guidance. These activities leave little time to promote either in-house or districtwide teacher development.

I will concentrate mostly on elementary-level school-based *kenshû* using data collected in Japan since 1989. The concept of *kenshû* is largely predicated on several assumptions (Sato & McLaughlin, 1992; Shimahara, 1997). The first assumption—that teaching is a collaborative process—is promoted, for example, by clustering the desks of teachers of the same grade level in the staff room, where teachers spend considerable time every day for work, meetings, and consultation. Teachers easily exchange ideas and seek each other's assistance. Peer collaboration among teachers of the same grade is also important at the middle-school level to coordinate strategies and tasks pertinent both to gradewide programs and to problems cutting across subject areas.

The second assumption, which stems from the first, is that peer planning is a critical aspect of teaching. At the elementary level, teachers have weekly grade-level meetings to review and plan lessons and extracurricular activities. Peer planning is used to develop a variety of events: an intraschool professional development program; the curricular program at each grade level or subject area; and schoolwide programs. Many of the activities involve collaborative teacher planning, supported by the ethos that schooling is a cooperative enterprise.

The third assumption is that the active engagement of teachers in a variety of school activities is an indispensable element of teaching and schooling. This is evident in schoolwide programs and in-house *kenshû*, which rely on teachers to implement them. Further, every Japanese school at both elementary and secondary levels is managed cooperatively by faculty. Teachers receive specific assignments to promote school programs, the school environment, the lunch program, public relations, counseling, *kenshû*, subject-area study activities, moral education, student guidance, and school events. This cooperative management by teachers provides smooth implementation of everyday routines and new initiatives in the programs. Japanese schools center around interdependence rather than separation, and teaching takes place with an audience of peers.

With these three assumptions as the premise, school-based *kenshû* offers a structure by which teachers transmit, reformulate, and share craft knowledge through practice and collaboration with peers. While these premises constitute the normative framework of the Japanese ethos of teaching, however, significant local variation exists depending on the quality of leadership and faculty in each school and district.

In-house Teacher Development Initiatives

The most common type of teacher-generated professional development, in-house *kenshû*, aims to improve classroom teaching through programs organized by teachers and free of external official control. A study promotion committee, one of the most important faculty task groups in the school, runs the professional development program. It typically consists of several teachers representing different grade levels, including the director of academic programs and the principal *ex officio*. The committee drafts a yearly study plan and presents it to grade-level groups of teachers for discussion. Once the study theme and plan are accepted by the entire staff, each grade-level group determines the process of implementation. The program generally consists of *kenkyû jugyô* ("study lessons"), scheduled throughout the year. These classes are observed by a large critical audience, including the entire staff and an invited advisor with expertise in the subject of the lesson. *Kenkyû jugyô* is a widespread popular practice embedded in the culture of teaching, an ethos that Japanese teachers cherish as a proven means to improve teaching.

Study lessons enhance pedagogical knowledge and skills through peer collaboration, review, and critique, and are grounded in the belief that collaborative construction, reflection, and analysis in teaching are central to professional growth. Study lessons, actual classes within the regular curriculum, are usually videotaped. Appointed staff take detailed notes of their observations, focusing on particular aspects of teaching. Preparation for each study lesson involves extensive peer participation lasting at least several weeks. On a rotating basis, a few teachers take the lead and the remaining faculty members collaborate in helping them prepare their lessons. After the demonstration, staff members meet to review their observations and critique the class, and an invited advisor makes critical comments based on his or her expertise. The advisor is usually a veteran practitioner from outside—a teacher with a fine reputation, a principal, or an instructional supervisor at the education center who is on leave from his or her school. During the review and critique session, the observed teacher and his or her collaborators defend the lesson—its plan, teaching strategies, and student interest in and comprehension of the materials presented. At the end of the academic year, records of study lessons are usually published in a school bulletin (LeTendre, Chapter 2, this volume).

Through preparing for study lessons and undergoing intense classroom observation by their peers, teachers critically reflect on and improve their teaching. Study lessons require the construction of a theoretical framework for a teaching unit, the sequencing of lessons leading to the study lessons, and sustained effort to develop teaching materials and strategies for the lessons. Perhaps more fundamentally, study lessons require a classroom culture conducive to these efforts. In short, this approach creates a collaborative model of teaching and curriculum development including reflection on teacher and student performance and analysis of the process and structure of teaching and learning. Study classes benefit everyone involved, the teachers and the observers.

Interschool Teacher Development Initiatives

The second type of school-based professional development consists of interschool programs organized by districtwide subject-area associations of teachers, or *kyôka bukai*, at both the elementary and secondary levels. Each city or city ward has *bukai* that organize a study program for its schools in each subject field. They also conduct other activities, including the review of curriculum and discussion of critical issues in the field. Study programs similar to the in-house study program in terms of lesson preparation, collaboration, review, and reflection-in-action rotate among schools and are open to all *bukai* members. Administrators, including principals and head teachers, participate in *bukai* activities such as in-house *kenshû* because they are considered "peers" with accumulated teaching experience.

Although the pattern of professional development activities just described is typical in Tokyo, there is some variation across the country. For example, in Tokushima Prefecture, in-house and districtwide professional development initiatives are designed by the subject-area associations of teachers at the district and prefectural levels as part of the prefectural study program for elementary and secondary teachers. Every year subject-area associations designate study schools in different subject areas. During the autumn study meetings, teachers at the study school sites prepare and present study lessons at all grade levels for observation and discussion by peer teachers from other schools in the district or prefecture. Preparation for study lessons is a prolonged process, usually 1 year, and includes the construction of a detailed instructional plan in each subject and "exploratory" study lessons, repeated several times by the teachers for critique and reflection within their schools. Teachers regard these exploratory study lessons as helpful in developing effective plans and strategies for the demonstration lessons presented at the study meetings. The board of education designates a professional development day to enable all the teachers in the prefecture to participate in the study meetings. A typical study meeting consists of an all-day program, including study lessons, presentations of case studies focused on the themes of study meetings, and a lecture by an invited guest.

In Tokushima, study meetings initiated by subject-area associations constitute the teacher development activities organized at different levels—district, prefectural, and regional. Study lessons are largely organized in conjunction with these study meetings, although individual schools with strong leadership may independently conduct study lessons as part of their own teacher development initiative. In Tokushima, regional study meetings occur once every 2 years and involve teachers in nine prefectures from the Shikoku and Chûgoku areas. In addition, there are national study meetings, which rotate among the 47 prefectures in the country.

A Case Study from Ômatsu Elementary School

As an illustration of how school-based professional development is organized, I will briefly describe the *kenshû* program that Ômatsu Elementary School implemented in 1998. Ômatsu, a small school located in Tokushima City, consists of two administrators and 12 classes, each staffed by a classroom teacher. The school focused on moral education as the study theme for professional development in 1997 and volunteered to serve as host for the Shikoku Regional Study Meeting on moral education held in November 1998. In the late 1950s, moral education was reintroduced as a formal instructional subject in the national curriculum at the elementary and middle-school levels and one period was allocated to it weekly. When student behavior became a national concern in the 1980's, education reformers again stressed the importance of moral education. As a result, moral education has gradually gained emphasis.

The responsibility of the host school of the regional study meeting is to organize study lessons and related events, including a lecture on the theme of the study meeting by an invited guest. When the study meeting was held at Ômatsu in 1998, the school presented moral education study lessons to over 300 invited teachers from the four Shikoku prefectures. All 12 classes from first through sixth grade participated in study lessons, followed by the school's very impressive, illustrative presentation of its moral education program. Participants also received a packet of materials, including a 168-page document titled "Program of Moral Education at Ômatsu" and a 121-page study-meeting bulletin, which included the framework for moral education at each grade level and units of lessons leading to the study lessons at the meeting.

For teacher development, the process is perhaps more important than the final *kenshû* meeting. This process involves prolonged planning, including construction of a moral education curriculum, development of the strategies to present moral issues to students, creation of exploratory study lessons, and consultation with the subject-area associations on moral education at the municipal and prefectural levels. In April 1998, Ômatsu faculty held a seminar to discuss how to construct a lesson plan; in May they organized three in-house exploratory study lessons presented by second-, third-, and fifth-grade teachers for observation, critique, and reflection. These lessons were preceded by a faculty review of the lesson plans. In June faculty organized two more study lessons and briefed the municipal subject-area association on moral education about their progress in preparing for study meeting. In July a sixth-grade teacher presented a study lesson, and faculty met to discuss how to prepare a draft for the study-meeting bulletin. In like manner, faculty organized three more study lessons, preceded in October by discussions on lesson plans. All this effort culminated in the Shikoku Study Meeting at Ômatsu in November.

The head teacher, who shared leadership with the director of the study promotion committee in developing moral education, explained the importance of a reflection meeting that occurred after each study lesson:

At the reflection meeting, we discussed various matters: the extent to which the goals of the lesson were accomplished; how children participated in the lesson; what approach the teacher used; how she interpreted materials on moral issues and presented them to children; how she elicited children's views and feelings on particular moral issues; how a lesson was developed to promote the moral education theme of the school. In short, these concerns centered on the question of the teacher's pedagogical approach to moral issues.

The Ômatsu faculty's participation in teacher development and preparation for the study meeting just described was very intense and may not represent a typical *kenshû*. But the strategies that they used reflect the *kenshû* experience for many teachers. The head teacher commented that genuine teacher development results from collaborative efforts to accomplish shared goals and suggested that teachers' initiatives at Ômatsu embodied such goals.

NATIONAL TEACHER NETWORKS

Teacher-initiated voluntary national networks designed to promote teaching also support professional development in Japan. According to a survey (Otsuki, 1982), more than 47 such teacher networks developed in the early postwar period, most of which are currently active. They are independent associations committed to a shared purpose, that is, promoting teaching, independent of government and external institutional control. Many of these national associations were initially formed in the 1950s by small groups of educators intent on developing an independent approach to teaching at a time when Japan's postwar education was undergoing drastic ideological and systemic transformation toward centralized control under the stewardship of the conservative government. Examples of well-known influential associations include the Association of History Teachers (the oldest in the voluntary teacher network movement), the Japanese Journal Circle of Teachers, and the Association of Mathematics Education (Fujioka, 1992). One far-reaching popular recent network is a loosely knit association of teachers initiated in 1984 by an energetic and gifted elementary school teacher. Seeking a broad, collaborative basis in elementary teaching called *hôsôkuka* (science of teaching), this network has become a national movement to advance teaching through sharing and critiquing individual teachers' practice (Mukoyama, 1985). Networks like these regularly hold conferences and workshops and publish magazines sold at commercial bookstores, thereby disseminating information about their innovative ideas and practices to teachers throughout the country.

Currently national teacher networks hold nearly 200 summer work-shops every year, suggesting extensive participation in self-initiated study activities "Comprehensive List," (Comprehensive list . . . , 1998; Sato, 1992). Teacher networks hold annual membership drive meetings during the summer, drawing both elementary and secondary teachers.

IMPLICATIONS FOR AMERICAN PROFESSIONAL DEVELOPMENT

As American policymakers and researchers repeatedly point out, teaching in the Unites States is generally characterized by the structural isolation of individual teachers, and teaching takes place without an audience of peers (Lortie, 1975; National Commission on Teaching and America's Future, 1996; Shulman, 1987). Many U.S. educators, however, have come to recognize the value of teacher collaboration and networking as strategies to promote teacher development and reflection. Lieberman and McLaughlin (1996) observe: "Teachers choose to become active in collegial networks because they afford occasion for professional development and collegiality and reward participants with renewed sense of purpose and efficacy" (p. 63; see also Clark, 2001; Lieberman & Miller, 2001).

In light of the American interest in collaborative professional development, the Japanese model of peer-driven *kenshû* may offer a viable and promising approach. In Japan, teaching for observation and analysis at the school and district levels involves peer collaboration and planning focused on curricular materials, teaching strategies, and student learning. Study lessons are possible when there are networks of teachers both within and outside individual schools that envision them as a profitable effort for teacher growth.

The Japanese approach to professional development also benefits by a supportive context. First, Japanese professional development activities receive the support of national, prefectural, and education agencies. Second, the stable national curriculum allows Japanese teachers to come together around a shared curriculum with the knowledge that they can draw on their lesson-development work during subsequent years. The required guidelines of the national *Course of Study* offer a certain freedom to Japanese teachers, making it possible for them to work collaboratively on their classroom lessons. Similar collaboration in the United States often involves a small number of teachers in the writing of local, regional, or state curriculum guidelines, a process that focuses more on setting objectives than on classroom teaching. Finally, the Japanese approach seems to evolve from a body of knowledge that ties teaching practice to the subject matter. Subject-area associations exist at the school district and prefecture levels as well as in professional associations at the national level. U.S. professional development activities often focus on generic strategies that cut across subject areas, and many teachers pursue graduate degrees in education without delving further into the subject matter they teach. Japanese teachers work to integrate content knowledge and pedagogy.

Although a Japanese-style peer-driven approach could become a model for professional development in the United States, its success would require significant changes in the administrative structure of the educational system. Now that educators in the United States recognize the value of teacher collaboration, the next step is to create a system that fosters it.

REFERENCES

Clark, C. (Ed.). (2001). *Talking shop: Authentic conversation and teacher learning.* New York: Teachers College Press.

Comprehensive list of educational study meetings for summer 1998. (1998, June 20). *Nihon Kyôiku Shinbun.* [Japanese Education Newspaper, Tokyo].

Fujioka, N. (1992, March). *Self-initiated in-service teacher education in Japan: Development and issues.* Paper presented at the Comparative and International Education Society meetings, Annapolis, MD.

Lieberman, A., & McLaughlin, M. (1996). Networks for educational change: Powerful and problematic. In M. McLaughlin & I. Oberman (Eds.), *Teacher learning: New policies, new perspectives* (pp. 63–72). New York: Teachers College Press.

Lieberman, A., & Miller, L. (Eds.). (2001). *Teachers caught in the action: Professional development that matters.* New York: Teachers College Press.

Lortie, D. (1975). *Schoolteacher.* Chicago: University of Chicago Press.

Ministry of Education. (1998). *Survey concerning teachers' long-term social participation.* Tokyo: Author.

Miwa, S. (Ed.). (1992). *Comprehensive study of teacher education curriculum under new certification law* (Research report). Chiba-shi: Chiba University.

Mukoyama, Y. (1985). *The law to improve teaching.* Tokyo: Meiji Tosho.

National Commission on Teaching and America's Future. (1996). *What matters most: Teaching for America's future.* New York: Author.

Organization for Economic Cooperation and Development. (1998). *Staying ahead: In-service training and teacher professional development.* Paris: Author.

Otsuki, T. (1982). *The history of postwar voluntary education movement.* Tokyo: Ayumi Shuppan.

Sato, M. (1992). Japan. In H. Leavitt (Ed.), *Issues and problems in teacher education: An international handbook* (pp. 156–168). Westport, CT: Greenwood Press.

Sato, N., & McLaughlin, M. (1992). Context matters: Teaching in Japan and the United States. *Phi Delta Kappan, 73*(5), 359–366.

Shimahara, N. K. (1997). The culture of teaching in Japan. *Bulletin of the National Institute of Multimedia Education, 14,* 37–60.

Shimahara, N. K., & Sakai, A. (1995). *Learning to teach in two cultures: Japan and the United States.* New York: Garland.

Shulman, L. (1987). Knowledge and teaching: Foundations of the new reform. *Harvard Educational Review, 57*(1), 1–22.

Teacher Education Council. (1998). *Reforms of teacher education for an emerging age: An interim report on teacher education enhanced through graduate study at the master's level.* Tokyo: Ministry of Education.

PART IV

Implementing and Reacting to Educational Policy: Responses from Within and Outside of the System

A S EDUCATORS IN BOTH JAPAN and the United States know, educational reform is not a one-dimensional, linear process. Various constituencies within the educational system often bring their own agendas while outside interests look for ways to benefit. In both countries, these forces sometimes complement, sometimes contradict, proposed reforms. The chapters in this part directly challenge the notion that Japan's centralized educational system necessarily makes it more "efficient" or more readily able to implement reforms. Perhaps more important, the authors also question the expediency of reforms that seek immediate results.

In Chapter 8, David McConnell presents an educational reform that involves three government ministries and educators at all levels—national, prefectural, and local—in changing English-language education. An evaluation of the program during the first few years would have found few successes. The gradual implementation of the program over more than a decade, however, shows more favorable results. On the other hand, Gary DeCoker in Chapter 9 describes a reform that was implemented more quickly and measured, not on actual results, but on its adherence to ideology. The enthusiasm for the deregulation of government bureaucracies originated in Japan's 1990s economic downturn, but when applied to educational curriculum, deregulation resulted in less, rather than more, flexibility in the high school curriculum. Although the change looks real on paper—a broader curriculum and more choices—the reactions of individual constituencies (schools, students and their parents, and private supplemental education) created results very different from what was intended by ministry policymakers. Students, in fact, use their flexibility to choose a more limited range of courses. Nancy Ukai Russell in Chapter 10 puts education into a broader context of private initiatives that exist around the formal system and profit from it—sometimes supporting, sometimes contradicting the goals of the formal system.

For U.S. educators, these chapters raise questions about the speed and expectations of reform, the involvement of each level of education in the planning and implementation of reform, the influence of ideology, and the interplay of reform efforts with the private sector. McConnell points out the importance of an incremental approach and concludes that meaningful change in education takes time; DeCoker adds the caution that quick fixes may result in unforeseen consequences. On the other hand, as Russell notes, the climate of rapid technological change may no longer allow for a deliberate approach to educational reform. The private sector, poised to meet the desires of parents who need immediate results if their children are to benefit, sometimes takes control of the country's educational initiative.

U.S. educators who looked to Japanese education over the last two decades for sources of its high achievement assumed that they would be able to select from Japan what would work in the United States. In the end, however, perhaps the most important educational influence from Japan will be in the private sector. Japan's *juku* are rooted in its past and have adjusted well to recent changes in Japanese education. Some have already entered the United States and innovations in information technology will make it possible for them to move more fluidly across national borders in the future. In fact, they may find the climate in the United States, where private initiatives are encouraged, more favorable than in Japan, where the Ministry of Education routinely rejects attempts by *juku* to gain accreditation necessary to operate as schools. As Americans rely even more on test scores as the sole measure of educational success, the private sector increasingly promotes itself as better able than public schools to respond to these clearly defined standards. These and other future issues are explored in Thomas Rohlen's Epilogue following this section.

CHAPTER 8

"It's Glacial": Incrementalism and Japan's Reform of Foreign Language Education

David L. McConnell

SINCE AT LEAST THE TURN of the century, foreign language education in Japan has been maligned by foreign critics for its overemphasis on rote memorization and grammar. One of the latest in a long line of detractors, American linguist Roy Andrew Miller (1982), for example, provides a typical assessment: "What are potentially the most valuable years for foreign language learning are totally wasted in the course of hour after dreary hour in the English classroom with Japanese teachers, most of whom drone away in Japanese explaining the grammar and pronunciation of a language that they themselves have rarely even heard and certainly cannot speak" (p. 233). Moreover, such characterizations seem to have become part and parcel of Japanese perceptions of their own national character. The lament that almost all students, despite going through 6 years of English instruction in secondary school, and perhaps 4 more in college, remain unable to hold the most basic conversation with a native speaker is still heard from Japanese in all walks of life. Though private English conversation schools and after-school classes (*juku*) have thrived almost in direct proportion to the exam-centered curriculum in public education, there has been an increasing feeling that public schools themselves must do more to promote the acquisition of conversational skills.

It was in this context that foreign language education in Japan received a shock treatment of immense proportions in 1987. Over 800 foreign college graduates were dropped into public secondary schools throughout the country to "foster international perspectives in Japan by promoting international exchange at local levels as well as intensifying foreign language education" (Council of Local Authorities for International Relations, 1988). The subsequent growth of this program has been extraordinary. With an annual budget approaching $500 million, the Japan Exchange and Teaching (JET) Program now brings over 6,000 college graduates each year, mostly from English-speaking countries such as the United States, the United Kingdom, Canada, Australia, New Zealand, and Ireland. After a short orientation in Tokyo, the Assistant Language Teachers (ALTs) are assigned to work under the jurisdiction of prefectural, district, or municipal boards of education. These offices in turn dispatch them to public secondary schools where they "team-teach" foreign language classes, usually with a Japanese Teacher of Language (JTL). Under the agreed-upon division of labor for the administration of the JET Program, the Ministry of Foreign Affairs is responsible for the recruitment of participants abroad, the Ministry of Education guides the educational portion of the program involving foreign language teaching at the local schools, and the Ministry of Home Affairs is responsible for the overall administration and coordination of the program (see McConnell, 2000, for a fuller treatment of ministerial rivalries and competing goals).

The JET Program was in part a response to foreign pressure on Japan to demonstrate concrete steps toward opening up Japanese society and integrating foreigners into Japanese institutions. It also reflected growing concern within Japan about whether ordinary citizens and workers were being adequately prepared for the new millennium. The announcement about the JET Program came on the heels of the Maekawa report (Advisory Group on Structural Economic Adjustment for International Harmony, 1988) and the "Ron-Yasu" (U.S. President Ronald Reagan and Japanese Prime Minister Yasuhiro Nakasone) summit, and shortly after the National Council on Educational Reform (NCER) report issued by Nakasone's own ad hoc council, which described "the need for internationalizing Japan's educational institutions" (Schoppa, 1991, p. 5). The JET Program thus represented an attempt to integrate a relatively insular and homogeneous population with a global society made profitable and important to Japan by her own economic progress.

The JET Program is a particularly useful lens for examining educational reform because its origins were almost entirely top-down. In a sense, national-level ministries embarked on a course of "forced diversity" without ever consulting those most dramatically affected by the policy, namely, local educational administrators and Japanese language teachers. Moreover, the scope of reform was substantial in that team teaching required at least some reorganization of practice at the school level. And unlike most top-down reforms, the utilization of which was left to the discretion of individual teachers or schools, this reform walked, talked, and even talked back.

In this chapter, I use the JET Program as a lens for examining more than a decade of efforts to reform foreign language education in Japanese public secondary schools. Drawing on Thomas Rohlen's (1983) notion of each administrative level as a distinct sociocultural subsystem with its own sets of priorities, I ask how this top-down educational policy innovation was disseminated throughout the school system, and how the distinctive political, social, and bureaucratic environments at local levels shaped policy implementation. The larger question I address is the relation between top-down and bottom-up supports for planned educational innovation in Japan.

The data come from a long-term qualitative study of the JET Program, which included 2 years of ethnographic research in Japan from 1988 to 1990 and four follow-up visits during the summers of 1993, 1995, 1996, and 1998. Understanding how the JET Program unfolded over its entire history is important because it allows us to separate out the substantive and lasting changes from those that were fleeting.

INITIAL REACTIONS, LONG-TERM HORIZONS

The initial wave of JET participants were treated like foreign dignitaries during their week of orientation at a five-star Tokyo hotel; all the major print and visual media in Japan covered the event, and the mayor of Tokyo and the heads of the sponsoring ministries attended the opening reception. But the concept of "internationalization," so easy to agree on in the abstract, began to break down as soon as the ALTs were dispatched to local boards of education and secondary schools. Some ALTs were shocked when prefectural offices began sending them on a one-shot basis to dozens of schools, where they were wheeled out like "living globes" in classroom after classroom. The realities of entrance exams and the poor conversational abilities of many Japanese teachers of English left most feeling underutilized at best and intentionally misled at worst. Some ALTs broke their contracts and returned home early. On the Japanese side, prefectural administrators complained bitterly, if privately, about the extra work and indigestion created by interaction with unpredictable foreigners. Teachers, who had never been consulted about the plan, were understandably ambivalent. Some began referring to the JET Program as "the second coming of the black ships," the term the Japanese gave to Commodore Perry's fleet when it arrived in Tokyo harbor in 1853. The Americans subsequently forced Japan to sign a treaty that led to the opening of Japan after two and a half centuries of self-imposed seclusion from the rest of the world.

To compound the expectations gap, a number of serious incidents involving ALTs—ranging from sexual harassment to drunk driving to suicide—shook program morale during the early years, and the JET participants themselves formed a quasi-union to pressure the Japanese government to improve working conditions. Moreover, there was no shortage of second guessing of the government's intentions in domestic and foreign media as well. Almost overnight the JET Program had become a political football for critics of all stripes. It seemed that only Japanese students, thrilled at the prospects of hearing native English, were excited by the JET Program.

Ten years later, however, when the dust had settled and expectations had been adjusted, the JET Program was being touted by Japanese officials and foreign participants alike as one of the most successful educational policies of the postwar era. By the year 2000, ALTs were based in nearly one-half of the nation's 15,000-plus secondary schools, and "team teaching" had become a household term for foreign language teachers in Japan. The satisfaction of JET participants has markedly improved; in 1999 nearly 95% said that they would recommend the JET Program to a friend, and less than 1 percent returned home prematurely each year. The JET Program has been credited with influencing not only the criteria for hiring new teachers but also the content of new foreign language textbooks and the new *Course of Study*. Even the addition of an oral component on some of the university entrance exams in English has been attributed to the influence of JET.

How can we explain such a seemingly dramatic transformation? Of course, Japan has a long history of importing foreign objects and ideas and transforming them in ways that are compatible with their own cultural sensibilities. But it is still an intriguing question to ask *how* the foreign language system as a whole has adapted to a program whose origins were entirely top-down. It has been said that the best way to find out how something works is to kick it, and see if it kicks back. The foreign participants "kick" Japan's foreign language education in a myriad of ways, both consciously and unconsciously, and it is in the nuts and bolts of how Japanese at each administrative level have adapted to the ALTs on an everyday basis that we can find real clues as to how educational reform plays out "on the ground" at the national, prefectural, and local levels.

A MINOR PERESTROIKA?
THE MINISTRY OF EDUCATION AND THE REFORM
OF FOREIGN LANGUAGE EDUCATION

What does the track record of the Ministry of Education reveal about its attempts to disseminate a top-down innovation throughout the entire public secondary school system? The question is intriguing because of the ministry's reputation as a bastion of conservatism and rigidity. The stubborn persistence of this image is captured in a political cartoon run in the *Japan Times* in April 1997. Four identical male Ministry of Education bureaucrats dressed in dark suits are shown musing, one by one: "Why should we in the Education Ministry waste taxpayer money funding research on cloning humans when we've already developed a perfectly good system for producing clones in the classroom?"(p. 20).

In light of this image, it is not surprising that Ministry of Education officials initially were quite ambivalent about supporting the JET Program. They rightly perceived that the Foreign and the Home Affairs ministries were attempting to leapfrog over their own jurisdiction, and while they agreed with "internationalization" in principle, they were reluctant to endorse the scope of change implied by JET and to give up administrative control of existing smaller programs. This reluctance, coupled with the rushed development and implementation of the JET Program, meant that top-down supports were very thin during the early years of the program. Many JET participants arrived at local schools to find that Japanese teachers of language had received little or no information about the JET Program and in many cases were terrified of having to interact with a native speaker who might expose their oral-communication deficiencies.

But a long-term perspective provides a more favorable picture. For one thing, in spite of the lukewarm initial endorsement, the rhetoric emanating from Ministry of Education officials is clearly consistent with the goal of making English-language education more communication oriented. The ministry's *Handbook for Team-Teaching*, published in 1994, for example, stresses the idea that the team-teaching classroom involves a substantial departure from the traditional classroom. Its official "demonstration videos" on team teaching also highlight this point. One team-taught class in this video features a lively class in which an ALT uses a make-believe bottle of "*nattô* juice" (fermented soybeans) to teach a lesson on likes and dislikes.

Consider, too, the following statement of the goals of the program by one Ministry of Education official at a Mid-Year Block Seminar in 1989:

> First, we should try to develop students' communicative competence and performance and their awareness of different cultures. . . . Second, we must develop the above skills in JTLs. There is a big gap between what Japanese teachers are doing and what the Ministry of Education wants to accomplish, and in order to bridge this gap we need ALTs. All 35,000 JTLs throughout Japan follow almost the same teaching procedure, one that focuses on linguistic competence—grammar, sentence patterns and pronunciation of new words.

These teaching methods have been firmly established through a long history, and JTLs are very stubborn, though not entirely wrong, in sticking to them. I believe we need to change them, and if JTLs become more receptive to the ideas of communicative competence, then they have become more "internationalized."

After this speech the ALT sitting next to me turned and cast a skeptical look. "I don't know," he said. "His speech sounded good, but maybe he was just telling us what he thought we wanted to hear." The question is worth exploring further. Other than serving as a "bully pulpit," what concrete steps has the Ministry of Education made in recent years to develop structural supports for the desired shift in foreign language pedagogy?

One of the Ministry of Education's most interesting moves came in 1990 when the Upper Secondary School Division hired a former ALT and a JET chairperson from Chiba-ken to serve as an ALT counselor. When Robert Juppé moved into the High School Education Section of the Ministry of Education, he became the first foreigner ever to work for this ministry. Over the next 3 years, Juppé developed a close working relationship with officials in his office, where he was widely respected for his work ethic and ability to generate creative proposals while maintaining a healthy respect for protocol. In addition to fielding calls and complaints from ALTs, he was often sent out to conduct team-teaching training sessions for JTLs, and he participated in the ministry-sponsored intensive one-month study programs for select JTLs. Most importantly, in the eyes of ALTs, both Juppé and his successor, Huw Oliphant, have given the Ministry of Education a human face (Robert Juppé, personal communication, June 2, 1996).

At roughly the same time that they hired an ALT advisor, the Ministry of Education embarked on an 8-year project to conduct research on team teaching and to groom centers of local expertise in team teaching. Under the plan, each prefecture selected one school to serve as a model for team teaching on a 2-year cycle. At the end of the term each school conducted an open house (consisting of demonstration classes, discussion groups, and research reports) and published a record of its accomplishments. The Ministry of Education used these reports in policymaking and in disseminating advice to local boards of education, and published summaries of the results from each of the 24 junior high schools and 23 senior high schools that participated in the first cycle in a special "team-teaching" edition of the ministry journal (Summaries, 1994). By 1998, the Ministry of Education had completed the fourth and final 2-year cycle. While the four schools chosen to serve as prefectural "models" for team teaching usually regarded the designation as a mixed blessing (due to the amount of extra work and the added pressure of having to make a highly visible public presentation at the end), many Japanese teachers found that significant professional growth resulted from the focus on improving team teaching and the opportunity to conduct mini-research projects in their school.

In conjunction with the pilot school project, Ministry of Education curriculum specialists had spent a large part of their time traveling throughout Japan to give advice on team teaching to local and prefectural curriculum specialists and JTLs. This kept Ministry of Education officials in tune with local developments and gave a "hands-on" quality to the national-local relationship that is useful when implementing top-down reforms.

Another interesting development occurred in 1994, when the Ministry of Education implemented revised curriculum guidelines under a new *Course of Study*. These guidelines gave junior high schools the option to restore English classes to 4 days a week instead of 3 and authorized the establishment of new classes, each with a different "communicative" focus, at the high school level. Under the new Oral Communication guidelines, high schools can now choose from a conversation course with a focus on speaking, a listening course, and a formal thinking and speaking course. So far very few schools have adopted the third course, as its goals are unclear, but the first two are quite popular. According to the head of a Ministry of Education committee formed in the early 1990s to assess trends and prospects for foreign language education in Japan, the JET Program provided an important impetus for these changes (Ikuo Koike, personal communication, June 3, 1993).

On the surface, the Oral Communication program appears to challenge the traditional aims and methods of English learning. Yet at the same time that Ministry of Education officials were promoting their new guidelines, they were insisting that ALTs use the approved textbooks. One Ministry of Education official explained the situation to ALTs this way:

> The textbooks are not useful for communication and we need to rewrite them, but Japanese teachers like to teach textbooks. You need to use the texts indirectly. If ALTs continue to reject textbooks, I'm afraid Japanese teachers don't want to invite you to their schools, so try to compromise.

Part plea and part threat, the comment reflects the delicate line the Ministry of Education has had to walk between acknowledging the ALTs' complaints about the limited utility of the textbooks and appeasing JTLs who prefer grammar translation out of tradition or because of its importance on the entrance exams. Nevertheless, the new guidelines have brought the

ALTs to a more central position in the curricular offerings of secondary schools.

Taken together, the above efforts suggest that the JET Program may have produced a "minor perestroika" at the Ministry of Education in the sense that officials are now publicly committed to promoting conversational abilities, and have begun several pilot programs that introduce English classes in public elementary schools. Formalizing this arrangement, however, involves surmounting legal barriers as well as resistance from many elementary school teachers themselves. Still, the fact that the topic is being openly considered seems like a quantum leap. Though one may certainly question the pace, I would argue that the Ministry of Education has moved slowly but unmistakably to make broader changes in line with its goal of facilitating a more communication-based approach to language teaching.

On the other hand, major structural changes are not in sight, and reforms will be minimal as long as the current entrance exam and textbook screening processes remain in place. Major reform of the examination system is unlikely, but the content of entrance exams may be subject to change. Tokyo University's decision to include a listening component for English on their entrance exam, for instance, was widely hailed as a major step forward. Given that assessment practices play a powerful role in shaping teaching strategies, the issue of including a listening component on entrance exams could be viewed as an important litmus test of change in Japanese foreign language education. Yet in 1996, while 41.4% of national universities reported that at least one department in the university included a listening component on entrance exams, the figure at private universities was only 18%, and for local public universities it was even lower (9.6%) (Robert Juppé, personal communication, April 1, 1998). One Ministry of Education official noted:

> ALTs are one part of the process of changing English education. We must change the textbooks, teacher training, and guidelines. But we can't change the whole education system so quickly. If we compare with 10 years ago, we've made lots of progress.

PREFECTURAL AND MUNICIPAL RESPONSES: THE CRITICAL ROLE OF THE CURRICULUM SPECIALIST

National-level bureaucrats in Japan by and large subscribe to a theory of administrative guidance in which they pressure prefectural officials, who in turn pressure local school officials, until the desired policy outcomes are achieved. But how are national-level directives received and interpreted by prefectural and municipal officials? First of all, we might note that most governors and mayors have enthusiastically supported the JET Program. In the first year of the program, every prefecture in Japan accepted ALTs, and the increase since then has been dramatic. By the program's 12th anniversary in 1999, over half of Japan's 47 prefectures employed at least 100 JET participants!

But the curriculum specialists shoulder the administrative responsibility for the ALTs, and their responses have been mixed. Coming directly from the ranks of teachers, the curriculum specialists are a key educational "conduit" between the national and local levels, and they typically spend much of their time advising school-based personnel on prefectural and national policy regarding their subject matter specialty. As Rohlen (1984) points out, the curriculum specialists "tend to be firm pragmatists who can navigate the tricky waters of education politics" (p. 159). They are almost always men. In addition, they are relatively young, usually in their mid-to-late 30s, and thus at an early point in their careers.

In the early 1990s I had an opportunity to follow closely the efforts of a curriculum specialist in charge of the JET Program in a prefectural board of education in southeastern Japan. Mr. Sato, who as a teacher in Japan would be referred to as Sato-sensei, was a graduate of Sophia University and had taught at several prefectural high schools. He had also served on the prefecture's High School English Teachers Study Group before joining the ranks of administrators. What impressed me the most about Sato-sensei's work was that he reinterpreted program objectives and shaped structure and content in ways that conformed to the bureaucratic priorities of his office while at the same time going to great lengths to implement the formal goals of the program.

First of all, there was clearly some "slippage" between the goals of promoting communication-oriented language classes and administrative and political priorities. For instance, the JET Program came at precisely the moment that this prefecture was attempting to make its public high schools more competitive in the college entrance exams, and English was one subject that had been targeted for improvement. Therefore, at the same time Sato-sensei was promoting the goal of team teaching conversational English, he was also engaged in several other projects to raise the exam scores of prefectural students in English, including the preparation of grammar-focused "practice exams" for all prefectural high school students. Because hosting an ALT might detract from the time teachers needed to prepare students for the entrance exam, Sato-sensei at first tended to avoid the more "academic" schools when placing ALTs in prefectural high schools. He still focused on high schools, however, because he had much more leverage over the shape of team-teaching in these schools than in junior high schools, most of which were operated by municipalities and thus were further from his jurisdiction.

In short, numerous factors made the climate of prefectural implementation unstable in small ways that cumulatively affected the course of reform. In some cases commitments to various sets of reforms were incompatible; they were dependent on others who had a different sense of urgency or they were constrained by procedural requirements. In addition, the bureaucrats charged with implementation at this level often lacked the level of English proficiency needed for the task. Finally, there was a lack of continuity. The curriculum specialists rotate every few years (nationwide, nearly 40% of curriculum specialists report that they are working with foreigners for the first time), and coupled with the constant turnover among ALTs, they are pressed to meet the demands of a continually changing group of actors. Given this climate, it is little wonder that the most common word I heard Sato-sensei use to describe his JET-related job responsibilities was "burdensome."

For all these reasons, the curriculum specialists employ a variety of methods to create a "soft landing" and minimize interruption to established routines and existing institutional priorities. They exhibit a tendency toward what Harry Wolcott (1974) has referred to as "variety-reducing behavior" (p. 269); that is, there is an inherent conservatism in the curriculum specialists' response to the ALTs because they are anxious to keep things manageable and to minimize the burden to themselves and others. Contradictions in policy and overlaps in jurisdictions and programs are often tolerated, and major changes in policy are avoided because new initiatives usually arouse controversy. While such "coping" is usually equated with a lack of principles, it can also be seen as a highly pragmatic response.

In spite of private ambivalence about the JET Program, however, Sato-sensei went to great lengths to promote the program in his prefecture. For one thing, he was committed to finding "base schools" for the exact number of ALTs that the governor and the superintendent had directed him to invite. And once they had arrived, he tried to ensure, not always successfully, that they did not leave prematurely, as this was viewed by his superiors in a very negative light.

Sato-sensei also worked to promote team teaching. Perhaps the most controversial arrangement in the entire JET Program was the requirement that ALTs serve as assistants to Japanese teachers rather than take responsibility for their own classes. The arrival of reform-minded native speakers into an exam-oriented school environment thus created a significant dilemma for Japanese teachers. The English as a Second Language training for the ALTs stressed the student as active learner, the teacher as facilitator, a focus on the content of language as opposed to form, a curriculum that is inherently interesting and relevant to students' lives, and classes marked by liveliness and spontaneity. Partly as a result of this training and partly due to their own view of the goals of education, most ALTs were vigorous proponents of the use of games and other "fun" activities in the team teaching of English. Yet this approach ran counter to Japanese sensibilities about age-appropriate learning, which stressed the serious and sober business of secondary school studies and the importance of repetition of a model delivered by the teacher. It also ran head on into teaching practices honed to entrance exam preparation and wedded to ministry-approved textbooks (Singleton, 1989).

Within this context, how did Sato-sensei maintain momentum for team teaching while not alienating either ALTs or Japanese teachers of English? Sato-sensei, firm in his conviction that team-teaching classes must be wedded to specific grammatical points, did not approve of anyone who deviated from the text, or who used the team-teaching class only for "fun and games" to entertain the students.

Under Sato-sensei's guidance, the prefecture sponsored a series of team-teaching workshops and seminars, leading to publication of a sourcebook of ideas for the communication-oriented English language classroom. Both of these projects were fraught with difficulty. In the case of the seminars, Sato-sensei decided to hold one in each of three districts in the prefecture, but finding schools that were willing to host the event involved some arm-twisting on his part. He faced a boycott of one seminar by a strong union-affiliated high school, and in one school, the JTLs were so unsure of how they should approach the team-taught "demonstration class" (a customary feature of such in-service workshops in Japan; see Shimahara, Chapter 7, this volume) that he had to make several trips to the school to coach them. In moderating the ensuing discussion, he faced the constant challenge of encouraging JTLs to speak up and preventing ALTs from dominating the discussion.

Compiling the team-teaching sourcebook was equally frustrating. Many of the initial ideas submitted were either too removed from the textbooks or followed the text so closely that they inhibited meaningful communication. Nevertheless, Sato-sensei was determined to bring this project to fruition. Observing Sato-sensei's dedication to the cause of team teaching, I was impressed that he did not give up in the face of resistance from JTLs and by his unwavering determination that Japanese teachers of English must improve their English ability. This conviction led him to conduct all team-teaching seminars in English and to insist that the team-teaching guidebook be written in English. When I raised the possibility that the team-teaching sourcebook would reach a wider audience if it were written in Japanese, Sato-sensei's response was simple: "They're English teachers," he said. "They ought to be able to speak and read English."

Sato-sensei's encouragement of team teaching was supported by numerous Ministry of Education initiatives. Most importantly, the revised *Course of Study*, which was to incorporate more communication-based activities, gave Sato-sensei's work a legitimacy in the eyes of teachers. He also attended briefing sessions on team teaching by ministry representatives, and coordinated the pilot school project in his prefecture. He was asked to participate in national-level orientation and mid-year conferences for the JET Program as a presenter, a role that caused him much anxiety. While he did not have a close personal relationship with any one ministry official, he knew many of the officials by name. At the same time, he came to know other curriculum specialists in his region quite well as a result of regional conferences on the JET Program, and he frequently called on them for advice. The interlocking matrix of vertical and horizontal supports was thus crucial in shaping his ability to coordinate this reform effort (see Le-Tendre, Chapter 2, this volume).

How typical was the experience of this prefectural educational administrator? This is a difficult question to answer due to the problem of breaking through the sound barrier in other boards of education. At one extreme Sato-sensei himself told me of a friend of his in a neighboring prefecture who was literally at wits' end (Sato-sensei threw his hands up in the air to signify despair) due to the governor's decree that an ALT be placed in every prefectural high school. On the other hand, not all curriculum specialists view the program with such misgivings. For a minority who are exceptional at English or who have lived abroad, the chance to use one's skills can be very rewarding. In fact, there are some curriculum specialists who have excellent working relationships with virtually all the ALTs in the prefecture. In such cases, the curriculum specialist almost singlehandedly is able to make the program successful from the ALTs' point of view, and such persons are in high demand as "experts" who travel around to various English teachers' meetings dispensing advice.

THE JET PROGRAM IN LOCAL SCHOOLS

Prefectural officials, of course, must turn the ALTs over to school-based personnel, and it is at the school level where the symbolic agreement, so easy to maintain when the concept of "internationalization" is kept at a certain level of abstractness, has the potential to break down. Japanese schools, like their counterparts elsewhere, are far removed from the administrative reach of national and prefectural policies. They are also quite distant in cultural terms from secondary schools in the ALTs' home countries. The environment of most Japanese secondary schools is one of close daily cooperation and interaction centered around the twin goals of preparation for entrance exams and the socialization of students toward norms of group process. In short, the model operating at the school level is one of propriety and organizational maintenance.

On the other hand, in spite of the shared administrative and normative framework for public secondary education, the variation in atmosphere between individual schools is considerable. One of the most remarkable features of the JET Program is its capacity to transport participants past the stereotypes of Japanese education; if there is one refrain that is sung by every ALT, it is that "no two JET experiences are alike." The social and academic environment in a small junior high school in a mountain village is a far cry from the realities of a large junior high school in a major metropolitan area; an ALT's experience in a fisheries or a commercial high school is likely to be quite different from that in a rigorous academic high school bent on sending its graduates to prestigious 4-year universities.

Not surprisingly, I discovered tremendous diversity in the reactions of JTLs and other school staff to the ALTs and the team-teaching enterprise. At one extreme were those who viewed the ALTs as a virus whose deleterious effects were to be controlled at all costs; these were the teachers who spoke of the JET Program as "the second coming of the black ships." At the other extreme were those "teachers-turned-social-critic" who saw the ALTs as a breath of fresh air, exactly what Japan needed to usher in the 21st century. In the middle were the majority of teachers, who felt quite ambivalent about the ALTs. One teacher, trying to put a positive spin on the "black ship" metaphor, noted:

> Black-ship benefits accrue to teachers when the ALT—only one cup keeps you up the entire night—awakens you from your peaceful slumber and causes you acute anxiety. You begin to wonder whether you should have been using more classroom English and to worry whether the students will respond well to the team-taught class. In a dither, you hasten to make preparations but when the preparations take too much time or the paperwork becomes too much of a bother, you begin to resist and eventually fall into the "expel the foreigner" camp. On the other side, however, is the "open up Japan" camp, which seeks to usher in a new era and thus gives wholehearted approval to the appropriateness of the ALT system. Most teachers, my-

self included, are probably somewhere in between these two extremes, fumbling along in a trial-and-error mode as we struggle to respond to this new system.

In any given school, therefore, one could count on some mix of outright resistance, confusion and ambivalence, and general acquiescence. At the level of classroom teaching, this manifested itself in a continuum of responses, from completely turning the class over to the ALT to utilizing him or her as little more than a "human tape recorder."

While such variation makes generalizations difficult, two major problems in the early years of the JET Program were the underutilization of ALTs and the lack of carryover from team-taught to solo-taught English classes. In the first instance, many ALTs found that Japanese teachers had little time or interest in planning or evaluating lessons together or in fully integrating them into school life. In some cases, this was due to the language barrier or to a fear on the part of the Japanese teachers that the ALT would expose their limited English ability. In other cases, Japanese teachers were genuinely preoccupied with other responsibilities, especially the important matter of student guidance. In addition, ALTs discovered that a team-teaching class was conceptualized as a distinct entity, something apart from the regular English classes. As a result, there was minimal carryover between team-teaching classes and regular English classes, even in areas such as the use of basic classroom English. Powerful cultural notions about when it is appropriate for Japanese to use English were at work here. The degree to which Japanese teachers marked off these classes as distinct, both linguistically and conceptually, revealed that team teaching was often viewed as a type of situational accommodation rather than as the substitution of a new pedagogical approach for an old one.

Given these formidable out-of-sight barriers to change, one might easily have predicted an early demise for team teaching. Long-term observers of the JET Program, however, cannot help but notice that team teaching is still alive and well in Japanese secondary schools at the start of the new millennium. Nearly every prefectural board of education in Japan now employs a full-time ALT liaison to oversee and coordinate team-teaching efforts in the prefecture, and many are included in the interviews prospective foreign language teachers must undergo. At the school level, more and more JTLs are "trying out" team teaching, and in many cases this approach has become quite routinized and accepted. There is much discussion now about methods of evaluating team teaching and better ways to integrate ALTs into school life, topics that were barely considered during the early years of the program. It seems as if Japanese teachers have acquired a sense of ownership of team teaching that would have seemed impossible even a decade ago.

What were the cultural and institutional supports that allowed for this gradual transformation and provided a highly intrusive top-down initiative with a chance of success? First of all, these efforts were aided by a general cultural climate within which "internationalization" is seen as prestigious and desirable and "not to do so or to resist doing so is a sign of the backwardness of a country bumpkin" (Befu, 1983, p. 262). On a related note, we cannot discount the fact that unlike many reforms, this one involved real people. ALTs could not be "put on the shelf" like other top-down initiatives. Furthermore, team-taught classes were extremely popular among Japanese students eager to hear native English and to get a break from the routine of exam study. In short, some characteristics that were specific to this policy probably contributed to its success.

An equally important consideration is that the Ministry of Education did not force boards of education to take ALTs, nor did boards of education require schools to do so; even individual faculty members who did not want to team-teach could usually find an excuse to avoid it. Persistent pressure was used, but there was always an "escape hatch" for those schools and individuals that needed more time to prepare themselves. At the same time, considerable resources and institutional support were provided at both the national and prefectural level, all aimed at creating a climate of intellectual debate about how to improve team teaching.

Over time, this approach enabled team teaching to permeate the environment of professional development for Japanese teachers (Shimahara, Chapter 7, this volume). For instance, prefectural English teachers' study groups all across the country took up the issue, conducting surveys and publishing reflections and advice from teachers who had tried team teaching. At both the school and the district level, the available framework for in-service training allowed Japanese teachers to conduct demonstration classes with ALTs and to benefit from extensive discussion by their colleagues. Select schools could participate in the Ministry of Education's pilot school project in the prefecture, and select teachers could participate in the national-level seminars. Both of these initiatives created a cohort of teachers who were intimately familiar with the strengths and limitations of the team teaching scheme. In sum, by harnessing the vast network of professional development opportunities, team teaching worked its way into the mechanism of craft at the local levels.

CONCLUSION

In important ways, this case study of foreign language reform illuminates the relation between administrative levels in policy implementation in Japan. It suggests, first of all, that our understanding of Japanese education as a "centralized" system needs to be qualified. To a large extent, power does remain in the hands of national-level administrators, but initiative and decision-making are delegated to the lower levels of the system. In short, the national ministries coordinating the JET Program seemed content to set minimum standards, provide a model, and then let prefectures and localities work out the details of implementation. Local boards of education also offered tremendous leeway to local schools, all the while hammering away to create momentum for reform. Far from being a command system, policy implementation seems to have worked through a combination of firm persuasion from the top and a general willingness on the part of the curriculum specialists and Japanese teachers to accept the authority of higher-ranking administrators while retaining the right to pursue their own interests in specific instances.

During the early years of the JET Program, foreign participants frequently took Japanese teachers and administrators to task for the slow and laborious pace of change. "It's glacial" became a disparaging phrase designed to call attention to Japanese resistance to change and preference for the status quo. Yet a long-term perspective provides a different view. At first the ALTs were largely outside the framework of exam-oriented English. But as the *Course of Study*, English textbooks, and even the content of entrance examinations were modified, and as team teaching began to permeate the world of professional development for teachers, the presence of the ALTs became more legitimate. A long-term view reveals that the ice was melting, slowly but steadily, and that teaching practices were changing.

While one may question the pace of change in Japan, it can also be argued that incremental change is preferable to the dizzying pace of innovation in the United States, where any given school district typically has dozens, if not hundreds, of independent, ongoing reform initiatives in its schools and classrooms. As Albert Shanker (1995) suggested, "the notion that standardization and routinization are evils and that teachers should be creative and innovative every minute of the day is disastrous" (pp. 52–53). It leads to confusion and fragmentation, to a continual reinventing of the wheel without any possibility of dissemination on a larger level.

The incrementalist framework proposed here suggests that gridlock in national-level politics doesn't always mean that schools are at a standstill. Indeed, my findings support Christopher Hood's (2001) revisionist interpretation of Leonard Schoppa's (1991) argument that educational reform is stalled due to "immobilist politics." Hood argues that in the mid-1980s Prime Minister Yasuhiro Nakasone inspired a set of slow but steady changes in the structure and content of Japanese schools that is only now beginning to be recognized. These include liberalization of the educational system (including more room for electives in high school), growing support for the private sector in education, more focus on the individual (including the 5-day-week and "lifelong learning"), and a smorgasbord of initiatives related to internationalization (see also Azuma, Chapter 1; DeCoker, Chapter 9, this volume).

The incrementalist approach has strong roots in the neo-Confucianist approach to learning. Rohlen (1992) argues persuasively that Japan is distinctive in its devotion to the idea that "self-cultivation through the disciplined pursuit of knowledge is the path to human perfection" (p. 328). The capacity of Japanese teachers to place themselves in the position of learner vis-à-vis the ALTs and to approach team teaching as an opportunity for "learning by doing" is consistent with Rohlen's description of Japan as a "learning society." Japanese teachers and local administrators have taken a top-down initiative in which they had absolutely no say, and over time they have mobilized knowledge and striven for mastery, while refusing to relinquish their own autonomy. That Japanese teachers have learned quickly, if not always smoothly, shows that lasting educational reform comes not only from "the big fixes" designed by educational researchers or career administrators but from a continuous striving to perfect daily practice and the conduct of one's life on the part of those closest to the classroom.

REFERENCES

Advisory Group on Structural Economic Adjustment for International Harmony. (1988). The Maekawa report. In D. I. Okimoto & T. P. Rohlen (Eds.), *Inside the Japanese system: Readings on contemporary society and political economy* (pp. 252–256). Stanford, CA: Stanford University Press.

Befu, H. (1983). The internationalization of Japan and *Nihon Bunkaron*. In H. Mannari & H. Befu (Eds.), *The challenge of Japan's internationalization: Organization and culture* (pp. 232–266). Tokyo: Kodansha.

Council of Local Authorities for International Relations. (1988). *JET program advertising brochure*. Tokyo: Author.

Hood, C. (2001). *Japanese education reform: Nakasone's legacy*. New York: Routledge.

Japan Times Weekly International Edition, (1997, April 7–13, p. 20).

McConnell, D. (2000). *Importing diversity: Inside Japan's JET program*. Berkeley: University of California Press.

Miller, R. (1982). *Japan's modern myth: The language and beyond*. New York: Weatherhill.

Ministry of Education. (1994). *Handbook for team-teaching*. Tokoyo: Author.

Rohlen, T. P. (1984). Conflict in institutional environments: Politics in education. In E. S. Krauss, T. P. Rohlen, & P. G. Steinhoff (Eds.), *Conflict in Japan* (pp. 136–173). Honolulu: University of Hawaii Press.

Rohlen, T. P. (1992). Learning: The mobilization of knowledge in the Japanese political economy. In S. Kumon and H. Rosovsky (Eds.), *The political economy of Japan, vol. 3: Cultural and social dynamics* (pp. 321–263). Stanford: Stanford University Press.

Schoppa, L. (1991). *Education reform in Japan: A case of immobilist politics.* New York: Routledge.

Shanker, A. (1995). Education reform: What's not being said. *Daedalus, 124*(4), 47–54.

Singleton, J. (1989). *Gambaru*: A Japanese cultural theory of learning. In J. J. Shields, Jr. (Ed.), *Japanese schooling: Patterns of socialization, equality and political control* (pp. 8–15). University Park, PA: The Pennsylvania State University Press.

Summaries of Reports from the 1990–1992 Team-Teaching Research Schools [Heisei 4–5 nendô Teimu Teichingu Kenkyû Shinshinkô Kenkyû Shuroku]. (1994). *Curriculum materials for secondary education* [Chûtô Kyôiku Shiryô], 4 (651).

Wolcott, H. (1974). The elementary school principal: Notes from a field study. In G. Spindler (Ed.), *Education and cultural process: Toward an anthropology of education* (pp. 176–204). New York: Holt, Rinehart and Winston.

CHAPTER 9

Deregulating Japan's High School Curriculum: The Unintended Consequences of Educational Reform

Gary DeCoker

THE RAPID INCREASE IN THE Japanese high school graduation and university entrance rates over the last 4 decades, coupled with the perception that the secondary education system contributes to various social maladies affecting adolescents, has led to numerous proposals to ease government control of the secondary school curriculum. But the goals and rhetoric of reform differ from the reality of high school students' preparing for college. Ministry of Education reforms begun in the early 1990s have created a decrease in high school course requirements and a bewildering variety of options in the university entrance system, yet flexibility for the typical Japanese high school student has actually diminished. Researchers have recently begun to recognize these unintended consequences, but the political appeal of deregulation continues to foster proposals that open up the system in ways that force students to decide early which colleges to pursue, often leaving them with few choices in their high school curriculum.

This chapter will present an overview of Ministry of Education reforms of the high school curriculum and university entrance examination system, followed by a discussion of the efficacy of these reforms as Japan struggles to adjust to recent demographic, economic, and social change. The third section presents an illustrative example from Yamagata Prefecture, and the conclusion compares Japanese and U.S. approaches to curriculum, testing, and university admission procedures.

JAPAN'S SECONDARY AND POSTSECONDARY EDUCATION

Japan's centralized education system allows for more precise articulation between the high school and university education systems than in the United States. Despite the Ministry of Education's ability to set curriculum and admission procedures, however, social, economic, and demographic change often seems to overwhelm planned reforms, especially given the increasing dynamism in the private sector of supplemental education.

High School and University Enrollment

Between 1960 and 1980, the percentage of young people graduating from high school rose dramatically from 47% to over 90%. In addition, the number of high school graduates making application to 2- and 4-year colleges also rose dramatically, from 242,000 in 1960 to over 900,000 in the early 1990s. At present, nearly 50% of Japanese young people enter some form of postsecondary education, compared with about 10% in 1960. During these years, under the guidance of the Ministry of Education, the university system expanded to meet enrollment demands. Ministry regulations specify the number of students each university may accept, and although the places for high school graduates to enroll kept pace with the burgeoning number of college applicants, much of the growth took place at the lower levels of the university hierarchy. The number of places available at prestigious universities grew less dramatically over the last 35 years, resulting in more pressure on applicants to top-ranking universities. Reports of Japan's examination hell and the pressure on high school students, in fact, describe primarily students seeking admission to these elite universities.

In the early 1990s, after 3 decades of dramatic expansion of Japan's university system, the 18-year-old population began a precipitous decline to about 1.5 million in 2000 from over 2 million a decade earlier. A decade hence, the number will dip below 1.2 million. This decline, coupled with the growth of lower-ranking universities and junior colleges, has begun to create a shortage of applicants, leading to competition among these institutions to recruit students. In other words, top high school students continue to compete for places at the most prestigious universities, but for the foreseeable future, the competition at the lower-ranking institutions will be between universities trying to recruit students rather than between students seeking enrollment. Some people within the university community see hope in the rising percentage of high school graduates who aspire to continue their education, but other observers note that Japan's stalled economy has reduced the economic incentive for students considering higher education.

The most realistic appraisal is that Japan's lower-ranking universities and junior colleges must make dramatic adjustments or risk closing.

The University Entrance Examination System

Japan's educational policymakers responded to the postwar rise in university enrollment by revising the university entrance examination system. The first major change took place in 1979 with the development of the Joint First-Stage Achievement Test (JFSAT). Prior to this date, each university offered its own entrance examination. To be more precise, in many universities each department conducted its own application process and administered its own examination, a system requiring applicants to take the examination at each university where they applied. The National Center for University Entrance Examinations, a Ministry of Education administrative institution, created the JFSAT to be taken prior to the examinations at individual universities, making these "second-stage examinations." The goal of this new system was to make the examination process uniform and to bring the entrance examinations closer in content to the high school curriculum. Students, in theory, could then concentrate on their high school classes and would feel less pressure to focus on supplemental test preparation. Based on their JFSAT scores, students also would have a more accurate view of their ability before applying to a specific university.

The JFSAT, consisting of examinations in the five basic subjects (Japanese, English, mathematics, social studies, and science), was taken by all applicants to national and local public universities. Private universities, however, did not use the JFSAT. Reaction to the examination was mixed, with criticism focusing on its failure to achieve the stated purpose of reducing examination pressure. Like most of the second-stage examinations, the JFSAT consisted primarily of objective questions, and in the conclusion of many observers merely added to intensity of the examination process.

In 1990, the National Center for University Entrance Examinations replaced the JFSAT with the National Center Test (NCT), ushering in many changes. First, some private universities began to require the test. Second, the NCT expanded the examination menu in an attempt to respond to the increasing variety of curricular offerings in Japanese high schools. Beginning in 1990 with 18 examinations in five subjects, the number of examinations increased to 31 in six subjects by 1997, the sixth subject resulting from the division of social studies into history/geography and civics. Third, universities no longer were required to use tests in all the subject areas. Instead they could allow their applicants to choose from among a selection of examinations offered each year. Under this "à la carte system," some universities require an examination in only one subject, others in all six. And many give applicants the option of choosing a specific examination, or sometimes two or three, from among a number of examinations in certain subject areas. For instance, the humanities department of Kyoto University, in its first application period of 1997, required the following National Center examinations: one from English, one from Japanese, two from mathematics, a choice of one of three from geography/history, and one of five from science. In general, private universities require fewer National Center examinations than do public universities. In both the public and private sectors, however, there are few universities that require only one center examination. At the other extreme, the number requiring six exams is also small. The overall trend, however, is to require fewer center examinations.

Many private universities, especially lower-ranking ones, have begun to experiment with other means of selecting students under a system called "nominated admissions." The profit motive often drives the experimentation. New or unique application procedures can increase the applicant pool, and for some schools, application fees are a major source of revenue, second only to tuition. Most private universities that use the new procedures set up various criteria such as participation in a sport, a certain grade point average, a recommendation of a principal, foreign language ability, or community service. Students applying for one of the spaces allocated for a specific criterion face some combination of a university-created examination, interview, short essay, portfolio, aptitude test, or a means of assessing ability in the arts, athletics, and so forth. In the public sector, however, fewer applicants are nominated students, and about half of these still take the NCT in addition to following other admission procedures.

Application procedures for nominated students vary greatly. Interviews can be perfunctory or highly competitive. Essays can be devoid of subject-matter content or highly contextualized. Sometimes questions are given in English and answered in Japanese. Examination questions in a specific subject area most often contain content taken from the corresponding course in the high school curriculum. Some universities, however, have begun using comprehensive questions that are taken from more than one subject area. In all cases, however, applicants arrive at the university knowing what type of test or interview to expect. Universities publicize their procedures, and *juku* provide students with additional information about requirements in each department of each university. *Juku* compile the most thorough information for student applications, and their participation in the university entrance system seems to have grown as a result of recent reforms (Russell, Chapter 10, this volume).

Japan's High Schools by Type

In 1948 the Ministry of Education established two types of high schools: "academic schools" and "specialty schools." Specialty schools, about 24% of the total, refer primarily to vocational schools such as agricultural, mechanical, and commercial. Academic schools, the remaining three-quarters, often divide their students into tracks on their entry into high school or on completion of the first year. Each tracked group is made up of about 40 students who take most of their classes together until they graduate. Some schools use these groups as a means of tracking students by ability, an increasingly used strategy over the last decade. For instance, a school might have four tracks that would take the same classes in the same curriculum, but to a different degree of depth. Another way schools use these groupings of students is to create tracks with different curricula. For instance, a school might have an international track, a computer track, or a college-entrance track in addition to its regular tracks. One of the most common means of tracking students is through the creation of humanities and science tracks, a division usually made after the first year of high school. Further grouping might be made based on the type and level of university to which the students aspire, thereby creating separate groups of students preparing for entrance to national and to private universities. The ability to divide students, of course, depends on the school's size and student-faculty ratio. Some private schools are able to create groups of about 15, allowing students sometimes to take classes in these small groups and sometimes in a larger group.

Specialty or vocational schools typically enroll students with lower academic aspirations and lower ability. As college enrollment rates have increased, however, some of these schools have begun creating a track for students who have decided to pursue college enrollment (i.e., an academic track within the specialty school). More commonly students are grouped by the type of career or vocational license they want to pursue. The academic rigor of vocational schools varies, as does their ability to attract students. The decreasing population of young people and the increasing college enrollment rate make it difficult for some vocational schools to survive. In order to offer these schools another option, in 1994 the Ministry of Education created a third category of school called "comprehensive schools." These schools typically are converted from existing schools, most commonly from vocational schools but occasionally from academic schools. Still, they enroll less than 1% of Japan's high school students. Comprehensive schools attempt to create a unique curriculum based on the perceived needs of a changing population of junior high school graduates.

The curricular offerings, however, depend greatly on the available re-sources of the school and the number of students enrolled. Some vocational schools do not have enough students to allow them to convert the entire school to the comprehensive program, so they create one or two compre-hensive tracks in addition to their existing vocational tracks. And in some cases the conversion to a comprehensive school can dramatically change the type of student applicants, creating a need for a more college-prepara-tory-style curriculum and a move further away from vocational programs.

High Schools and Their Curriculum

The Ministry of Education promulgates a new *Course of Study* about every decade, based on the recommendation of various advisory councils (see Azuma, Chapter 1, this volume). By the implementation date, all schools must revise their curriculum to meet the new version. Since World War Two, Japan has seen eight courses of study, with dates for their implemen-tation at the high school level of 1948, 1951, 1956, 1963, 1973, 1982, 1994, and 2003.

The high school *Course of Study* includes a list of required courses and a total number of credits allocated to each—a credit being the equivalent of one 45-minute period per day for the entire school year. As can be seen in Figure 9.1, from 1948 to 1973 the number of credits required for gradua-tion from a 3-year academic high school remained at 85. In 1982 the num-ber became 80. The current proposal for 2003 further reduces the number to 74. This reduction of six credits results from Japan's transition to a 5-day-school week. The number of credits in required subjects has changed more than the total number of credits for graduation. In 1956 the number of credits of required subjects increased from 38 to 45. In 1963 it jumped to its postwar high of 68, and then back to 47 in 1973. The 2003 revision calls for a total of 34 credits of required subjects. The increase in 1963, however, is somewhat deceiving because it is the only year in which foreign language classes (most often English) were required by the Ministry of Edu-cation. In subsequent years, most schools, regardless of the changes in the *Course of Study*, continued to require their students to take English be-cause of its importance on university entrance examinations.

The best way to understand the changes in the required subjects is to look at the four major subject areas, those that are tested along with En-glish on the entrance examinations, that is, Japanese language, social stud-ies, mathematics, and science. The total number of required credits for these subjects over the last four revisions went from a high of 43 in 1963 to a low of 15 in 2003. On the surface, therefore, it appears that Japan's high school curriculum has become more flexible since 1963. The 1973

Figure 9.1. Academic High School Curriculum: Number of Credits Required for Graduation

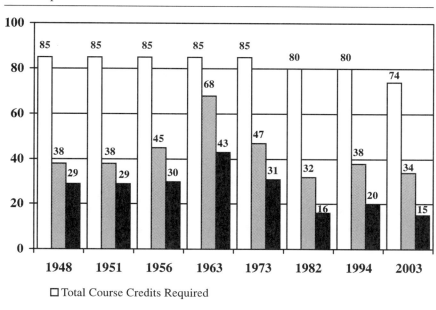

□ Total Course Credits Required

▨ Credits in Required Courses

■ Credits in Required Courses in Japanese, Social Studies, Science, & Mathematics

numbers, however, are actually a return to the 1956 amounts. The first major drop in credits for required courses really took place in 1982. According to Ministry of Education educational reform documents, the move toward flexibility in the high school curriculum began in 1973, but in fact, 1982 might be considered a more accurate beginning point. In any case, although the rhetoric of flexibility has continued to dominate the Ministry of Education's reform efforts for the last 3 decades, a more important question remains: How have Japan's high schools and their students used the increased flexibility?

The requirement of English in the curriculum of most high schools presents an answer to this question. Since 1973 schools have had the option of not including foreign language in the curriculum, but because of its importance in entrance examinations, most of Japan's high schools require

English. Without it, they would loose their credibility with students and parents. A similar situation exists in the other four examination subjects. Over the years that the Ministry of Education has decreased the number of required credits in these subject areas, academic high schools have not followed suit. Guided by the entrance examinations, these high schools continue to require more courses than do the ministry guidelines. They also require more total credits.

The government's 3-decade attempt to create a more diversified high school curriculum is striking given Japan's centralized educational system. Outside observers might expect the change to take less time. Shimahara (1995), however, points out that there are many constraints on the Ministry of Education's power to implement its reform agenda at the high school level. First, the entrance examination system defines the curriculum of most academic high schools. Second, prefectural boards of education exercise substantial control over Japan's high schools. In some cases, for instance, prefectural education policies seem to work directly against the Ministry of Education's goal of diversifying the curriculum. These issues will be explored in the next two sections.

THE UNFORESEEN IMPACT OF THE REFORM OF THE UNIVERSITY ENTRANCE EXAMINATION SYSTEM

Because schools set their curriculum and students set their educational agenda with an eye sharply focused on the university entrance examinations, the Ministry of Education has attempted to reform the high school curriculum by changing the nature of the examination system and through various directives to the universities. Some are mandatory, such as the requirement that the public national and local universities use the NCT; others are strong suggestions, such as the promotion of nominated admission procedures.

The increasing number of National Center examinations has created an incredible variety among university examination requirements. In the social sciences there is an exam for every course in the high school curriculum. In mathematics, science, and Japanese language there are examinations for the first one or two levels, but not for the advanced or vocational courses. In foreign language, there are examinations in English, Chinese, French, and German. As described above, some universities require specific exams; others offer a choice between examinations offered in specified subject areas. Some use only one of the subject areas; others use all six. The complexity of the system, for high school students and for their teachers, is astounding. A table listing the NCT requirements of the departments of national and local universities takes up 95 dense pages in one *juku* publication. And, of course, the NCT is only part of the admission procedure. Students must also factor in the second-stage exam and the possibility of nominated admission. The end result of this complexity is that each student, depending on his or her college aspirations, needs a unique high school program. These programs include course curriculum and also strategies for approaching the various types of examinations: objective, essay, interview, and so forth.

Looking first only at the NCT, social studies includes nine examinations broken into two subject areas: six in geography/history and three in civics. Universities that require an examination in social studies most often require a selection of one exam in each of the two areas, but some universities give a choice within only one area, and still others require a specific exam in one or both areas. When there is a choice among examinations, students usually look to the second-stage examination of the university. In the case where a specific social science exam is required, students typically choose the same examination on the NCT, thereby allowing themselves to focus on the same content for both examinations. Once the students have decided on the specific examination(s), then it naturally follows that the high schools try to prepare them, sometimes through manipulation of the curriculum. For instance, teachers might skip sections of the textbook that do not have relevance for the university examinations. Or a school preparing students for the Japanese history entrance examination might use the world history course to conduct additional examination preparation in Japanese history. At a visit to a private academic high school, I showed a group of social studies teachers a list of the school's courses that I had received from the principal. The teachers began a discussion of some discrepancies on list. Finally one blurted out, "Oh, this is the list we put together for the Ministry of Education visit." They promptly discarded it and produced a document showing the actual curriculum.

A parallel strategy in the preparation of students for a specific examination agenda results when students, realizing that they may need to take exams in only two or three subject areas, begin to focus on these subjects at their *juku*. This narrowing of focus directly conflicts with the Ministry of Education goal of broadening the high school curriculum. In fact some researchers are beginning to argue that the narrowing of curricular focus by many high school students is the direct result of recent Ministry of Education efforts. In other words, the more flexibility high schools and students have to create their own individual courses of study, the more narrowly they will tailor their courses to examination preparation. And the increasing flexibility given universities to choose exams from the NCT has exacerbated the problem. As universities reduce the number of required examinations, their future students focus on even fewer subjects, and enter college with less curricular breadth. To compensate for this, many colleges have begun to provide remedial work for their entering students. Of course, the problem could be eliminated by requiring a wider array of examinations, but in a time of intense competition for a shrinking number of high school seniors, not all universities have this option.

Researchers at the National Center for University Entrance Examinations have begun studying the effects of the changing entrance examination environment on the high school curriculum (Arai, 2000). In 1995 and 1999, they surveyed college sophomores from various academic departments at national, local public, and private universities. The research points to a trend among high school students toward narrowing the curricular focus to match college aspirations. For instance, under the 1994 *Course of Study*, high school students had a choice between a Japanese history and a geography course. Between 60% and 65% of the sophomores who were majors in the sciences chose geography in high school, but of the majors in the humanities, education, and social sciences, the percentage was about 40. Of the social sciences, geography is most like a natural science, and university science departments often require it on their examination. Similar differences in course selection existed in math and science, where science majors in the 1999 study typically took the more rigorous Mathematics C and Mathematics III in high school. In science, where high school students chose two subjects from a list of five (integrated science, physics, chemistry, biology, and earth science), most of the college students surveyed took chemistry. For the second course, nonscience majors typically took biology, and science majors took physics.

The Ministry of Education and the universities currently are debating the influence of the NCT on high school course selection, but major changes do not seem likely, in part because the university community is not in agreement. The ministry tends to prefer influencing the high school curriculum through the *Course of Study*. For example, a general science course had been required under the 1973 and 1982 guidelines. In 1994, when the requirement was dropped, few students enrolled in integrated science because most universities require tests in a specific science curriculum. The 2003 *Course of Study* requires either basic science or integrated science in order to ensure that students have a broad science background. In similar fashion, world history became a requirement under the 1994 guidelines and this continues in the 2003 version.

Universities, too, have become concerned with high school course selection, but the quality of the university influences its preferences for reform of the NCT. The narrowing of focus among high school students has allowed students to better prepare for their examinations, and as a result, increasing numbers of students receive high test scores. The resulting clustering of students at the top of the scale reduces the NCT's ability to differentiate between applicants, making the second-stage examinations offered by the universities a key criterion for entrance into the best universities. The top universities, pointing to a decline in the overall quality of applicants, are pressuring the ministry to increase the rigor of the NCT. But universities of lower quality, confronted with a decline in the 18-year-old population, worry that a change in the NCT might lower their applicant pool. The Ministry of Education, for its part, remains committed to the idea that the examinations should be based on the content of the high school curriculum. To create NCT examinations that include content not taught in high school would reinforce the need for students to enroll in *juku*. And one of the major goals of the NCT is to reduce the pressure of the entrance examination system and the influence of *juku*. The 2003 curriculum (with even fewer specific high school course requirements), the increasing competition among universities for applicants, and the ability of the *juku* to adjust to the changing environment will continue to make it difficult for the ministry to achieve its long-standing goal of broadening the curriculum of the college-preparatory student.

FLEXIBILITY AND INDIVIDUALITY IN YAMAGATA PREFECTURE

A good example of the Ministry of Education's difficulty in instituting reform comes from Yamagata Prefecture. In 1988 the Prefectural Board of Education instituted a 5-year program focusing on increasing the university entrance rates of 16 academic high schools. When the program began, Yamagata's high school graduation rate had consistently ranked among the country's highest, yet its university entrance rate was near the bottom of the 47 prefectures. In addition, Yamagata University, the national university in the prefecture's capital city, enrolled far more students from outside the prefecture than from Yamagata. The prefecture's low ranking in college attendance probably resulted from a number of factors; for example, the prefecture had only one 4-year university, and the income level of its residents is lower than that of most prefectures. The Prefectural Board of Education, however, placed some responsibility on the low level of scholarship among its academic schools, and they created an "Activation Program" aimed at these schools.

In the beginning, each of nine schools received three million yen (about $27,000) per year. The Board of Education directed that schools use the funds to improve university entrance rates through various means including improved student guidance, development of effective teaching materials, cooperative exchanges with successful high schools, lectures on university and career opportunities, and academic training camps. Each school developed its own programs independently. The results were measured simply by the percentage increase in university enrollment. After 2 years, the first nine high schools netted a 22.7% increase in the number of students accepted to national universities. One school went from 75 to 139, an 85.3% increase. Two others increased over 40%. The rest were less dramatic, but all except one school made increases, and that school declined only by one, from 65 to 64 admitted students. Based on these results, the prefecture extended the participation to seven more schools. At the end of 5 years, the entrance rate for the entire prefecture went from 22.2% to 25.6% and the prefectural high schools to 27.1%, cutting in half the gap between them and the national average. The program received a good deal of attention in Yamagata and throughout the northern region, and rural prefectures across the country began using it as a model for their own efforts to increase their university entrance rate.

Ironically, the prefectural education officials and high school administrators used Ministry of Education phrases such as "developing the unique characteristics of the schools" when describing the program. As a result, the program seemed to follow the Ministry of Education's efforts to broaden the curriculum. The actual result, however, did not lead to a more flexible and diverse curriculum. In fact, one Yamagata prefectural education official who was directly involved with the program told me that the 16 schools did not change very much. The increase in university enrollment probably came more from a change in consciousness than from changes in the curriculum. At best, some teachers visited elementary and junior high schools and began to think differently about the way they teach. But the curriculum, he said, remained largely unchanged. For example, Tsuruoka Minami High School and Sakata Higashi High School, two of the original nine schools in the program, both require far more than the 80 credits that the Ministry of Education requires for graduation and take similar approaches toward preparing their students for university entrance examinations.

At a visit to Tsuruoka Minami in the late 1990s, I learned that students in the academic track must complete 105 credits for graduation. Of these, most are required courses. The only choices exist in history/geography, science, and the arts, but course selection here, too, is rather narrow. The only other decision students make is whether to enter the science or the humanities track after the first year. The courses are almost the same for the first 2 years, however, so the actual difference in courses comes only in year 3. Throughout the first 2 years students also use the same textbooks, regardless of their track. In English and math courses, however, students are split into three levels. Those in the highest-level classes finish the textbook sooner and move to supplementary books. In the future the school plans to use different levels of textbooks in English, although the course titles would not change. According to the principal, students consider their university aspirations when exercising their few curricular choices.

Tsuruoka Minami also offers students many supplementary classes to prepare for university entrance examinations. During most of the summer vacation, school remains in session for special examination-preparation courses. About 80% of the students attend, paying a minimal tuition to cover the cost of materials and a small stipend for the teachers. During late spring and autumn, students can also participate in an after-school program, choosing from a variety of courses, each of which meets for 65 minutes. The school teachers and administrators feel obliged to offer these programs because of the lack of *juku* in the area.

In addition to supplementary classes, the school offers a variety of practice examinations that they purchase from private companies. These tests, which mimic the university entrance examinations, provide a national ranking of each student, and most students choose to take these tests, even though the schools must offer them on the weekends due to a Ministry of Education rule that forbids using school time for practice examinations. In each of their first 2 years, students at Tsuruoka Minami take four of these tests. From April to December of the last year of high school, however, they take practice tests every month. In addition, during these months, the school offers special sessions to help students prepare for the newly implemented essay examinations that many universities have begun to use. This preparation takes place outside of class time in small groups of students working with one teacher. Each year the students also take six term tests, prepared by the teachers. Students are ranked by the results of these tests, and the rankings are posted in the school and sent to parents.

The strategies used at Tsuruoka Minami are not unique. Most academic schools take a similar approach toward readying their students for the examinations. But it is ironic, given Ministry of Education reform efforts aimed at creating flexibility in the high school curriculum, that the Yamagata program encouraged its best prefectural schools to go further in the direction of examination preparation. Realistically, however, if increasing the university entrance rate of graduates is the goal, a high school has few options. And in rural areas, schools must offer opportunities similar to those urban students can find at *juku*. In addition, these schools often look to successful urban schools for insights into examination preparation. A principal at one of the leading private schools in suburban Tokyo told me that he meets with many delegations of teachers and administrators who come from rural schools to study his school's strategies. A representative from a leading *juku* also told me that he has received similar delegations. Regardless of the Ministry of Education goal of lessening the pressures of examinations and diversifying the curriculum, rural prefectures like Yamagata have no choice but to take the successful urban schools and *juku* as their models.

CONCLUSION

Although the difference between the Japanese and American approaches to curriculum, testing, and university admission makes a direct comparison difficult, various issues can be explored. Japanese students take entrance examinations during the high school and college admission process. In addition, domestic and international researchers test random samples of Japanese students, and in 2002 the Ministry of Education began giving achievement tests to 7% of Japan's 5th and 9th grade students. Despite these tests, nothing similar to U.S. state proficiency tests exists to provide the general public with comparative data on students, schools, and prefectures. Students, instead, may elect to take numerous tests produced by *juku*, either at the *juku* themselves or at their high schools on weekends. The *juku* then publish the results in a variety of formats, including comparative percentiles and estimates of each student's level of potential university enrollment. Individual high schools and *juku* often publicly display this information about their students. These tests serve college-bound students, and therefore they exert more pressure on students of a higher academic level. The examinations in most U.S. states, however, focus on the student of lower ability who must pass in order to receive a high school diploma. Few states have tests that challenge their top high school students. In addition, tests are routinely given during the school day, upsetting the normal class schedule for a number of weeks each year.

The Japanese system also seems to put more constant pressure on middle- and high school students. Because the public views its high schools and universities in a hierarchy based on perceived differences in quality, students must determine a level at which to prepare. *Juku* and other privately produced examinations, taken by many students every few months, provide the most common measure of ability, and after each sitting, point the student to a specific slice of the school hierarchy (see LeTendre, Chapter 2, this volume). For the Japanese student, the results of the practice examinations provide fairly immediate feedback and make it obvious that each increment of preparation may result in entrance to a slightly higher level university.

College-prep students in the United States, lacking such a precise system, feel less academic pressure. Although they may be anxious about the SAT or ACT tests, their preparation—vocabulary building, test-taking strategies, and general academic skills—typically does not require a sustained effort comparable to that of Japanese college-bound students, and their preparation work is not directly related to their school curriculum. Some elite universities in the United States, recognizing the importance of content knowledge, have begun to make use of the SAT II Subject Tests, but still only a small number of U.S. universities actually require them. U.S. high school students, too, can choose more rigorous honors courses and take the Advanced Placement examinations, but these tests typically fall at the conclusion of the academic year. Few indicators along the way offer American students the kind of consistent challenge that Japan's college-bound students receive.

Of course, American students must work to achieve a respectable grade point average. But these days, with dozens of valedictorians and students achieving grades above the 4.0 average, academic success as measured by grades seems attainable by many students. Admission officers at Harvard and other top U.S. schools complain, somewhat tongue-in-cheek, of having only 4.0+ valedictorians to choose from. This situation may be a blessing for Harvard, but not for its applicants who must find other ways to distinguish themselves. Over the last decade or so, co-curricular activities and community service have become the most popular means of enhancing a college application. American high school students now must weigh the value-added benefits of each additional activity, and they often jump from one thing to the next in order to enhance their resumés. While Japanese students go from school to the *juku*, American students go from sports to play practice or from Habitat for Humanity to a part-time job.

The increasing support for educational standards among the American public indicates a desire for a more precise means of measuring student success. And for some American teachers, Japan's system probably looks good because it changes the teacher-student dynamic, shifting the focus from teacher-determined grades to student ability as measured on a standardized examination. The Japanese public, however, still laments the pressure that the entrance examination system places on college-bound students. In response, many Japanese colleges, at the behest of the Ministry of Education, continue to develop means of circumventing the examination system through nominated-admission procedures that place more emphasis on a student's co- and extracurricular activities, the very things that occupy the time of so many American high school students. But in Japan there is an important difference: The focus is typically on one activity rather than the wide range of activities that occupy U.S. students.

President Bush's program for yearly statewide testing extends the pressure from high schools into elementary and middle schools by threatening to close poor-performing schools. The Japanese public, on the other hand, focuses its attention more on the quality of academic high schools and judges them by the university enrollment of their graduates. In turn, a school's ability to attract students in the marketplace determines its viability. For schools that are declining in enrollment, the Ministry of Education has created the possibility of renewal through curricular reform. Some vocational schools, by changing themselves into comprehensive schools or including these tracks, have seen a higher university enrollment rate for their graduates, thereby increasing their status. In Bush's proposal, however, the states would be required to close poor-performing schools and to replace them with various public/private or pure private initiatives geared to improving test scores.

In summary, the Japanese continue to focus on incremental reform through the revision of the *Course of Study* and the National Center Test. In this somewhat controlled environment, the private sector adjusts and repositions itself to meet the needs of its clients. In the United States, by contrast, the private sector is being enlisted to assist or sometimes to replace the public schools (see Russell, Chapter 10, this volume). As the goals of the U.S. educational system become more precise as measured on standardized achievement tests, the private sector will increase its ability to produce gains in the test scores. The question remains whether private involvement will complement or displace the efforts of the public schools. In the freewheeling U.S. educational marketplace, private initiatives seem often to supersede the public schools. In Japan, where the government exerts far tighter control over the private sector, the relationship probably will continue to be somewhat more complementary.

Future reforms of the examination systems in both countries will probably continue to be incremental. In the United States, the federal and state governments seem intent on using examinations as a means of reforming the educational system, even though many K–12 and university educators warn of their negative influence ("Belden Russonello," 2000). Many ad hoc groups recently have formed to advocate changes or to directly oppose state and national testing programs. For instance, a group of prominent American research universities formed the Standards for Success project to explore the influence of proficiency testing on student preparation for college (Hebel, 2001). Their goal is to come to a consensus on what an incoming college student should know and be able to do. Given the enthusiasm for testing in Washington and in state capitals and the disparity in approaches among the 50 states, however, their ability to exert an immediate, unifying influence on the high school curriculum is dubious. American education, for the foreseeable future, will be guided by tests rather than curriculum. And for U.S. universities, the lack of consistency in the K–12 curriculum across the nation will result in the continued use of a variety of admission procedures as colleges try to make accommodations for students of diverse backgrounds.

In Japan, even though the Ministry of Education seems to prefer more dramatic reforms, the universities cannot agree, and the *juku* seem to take reforms in different directions. Nevertheless, the contrast with the United States is great. The ministry, rather than supporting or requiring standardized tests, restricts their use by high schools. And despite the government's desire for curricular flexibility, the newly implemented *Course of Study* still presents a well-balanced, academically challenging curricular model for the nation's schools.

Acknowledgment. This chapter benefited from a discussion with colleagues at the Midwest Japan Seminar meeting at Miami University of Ohio in January 1999.

REFERENCES

Arai, K. (2000). *Gakusei wa kôkô de nani o manandekuruka.* [What are high school students studying?] Tokyo: National Center for University Entrance Examinations.

Belden Russonello & Stewart Research and Communications. (2000, November). *Making the grade: Teachers' attitudes toward academic standards* (Findings of National Survey of Public School Teachers for *Education Week*). Washington, DC: Author.

Hebel, S. (2001, February 9). Universities push to influence state tests for high-school students. *Chronicle of Higher Education,* pp. A23–24.

Shimahara, N. (1995). Restructuring Japanese high schools: Reforms for diversity. *Educational Policy, 9*(2), 185–200.

CHAPTER 10

The Role of the Private Sector in Determining National Standards: How *Juku* Undermine Japanese Educational Authority

Nancy Ukai Russell

JAPAN'S *JUKU*—MORE FAMILIARLY known as cram schools, but including a wide assortment of for-profit academies and private after-school lessons—have long been seen as a fascinating cultural phenomenon. Toddlers preparing for kindergarten entrance exams and teenagers cramming at late-night classes strike observers in Japan and abroad as both an educational curiosity and academic overkill.

Despite their notoriety, however, *juku* have been a mainstream activity for Japanese middle-class youth since the 1960s, when double-digit economic growth fired popular interest in education and the concept of extra-curricular lessons. The "boom" in *juku* enrollments peaked in the 1980s, during the height of Japan's economic prosperity. But even during the recession that began in the 1990s, and despite a steep drop in the youth population due to low fertility rates, *juku* remain a thriving business. According to the most recent government surveys, nearly 70% of students will have enrolled in a private tutoring class by the time they have left ninth grade. The largest *juku* companies are traded on Japanese stock exchanges, and the *juku* industry generates 1.4 trillion yen ($12 billion) in revenue annually (Yano Research Institute, 1994). Some 6.5 million children are estimated to attend *juku* in Japan.

Meanwhile, over the past 15 years, the United States has developed a similar "test prep" culture of its own. Behavior and practice that not so long ago were thought to describe "educationally driven" societies such as Japan have quickly become a part of American educational life. It is American parents, now, as well as Japanese, who study annual media rankings of schools and compare the array of educational products and services offered by a variety of companies. A booming industry in the United States offers—just in the arena of test preparation—online diagnostic tests, private academic tutoring, SAT prep courses, and personalized guidance on how to navigate the college-application process.

Suddenly, *juku* appear less the odd phenomenon and more an exemplar of economic activity that provides a form of consumer choice to families that desire ever more educational options for their children. And to the extent that greater numbers of families go outside the public school system to purchase supplemental education, *juku* provide not only educational choice but a form of shadow competition to the public school system as well (Bray, 1999).

What does this mean for official standards? In the case of Japan, private tutoring helps to erode the authority of the public school system because private learning need not align itself with official education standards. By purchasing private lessons to help raise their children's score on high-stakes tests, parents demonstrate that the public system and its standards are, on their own, inadequate preparation for the reality of entrance examinations.

On the other hand, situations are developing in which private tutoring businesses may help to support official standards. Such a scenario is beginning to unfold in the United States, where private companies see a potential market in the nation's public school systems whose students perform poorly on standardized tests. Such tests are increasingly administered by state education departments to monitor school instruction and student achievement. Business firms hope to sell test preparation programs that will bolster student performance. The rapid development of the Internet and the ease of transmitting information may hasten this process. This recent development will be discussed in the conclusion.

In this chapter, I will discuss the nature of *juku* in Japan, including a description of the users and providers of supplemental learning and the commercial and educational nature of the *juku* phenomenon. Then I will explore the possible impact of *juku* on curricular standards in Japan and the United States. As long as *juku* are remedial in nature and used as a catch-up device, the integrity and authority of national standards are not threatened. The most academically accelerated *juku*, however, offer highly focused examination training courses that surpass the public school curriculum and render it less relevant to students preparing for highly competitive entrance exams.

In fact, despite predictions of their demise due to lower fertility rates and a steep decline in the school-age population, *juku* continue to play a pivotal role in Japanese education. One reason is found in the rising proportion of urban families who are applying for admission to private elementary and middle schools. Since the most selective schools require entrance examinations, going to *juku* for test preparation has become part of standard procedure. This phenomenon is not separate from the question of national standards. Rather, the movement to private schools and the role of *juku* in this process may represent in some ways a profound rejection of Japanese national standards and public education itself. It sharpens recurring questions about social inequality and the uneven ability of families to purchase advantage for their children.

Questions the reader should keep in mind include: How do *juku* fit into the centralized world of Japanese education and national standards? What impact does such extracurricular educational activity have at the classroom level? If many families privately supplement their children's education, what becomes of the function of national standards, one of whose purposes is to promote a common knowledge base and a foundation for equality of education? These questions are important for Japanese and U.S. policymakers alike. If, indeed, for-profit, external institutions are helping to create a different, perhaps higher set of standards acknowledged by a significant proportion of the population, a separate educational agenda will evolve alongside state policy. Yet, because *juku*-type classes are a voluntary activity, privately paid for by families, the phenomenon is a complex one for policymakers.

A COMMON AFTER-SCHOOL ACTIVITY

Like many middle-class children in the United States, Japanese children attend after-school classes and activities, but with much less emphasis on organized sports. Some children participate in a category of private lessons called *keikô-goto*, which focuses on instruction in cultural traditions. Girls tend to study abacus, calligraphy, and musical instruments, while boys are guided toward the martial arts. It is the academic after-school lessons, however, called *juku* and *yobikô*, that are the focus of society's concern. They are such an established part of family budgets that Japanese financial institutions and government bureaus collect data for the category "tutorial fees." In fact, tutorial fees account for an increasing proportion of Japanese monthly household expenditures. From 1972 to 1990, average monthly household spending on tutorial fees rose over five times, from 4,763 yen ($41) to 27,163 yen ($233) (Hashimoto & Heath, 1995). There are now about a dozen *juku* and *yobikô* listed on Japanese stock exchanges. Various estimates place the number of *juku* nationwide at 50,000 (Nomura Research Institute, 1994). But when small, home-based tutorial classrooms are folded in, the number swells to 150,000. By comparison, the largest after-school franchise system in the United States, Sylvan Learning Centers, has nearly 800 classrooms—although comparisons of bricks-and-mortar classrooms provide only one part of the picture, given the proliferation of other educational delivery methods, such as distance learning.

The Japanese government reported in 1994 that an average of 24% of elementary school students and 60% of middle-school students use *juku*. Participation traditionally has been higher in urban areas, but the government survey showed that rural enrollments are rising, spreading the phenomenon more evenly throughout Japan (Ministry of Education [MOE], 1994). For middle-class and upper-middle-class children, attending *juku* is the norm. But even among lower-income families in urban areas, participation appears to reach 40% by the time students reach the ninth grade (Sengoku & Iinaga, 1990).

Juku attendance commonly begins during the mid-elementary years, when parents enroll their children in low-pressure classes after school to strengthen study habits or to introduce curricula, such as English, not offered by public schools. The most popular *juku* among elementary school families is the Kumon Educational Institute, the country's largest *juku* in terms of annual revenues. Famous for its worksheet curriculum for arithmetic and Japanese language, it is delivered to 800,000 students through a nationwide network of 18,000 franchises (Russell, 1997).

By sixth grade, however, *juku* attendance rises to 42% as students begin to prepare for high-stakes entrance examinations into high school. These exams, which mark the end of compulsory education, are administered at the end of ninth grade. In ninth grade, consequently, *juku* participation rises to its highest point, 67%. Once high school entrance exams are taken and students have matriculated in high school, *juku* enrollments drop to approximately 30%. This decline may be due to the fact that students attend high schools that are highly differentiated academically and that take over the exam-preparation role that private *juku* previously served. Also, the 30% *juku* enrollment rate is close to the proportion of Japanese high school students who proceed to a 4-year university.

It is at the high school level that a narrowly focused test preparation academy called *yobikô* becomes prominent. *Yobikô*, which literally means "preparation school," assist high school students getting ready to take university entrance exams. *Yobikô* also prepare graduates of high school who failed to pass the exam of their desired university on the first try and who enroll at a *yobikô* fulltime to take the following year's exams. These test repeaters, called *rônin*, routinely make up one-third of the entering classes at colleges and universities. At the most selective national universities, such as Tokyo University and Kyoto University, *rônin* comprise well more than 50% of the freshman class (Amano, 1996; Tsukada, 1991). Test repeaters, therefore, represent a large proportion of entering classes at Japanese universities, and provide a steady stream of customers to *juku* and *yobikô*. But *juku* or *yobikô* usage is not limited to the highest achievers. *Juku* cater to students heading for community colleges as well as to the most elite schools. Like different levels of sports training, there are coaches appropriate for all levels of educational ambition.

CHARACTERISTICS OF *JUKU*

The term *juku* originates from the Chinese character that means "the smallest scale of school run by a teacher from his home" (Rubinger, 1982). A historical category of private school, called *shijuku*, flourished in late-19th-century Japan. These schools offered instruction in heretical subjects, such as foreign languages or Western science, to ambitious young men who traveled long distances to study under particular *shijuku* teachers. Although today's *juku* bear little resemblance to the *shijuku* of more than a century ago, three key characteristics persist and continue to distinguish modern *juku* from mainstream, officially sanctioned education:

1. *Administration. Juku* administration is private. *Juku* operate in a separate educational sphere from mainstream schools sanctioned by the Japanese government. *Juku* operate either as a business enterprise, overseen by the Ministry of Commerce, or as a special educational institution (*gakkô hôjin*) that receives special legal and tax treatment and falls under the jurisdiction of the Japanese Ministry of Education. In either case, *juku* are not required to follow the official requirements for compulsory education and can create their own professional practices, curriculum, and educational standards.
2. *Curriculum.* Because of their private nature, *juku* can teach unorthodox subject matter, produce their own textbooks, and use pedagogies not encouraged in public schools. Unlike public schools, *juku* can be non-ideological about controversial topics such as preparing for high-stakes exams, for example, and teaching to the test.
3. *Constituency.* Usage of *juku* is private. It is voluntary and fee-based, and participation is fluid.

The Commercial Aspect

The profit incentive and the commercial mechanisms that support it, such as advertising, market research, and product improvement, are key to understanding the success of *juku*, their persistence in Japanese education, and why their negative influence on Japanese standards grows. The profit motive injects a powerful market dynamic into the sphere of supplemental education. *Juku* must compete among each other for students in a marketplace where parents have choice as educational consumers. In order to survive, *juku* must develop, polish, and promote an educational product, deliver it efficiently in an easy-to-use style, monitor its use, and respond to complaints. Not to do so means to fall into decline and perhaps go out of business. Public schools, with their broader mission, are less apt to behave in such a consumer-oriented manner and are unable to respond as flexibly as *juku* on matters such as curriculum, discipline, or staff policies.

Since *juku* are able to sell educational services and products without direct guidance from the state's educational authorities, they are the source of much educational innovation in the areas of curriculum, delivery of educational material, and pedagogy. Their educational services often present a strong contrast to conventional school offerings, enhancing their appeal to parents who may be dissatisfied with school programs alone.

In curriculum, for instance, the Kumon mathematics program departs from the norm. It is a self-paced, 5,000-page worksheet curriculum that emphasizes progression through a sequential set of skills through drill, practice, and correction of worksheet problems. At the time that it was developed, in the 1950s, the drill-and-practice curriculum was considered a novel approach because Ministry of Education guidelines for mathematics study emphasized problem solving and small-group learning.

Juku employ unorthodox ways of delivering content, including distance education methods. The Ministry of Education considers Japan's largest *juku* to be the Benesse Corporation, a correspondence education firm, with a customer base of 3.6 million. Benesse is the nation's largest private user of the Japanese postal system.

Other *juku* have experimented, since the 1980s, with electronic telecommunications to transmit instructional materials. The Nagase Corporation delivers lessons via digital satellite broadcast directly into franchise *juku* or into students' homes. In the case of home delivery, students purchase a television set top box that enables them to order pay-per-view lectures on particular subjects or watch real-time lectures given by instructors in Tokyo.

Unlike public schools, *juku* can go out of business if their products do not stay competitive with those offered by rival *juku*. Kumon continually monitors its enrollments and curriculum through monthly reports submitted by its 18,000 franchise operators. It also pays a focus group of its elite instructors to serve as curricular advisors. They report to company managers on student reaction to new products, technical details in the worksheets, and areas of parental concern.

Juku aggressively market their products, using customer referrals, direct mail, newspaper inserts, and the Internet. Advertisements arrive at strategic times during the school year, particularly before important tests. They contain information such as the names of prestigious schools to which recent customers have gained entrance, as evidence of the quality of the test-preparation program. It is understood that big *juku* quietly waive the tuition of students who score high on diagnostic tests because they are certain to gain admission to a competitive school, thus boosting the reputation of the preparatory school. In the words of one Tokyo mother, "The bigger the *juku*, the more you can expect that you are subsidizing the top students."

These are some of the ways in which *juku* behave like commercial entities to compete in the marketplace of private education. But their commercial mission—to provide an educational service to parents and students—places them in school-like roles as well. *Juku* that operate classrooms must, like schools, hire and train teachers, select or publish textbooks, and consider educational topics such as the social and academic atmosphere of their classrooms.

Hiring and Recruitment of Teachers

Who are the teachers of *juku*? At *juku* for elementary school children and the lower years of middle school, women predominate. The two biggest mass market *juku* in the country, Kumon and Benesse, together employ more than 40,000 housewives as franchise owners and part-time correspondence course staff.

The phenomenon of Japanese housewives is an interesting one because it highlights several social factors peculiar to modern Japanese society. Women have far fewer job opportunities than men, are more apt to stay home and work part-time while their children are small, and in the Japanese social scheme, are expected to have a high interest in education as mothers. *Juku* capitalize on this underutilized human resource. The importance of women as a source of cheap labor should not be underestimated.

The women hired by *juku* are not licensed instructors but have passed qualification tests administered by the company and have received some sort of in-house professional training. They also may attend continuing-education lectures and take tests in order to teach at a more advanced level or to receive higher compensation. In the case of Benesse, an army of 24,000 Japanese housewives known as "*akapen sensei*" or "red-pen teachers" correct papers for the firm from their homes. They work a minimum of 4 hours per week and in 1998 were paid 200 yen ($1.80) per page, correcting an average two pages per hour. One Tokyo mother, for example, a 4-year college graduate, became an *akapen sensei* after finding a Benesse flyer in a coffee shop. She applied to the company by postcard, took a qualifying examination, and was approved by the firm to mark papers for middle-school English, history, and Japanese language, as well as all five elementary school subjects. She was hired after an interview and worked her way up to earning 50,000 yen ($450) a month after 7 years' experience.

In contrast to these mass-market *juku*, which reach younger populations of students, teachers at serious exam-preparation *yobikô* tend to be mostly male, which mirrors the gender imbalance in *yobikô* enrollment. Nationwide, *yobikô* enrollments are 85% male and 15% female (Tsukada, 1991).

The Ministry of Education estimates that only 15% of *juku* teachers have professional teaching experience. Other research indicates that a high proportion of *juku* teachers are moonlighting public school teachers, retired teachers, or graduate students. According to a U.S. Department of Education study (1987), one-third of *juku* teachers are university students, 4% are teachers at high school or in higher education, and only 1% are elementary or lower secondary school teachers. About half of the remaining teaching staff have teaching certificates but no experience in regular schools.

In the short-term, test-focused world of coaching schools, parent satisfaction with exam results is more important than the academic or professional credentials of a teacher. The glossy brochures of the biggest *juku* frequently do not indicate the teaching background of faculty. It may be that schools do not want families to be aware of the unevenness of credentials and qualifications of their tutors and instructors, who may come from a variety of backgrounds. In some cases, the faculty themselves, some of whom are moonlighting, may prefer it this way.

It is unclear exactly how many teachers are employed by *juku*. Home-tutoring businesses may be run by individuals while small- and medium-sized *juku*, which are defined as having enrollments of 2,000 or fewer students, may have a faculty of several dozen. The latter category forms the bulk of the *juku* industry, accounting for about 80% of all *juku* in the country. The largest *juku*, with nationwide chains, can have as many as 200 teachers on the payroll.

Average salaries appear to be comparable to public school salaries, without the job security. The top instructors, however, who can become nationally known media figures, may earn many times the average. Good *yobikô* teachers at Kawaijuku, a famous *yobikô*, earned 30,000 to 50,000 yen ($270 to $450) for each 90-minute block of instruction. An investment survey on educational services in Japan reports that the best teachers are independent, hard to retain, and similar to free agents in professional sports.

Textbooks and Materials

A variety of *juku* publishers supply a wide range of textbooks and curricular materials to the students. The largest *juku* publish their own curricular materials for their customers' use, but may also sell them in bookstores. Big educational publishers such as Gakken publish drill books and supplemental texts. Some *juku* publishers do not operate schools but publish materials that can be used alongside government-approved textbooks. Other private groups, such as religious organizations, sell their in-house textbooks to *juku* if demand exists.

Juku publishers take great liberty with text format and content. Kumon's 5,000-page worksheet series begins with simple mazes and ends with differential calculus. One publicly traded firm, Wao Corporation, is distinguished by its computerized study sets. Such firms operate their own curricular departments, which monitor the official textbook approval process as they create supplemental materials.

Few *juku* use government-approved textbooks as their sole text. A government survey found that 65% of *juku* used textbooks written by *juku* industry publishers; another 17% use "materials made in-house." Only 4% use school textbooks (MOE, 1994). Benesse, the correspondence firm, is an example of how private *juku* firms adapt their materials around government standards. It produces its colorful, coupon-laden workbooks to closely correspond with government-approved textbooks used in public schools. When a new child enrolls by mail, the firm uses the postal code on the customer's envelope to identify the school district. The child is subsequently mailed company-produced problem sheets that correspond to the locally used textbook, providing a customized study aide.

The Curriculum

Ultimately, the content of the entrance examination determines the patterns of *juku* usage and the topics that are studied. Mathematics, Japanese language, and English—the critical examination subjects—are the top three subjects studied by all *juku* students, regardless of age (MOE, 1994). Science and social studies receive less (but increasing) attention as students progress through the grades.

Mathematics outdistances all other subjects in elementary school, perhaps because parents believe that a strong foundation in arithmetic skills is important to future success in mathematics study and because of the general belief by Japanese parents that success in mathematics can be attained through personal effort. The Kumon mathematics program, which is used by 8% of elementary students nationwide, appears to be the program of choice for elementary-age children who study mathematics at *juku*. English is introduced as a compulsory subject at the public middle-school level. It is a difficult subject on entrance exams and is the most studied *juku* subject by middle-school students.

In choosing a *juku* for their children, parents are also selecting an after-school peer group. The twice-weekly routine of most *juku* students generates an alternative social setting. When asked in the 1994 ministry survey, "What were the benefits of attending *juku*?" 41% of upper-elementary students and one-third of middle-school students said "making friends." One mother of a middle-school student said that her daughter was teased at school and that the *juku* provided an opportunity to meet new friends. "She was happier at *juku*, and even if she stayed home sick from school, she didn't want to miss *juku*," the mother said.

Assessment of Academic Program

If the *juku* is small and privately run, assessment may be somewhat subjective, with parents measuring results by a change in the child's attitude at home or better grades at school. At large corporate-run *juku*, however, assessment of student progress is more quantified due to the need of large companies to systematize and replicate their learning program on a larger scale. The Kumon company asserts that its worksheet data show that after one year of Kumon study, 50% of children who are in the top half of their class have surpassed grade-level work. Children in the top quarter of the their class are studying 0.75 years ahead, while children in the bottom quarter of the class move beyond grade-level work within 2 years.

In middle school, "general skills" *juku*, such as Kumon and Benesse, experience a falloff in enrollment, replaced by purchase of lessons in test-coaching *juku*. Their success is more easily measured—whether students are able to pass the exam of their desired school or whether customers are satisfied that preparation was carried out to the fullest extent possible.

Assessment at test-preparation *juku* is quantified and straightforward. Programs are customized to meet the individual goals of students and regular practice tests enable families to monitor the child's progress until the test is taken.

EXAMPLE OF AN URBAN, UPPER-MIDDLE-CLASS FAMILY

The range of how *juku* are used by families able to afford a steady stream of lessons can be seen in the experience of one upper-middle-class family in Tokyo with three children. The oldest son, a public elementary school student, was enrolled in 3 years of lessons at a *juku* in order to prepare for three private middle-school exams to be taken at the end of sixth grade. In this case, the child had taken Kumon lessons from early elementary school, but began a focused course of exam preparation from the fourth grade. The mother, a junior college graduate, learned of the *juku* through word of mouth, and liked the fact that the *juku* was nearby and that it specialized in closely monitoring the entrance exams of area schools. The *juku* operated three branches in Western Tokyo and tried to be the dominant *juku* in its region by keeping an expert faculty together and offering multiyear programs that guided students together.

At the beginning of fourth grade, the child rode his bicycle to the *juku* twice a week, on Wednesday and Saturday, to study math and Japanese language for a weekly total of 5 hours. One practice test was taken each month. Tuition was 30,000 yen ($270) a month. In fifth grade, weekly *juku* study increased to 12 hours and two subjects were added: science and social studies. He began to take his dinner to the *juku* and continued to take one practice test a month, at the same tuition level. Now that he was spending approximately 50 hours each month at *juku*, the social aspect of attending after-school lessons grew in importance. In this case, the boy liked *juku*, his mother said, because there were few students from his public school, adding variety to his social life. An added benefit was the small class size—20 students at *juku*, compared with 35 at school.

Sixth grade, the exam year, was the critical period. The child enrolled in the *juku*'s special test-coaching course. His target school was known to have more multiple-choice questions on its entrance test, so the test-preparation curriculum was assigned accordingly. The time dedicated to attending lessons remained the same, 12 hours spread over 3 days a week, but the frequency of practice tests increased to weekly, every Sunday morning, and monthly tuition more than doubled, to 69,000 yen. On the morning of the exam for his first-choice school, the child woke up at 5:00 A.M. in order to arrive at the *juku* at 6 A.M. to do some last-minute studying. He took the test later that day, achieved a high enough score to gain admission, and subsequently enrolled in a 6-year program at Keio Central Middle School, which is attached to the elite university of the same name.

At the same time, the boy's elementary school–age brother was attending a less academic *juku* operated by a former schoolteacher known for his informality. The purpose was not to study for a private school test but to keep the child interested in learning. The youngest child in the family, a girl, was enrolled in *juku* when she was 4 and 5 years old to prepare for private elementary school tests. She attended *juku* lessons once a week to learn rhythm exercises, drawing, pattern recognition, and bead stringing. In summer she attended a *juku* to prepare for three private elementary school entrance exams. The daughter did not pass any of the exams and subsequently was enrolled in the local public primary school.

HOW *JUKU* UNDERMINE PUBLIC SCHOOL AUTHORITY

In order to think about how *juku* have an impact on educational standards, it is useful to separate them into three category types: remedial, enrichment, and exam-focused, according to the relation that they bear to the school curriculum. Remedial (*hoshû*) *juku* help the child stay current with the schoolwork assigned in class. Enrichment (*gakushû* and *sôgô*) *juku* are designed to provide a supplement to the school day, fill in academic gaps, and, often, to accelerate beyond the standard curriculum. The test-focused *shingaku juku* and *yobikô* are designed expressly to help children attain the highest possible score on entrance examinations of particular schools. Characteristics of these categories may overlap, but this framework provides a sense of how *juku* fit into the landscape of national standards.

In the case of remedial *juku*, users tend to be weaker students who struggle to keep up with the pace of classroom work. Such *juku* are not a threat to official standards because users are behind in learning the curriculum and *hoshû juku* try to help them catch up. The Ministry of Education is less concerned about the existence of remedial *juku*, and the Japanese media pay little attention to this category. Few parents care to openly admit that their child needs remedial work and the *juku* themselves do not necessarily desire a reputation as institutions that cater to lower achievers.

The enrichment *juku* support and reinforce the standards by filling in the academic and pedagogical gaps that parents perceive. They also are linked to higher achievement in the classroom. Whitman (1991) cites a 1986 study in which it was found that the percentage of students attending *juku* for mathematics study rose with each grade level, and that higher-achieving students had a correspondingly higher rate of *juku* enrollments than did middle- or low-achieving math students. This was particularly evident in the seventh- and eighth-grade classes, when half of the top-achieving students attended *juku*.

Enrichment *juku* seek to have their students accelerate beyond the school curriculum. If students can surpass the standards, classroom study will become a place of academic review. Children appeared to confirm this in the 1994 ministry survey, saying that the second most important benefit of attending *juku* was that they could "go beyond school lessons." Enrichment *juku* also provide curricula not offered by public schools. Some parents enroll their elementary school–age children in *juku* to study English, for example, which becomes compulsory at the middle-school level. When *juku* accelerate students to the extent that school becomes a place for review, *juku* begin to threaten the authority of public education, and the state system is no longer a place of educational leadership.

Shingaku juku and *yobikô* are the most subversive threat to educational standards. As long as entrance examinations are key to academic and future career success, and *juku* or *yobikô* can help students improve their exam scores, private educational services will continue to be in demand. They highlight the tenuous authority of national standards when unofficial standards, such as a high-stakes entrance examination, set the learning bar higher.

A concrete example of the growing might of *juku* in the educational process in Japan can be seen in the trend toward private schooling in Japan since the mid-1990s. The most sought after schools combine the middle and high school years into a continuous 6-year program, enabling students to attend the same school for 6 years uninterrupted by an entrance exam that normally is taken at the end of Japanese middle school. Such private schools claim that, in the absence of the test, they are freer to offer interesting curricular and cultural activities and respond more sensitively to individual needs. Such schools also have a good track record in placing their graduates in competitive universities. Amano (1996) demonstrates that the composition of students who gain admission to the most selective university in Japan has changed dramatically over the course of 25 years from predominantly public school graduates to predominantly private school students. Of the top 20 high schools in the country that sent students to Tokyo University in 1964, five were private schools. By 1979, the private school figure had grown to 11, and by 1989, 25 years later, 75% of the top-sending schools to Tokyo University were private and only 5 were public, the reverse of the 1964 ratio. If one accepts the premise that attending a test-focused *juku* is a requirement for successful admission to a private high school or selective university, then it seems clear that studying at *juku* is an integral component of educational success in Japan.

JAPANESE GOVERNMENT INACTION

The Japanese education system has received international recognition for the high average level of students' academic achievement. It appears, however, that some of the praise that flows to the government should be shared by the nonformal learning sector and the families who are its patrons. That this does not occur reflects more on the political, ideological, and cultural conditions that characterize contemporary Japanese education than on the reality of *juku* influence.

The government has reacted meekly to the challenges that *juku* bring to its own educational authority. Political proposals to convert respected *juku* into accredited private academies have failed (Schoppa, 1991), and education officials, in the absence of a clear policy on *juku*, make headlines merely by carrying out official surveys on parental usage of *juku*. Government action tends to be limited to public announcements urging parents not to purchase private lessons in the interest of allowing their children to experience a less harried, more play-oriented childhood.

The educational reality, however, is that as the Ministry of Education continues to reduce curricular rigor in order to lessen the academic pressure that society blames for school and juvenile problems, the examination system continues. From a business point of view, recent government policies such as the 5-day school week benefit *juku*. In the 1998 official *Course of Study*, the ministry reduced class hours in elementary and middle school by 10% and eliminated certain skills, such as the study of calculation of volume, from elementary school math. The number of English vocabulary words to be taught in middle school was reduced from 1,000 to 900. The common response of *juku* is to exploit parents' concerns that official standards are growing ever more distant from the entrance exam realities of Japanese universities, and to offer more English lessons to fill in the gap. The result is that Japanese parents take advantage of the benefits of a stable public system and supplement the gaps through private purchase of *juku* lessons (Rohlen, 1980).

COMPARING THE *JUKU* PHENOMENON IN JAPAN AND THE UNITED STATES

Much has been made of the real differences that exist between the Japanese and American educational systems. The centralization of education in Japan and its system of national standards and state-approved textbooks is often contrasted with that in the United States, which gives educational authority to the states and our 16,000 local school boards. When it comes to supplemental education, however, the differences between the two countries diminish. Education is one of the most important inputs for the formation of human capital, and when options outside formal education are made available to parents, Japanese and American families behave similarly. Supplemental lessons become an important consumer commodity for wealthier families. They are something a family might consider purchasing if it appears that the existing system is not meeting the needs of their child. For-profit education companies can be successful in fulfilling their narrow educational missions with flexibility, experimental methods, and new technologies.

In fact, although the United States has come to supplemental learning decades later than Japan, the private tutoring phenomenon is now full blown. We have become much like Japan in this regard, with media stories about astronomically priced SAT tutors, small children getting coached beginning in elementary school, and scandals in which cheating on high-stakes tests takes place.

Japan has a more established pattern of usage, thanks to a 40-year-history in the postwar era. The tradition of *juku* is accepted among families as a normal childhood activity. College-educated parents probably attended a *juku* and perhaps earned pocket money as *juku* tutors. For most Japanese children, participation begins in the lower- or mid-elementary years in a relaxed after-school environment that evokes a homework club. Enrollment in a test-coaching *juku* begins in middle school and peaks in ninth grade. This pattern has changed in urban areas in the 1990s as parents apply to private schools for their children and purchase test-coaching lessons earlier.

The U.S. phenomenon follows this example in some respects. As in Japan, private tutoring has taken off in the United States thanks to the competitive pressures of high-stakes examinations. The two leading test-preparation firms in the United States, Princeton Review and Kaplan Test Prep, profit from the weight given to SAT scores in college admissions offices.

Like Japan in the 1960s, education is now the number-one concern of American parents, who see higher education as key to the future economic success for their children. And, as in Japan, American tutoring firms benefit from the inability of public schools to address a controversial issue such as test preparation with the single-mindedness of a for-profit business.

Unlike Japan, however, America's dual-income and single-parent family members are unavailable to shuttle children to classes, and because of safety issues and a lack of public transportation, these children cannot go to classes by themselves after school as is the case in Japan. Furthermore, U.S. families are much less likely to see supplementary education as a continuous, ongoing process, but instead tend to view it as a short-term, stop-gap measure when poor report cards come home (Ukai, 1994).

Another difference is that the Japanese Ministry of Education controls more closely the boundaries, materials, and internal processes of its official domain. Textbooks, curricula, professional development, pedagogy, and distribution are under strict official oversight within Japanese schools, even if a vastly different world of *juku* exists outside. In the public classrooms of Japan, it is inconceivable to have corporate-produced teaching materials, *juku* offering free tutoring in exchange for the opportunity to try out their methods, or parents saving supermarket receipts to bring computers into classrooms.

The result is that the private-tutoring phenomenon in the United States has a distinctly American twist. Firms sell enrichment, remedial, and test-preparatory services, but also bolster their product lineup with services that meet the demands of a U.S. market.

Princeton Review, Kaplan, and Achieva College Prep Centers (Edwards, 1999) offer college guidance packages that range in price from $400 to $5,000, taking advantage of parental anxiety and the inability of over-burdened high school counselors to provide close assistance in a process that is growing more competitive and strategic. The market price appears to be $2,000 for a senior-year package, whether offered by a company or a private counselor. Private companies in the United States are experimenting with new tutoring concepts that apply the latest networking technology. A national online tutor referral service, tutor.com, invites students to tap their zip code into their web site and receive names of local tutors who can be selected according to subject, price, and qualifications. Scholastic, Kaplan, Houghton Mifflin, Encarta.com, and numerous Internet and educational firms belong to this partnership. The venture claims to have registered 18,000 tutors nationwide; National Education Association members are invited to register at a reduced price.

U.S. tutoring companies also are moving quickly to position themselves in the burgeoning "education industry" that offers new products to nontraditional markets, including public schools (Fromm & Kern, 2000; Herman, Craig, & Basel, 1997; Newman, Rynearson, & Evans, 2000). For example, Kaplan, in addition to offering traditional test preparation, has partnered with Apex Learning, an online educational services firm founded by Microsoft cofounder Paul Allen. It offers Advanced Placement courses and AP exam review materials to public school districts. The education secretary for the state of South Dakota, which has become a customer, said that the company's online materials will help distribute education more equitably in a state where district size ranges from 39 to 18,000.

Low-achieving schools in poor districts also represent a sizable market, since the schools receive Title I federal funds to improve achievement. Sylvan Learning Systems was one of the earliest firms in this business, subcontracting its tutoring services to low-performing schools in Baltimore and Chicago in the mid-1990s. Even merely adequately performing schools may present a business opportunity as the Bush administration places greater emphasis on testing for increased accountability in student performance (Steinberg, 2001).

A division of Princeton Review, homeroom.com, promises to assist teachers who must grapple with evolving standards and new curricula that are not aligned with textbooks and state assessments. In a message on homeroom. com's web site, John Katzman (2001), the founder and president of Princeton Review and CEO and cofounder of homeroom.com, says the new company will evaluate textbooks and state standards in order to help students learn the skills "his teacher cares about most." The statement continues:

> By quietly integrating state standards and exams into the class, teachers can be sure their students will perform well on them without weeks of test-prep. It's not a second curriculum, like some educational software and web sites. Homeroom.com molds itself around your state, your textbook, and your students' strengths and weaknesses.

This frontier area in public education, in which private businesses sell educational services to families as well as to the public schools, bears close watching in future years. The U.S. tutoring industry has become an estimated $6 billion-a-year business in annual revenues (Fromm & Kern, 2000); comparable figures put the Japanese market at $12 billion with 6.5 million students. Tutoring employs more than 10,000 people part-time and full-time in the United States, largely young college graduates, it appears, and more than 40,000 women, mostly homemakers, in Japan. Tutoring, and the burgeoning educational industry of which it is a part, are major educational service providers and employers, and a central part of the educational process. As a supplemental institution, they contribute to the erosion of the authority of public schools. The growing acceptance of market-driven approaches in education will only strengthen this trend.

REFERENCES

Amano, I. (1996). *Nihon no kyôiku shisutemu: Kôzô to hendô* [The Japanese educational system: Organization and change]. Tokyo: University of Tokyo Press.
Bray, M. (1999). *The shadow education system: Private tutoring and its implications for planners*. Paris: International Institute for Educational Planning.

Edwards, T. M. (1999). Guidance for sale: Achieve does it all—life tips, tutoring, testing and college counseling: Is this a good thing? *Time, 154*(18), 68–70.

Fromm, J. A., & Kern, R. V. (2000, Fall). Investment opportunities in education: Making a profit while making a difference. *The Journal of Private Equity,* pp. 38–51.

Hashimoto, K., & Heath, J. (1995). Income elasticities of household expenditure by income class: The case of Japanese households. *Economics of Education Review, 14*(1), 63–71.

Herman, J., Craig, R., & Basel, K. (1997). *Educational services industry.* Chicago: Everen Securities, Inc., Equity Research.

Homeroom.com (2001). Commentary. Retrieved January 29, 2001, from the World Wide Web: http://www.homeroom.com/press/texas_results.asp/

Katzman, J. (2001). Commentary. Retrieved January 29, 2001, from the World Wide Web: http://www.homeroom.com/commentary/katzman.asp/

Ministry of Education. (1994). *Gakushûjuku nado ni kansuru jittai chôsa* [The essential survey of academic *juku*]. Tokyo: Author.

Newman, A., Rynearson, K., & Evans, T. (2000). *What is the education industry?* Retrieved February 15, 2001, from the World Wide Web: http://www.eduventures.com/research/industry_overview/what_is_edu_industry.cfm

Nomura Research Institute. (1994). *Gunyû kakkyo no gakushûjuku gyôkai* [The academic *juku* industry: Rivalry of the powerful]. Tokyo: Author.

Rohlen, T. (1980). The *juku* phenomenon. An exploratory essay. *Journal of Japanese Studies, 6*(2), 207–242.

Rubinger, R. (1982). *Private academies of Tokugawa Japan.* Princeton, NJ: Princeton University Press.

Russell, N. U. (1997). Lessons from Japanese cram schools. In W. K. Cummings & P. G. Altbach (Eds.), *The challenge of Eastern Asian education: Implications for America* (pp. 153–170). Albany: State University of New York Press.

Schoppa, L. (1991). *Education reform in Japan: A case of immobilist politics.* New York: Routledge.

Sengoku, T., & Iinaga, K. (1990). *Nihon no shôgakusei: Kokusaihikaku de miru* [Japanese elementary school students: An international comparison]. Tokyo: NHK Books.

Steinberg, J. (2001, January 26). Adding a financial threat to familiar promises on education. *The New York Times,* p. A17.

Tsukada, M. (1991). *Yobikô life: A study of the legitimation process of social stratification in Japan.* Berkeley, CA: Institute of East Asian Studies.

Ukai, N. (1994). The Kumon approach to teaching and learning. *Journal of Japanese Studies, 20*(1), 87–113.

U.S. Dept. of Education. (1987, January). *Japanese education today.* Washington, DC: Author.

Whitman, N. (1991). Teaching of mathematics in Japanese schools. In E. R. Beuchamp (Ed.), *Windows on Japanese education* (pp. 139–174). New York: Greenwood Press.

Yano Research Institute. (1994). *Kyôiku sangyô hakusho* [Education industry white paper]. Tokyo: Author.

Concluding Observations:
Wider Contexts and Future Issues

Thomas P. Rohlen

URING THE 1970s AND 1980s an emerging body of American and European scholarship on Japanese education produced a considerable amount of fresh understanding about classroom instruction, school organization, the examination system, and policymaking at the national level (Lewis, 1995; Peak, 1991; Rohlen, 1984b; Stevenson & Stigler, 1992). While useful and very interesting as research and clearly of comparative relevance, the emerging picture had a number of significant gaps. We still knew little or nothing about how national-level policy initiatives were translated to the local level. We knew little about the institutional context of teaching and professional development. We could not with confidence say how this particular national system retained such a seemingly high level of coherence and coordination. We also knew very little about the actual processes of change and reform in the system. Nor did we have much in the way of comparative studies of such topics as textbooks and their production.

Beginning with a very lively 3 days of discussions at the Green Gulch Zen Center in the fall of 1998 where the authors and a number of other experts from Japan and the United States discussed these questions and continuing with the chapters in this book, these gaps have begun to be filled in with significant new material. I have learned a great deal about a convergent set of institutional mechanisms and practices that together define the way the larger Japanese system works in practice. Standards, national guidelines, teachers' manuals, professional development, curriculum design, and textbooks are obviously all a part of the coordination and control of any national system of education. The authors of these chapters show how these elements are linked in Japan to organizations of teachers, to classroom instruction, and ultimately to students' learning.

Neither organization charts nor formal rules provide very much information about how things really work in this less-visible realm, one of complex hierarchical and horizontal linkages and interactions whose real nature can be grasped only through close observation. This book represents a major step in elucidating this realm and clarifying the processes that give it its special character. The insights offered in the preceding chapters allow us to answer many critical questions that previously had been susceptible to overly facile and often erroneous treatment based on a popular perception that Japanese education is a centralized and largely top-down system.

These questions include: How can a seemingly vague set of national guidelines result in high levels of national coordination? What kind of production system lies behind Japanese textbooks and explains why they are so practically tailored to classroom use? How is it that a reputedly highly centralized national system like Japan's can achieve such a high degree of teacher participation in improvement and change efforts? How is flexibility built into a governance system that formally appears top-down? How does change occur in Japanese education, and why can it seem so glacial? At a time when public pressure for administrative reform and innovation is at a post-Occupation high, what are the prospects for change under the Ministry of Education's (MOE) new initiatives? What are the countervailing forces limiting such changes?

Some readers of this book will no doubt already have formed their own impressions of what is notably distinctive or "Japanese" in its education system. Those who have assumed that the Japanese bureaucracy possesses a high degree of top-down power (Cutts, 1997; Horio, 1988; Yoneyama, 1999), for example, may be surprised by the evidence presented in the preceding chapters of considerable local latitude and teacher participation in shaping educational content. But, on the other hand, those who have noted how authority works in Japan via relatively subtle and perfected means of underspecified direction—goal setting rather than order giving (Itô, 1969; Ouchi, 1982), and intermediate-level feedback mechanisms—Quality Circles, for example (Cole, 1989; Rohlen, 1975, 1984a)—may feel quite at home with the portraits presented in this book of how the top and bottom of education are related.

To summarize the essential elements of the picture that emerges from these studies, I propose to discuss the dimensions of time and space as they define the basic administrative approach to national coordination, and then to compare Japan and the United States in terms of how the two very different systems address the issues of change and reform. Following this discussion, I propose to present some of the analytic challenges one confronts when thinking comparatively about Japanese and American education, and, finally, I will look into the future of education in the two countries as we enter a period of rapid technological change and shifting balances between public authority and private initiatives in a more global environment.

NEW INSIGHTS INTO JAPANESE EDUCATION

We need to begin by thinking about the enormity of the challenge of relating the Ministry of Education's policies and intentions to over a hundred thousand classrooms and millions of K–12 students in 47 prefectures and the 12 largest cities. There is no best way for a central policymaking body to do this, of course, but over time a formula develops that defines the system of implementation in practice. In the abstract, however, a rather extensive range of options exists for the development of such a system. If we think of the possible variety as framed by several extreme or polar types of approaches, it may help us better understand the Japanese case and also compare what has evolved in Japan with the American situation. At one extreme would be approaches that use the coercive power of central authority to essentially direct and command a system. Implementation in this approach, in other words, follows directly the intentions of the governing authority, and as in the classic organizational design, is essentially top-down. Typically the ingredients of this approach include highly specified policies and close supervision, coupled with adequate incentives and punishments. The authority of the law strictly enforced would be another aspect at this extreme end of the range, one designed to exercise control in a linear and direct manner according to the letter of the law. At the opposite polar end of such a spectrum we can imagine a system in which the central ministry is active in producing studies, policy pronouncements, and so forth, but in practice the degree of its connection with lower levels and its authority to directly implement change are minimal. The term *loosely coupled* comes to mind as a description of this later arrangement. Vertical communications at this extreme would generally be characterized by a "don't ask, don't tell" spirit. Local and classroom autonomy would be the defining result.

Neither of these extremes, obviously, characterizes the current Japanese educational system, but where on the spectrum would we place its system knowing what we have learned from the preceding chapters? The answer, as I see it, is that in formal structure and legal authority the Japanese case falls closer to the first, highly organized and coercive pole, but in procedural style it falls on the other side, where extensive autonomy is granted to lower levels. That is, it fits neither extreme type, but is a mix of intermediate possibilities. The many mechanisms discussed in this book (see especially LeTendre, Chapter 2, this volume) form a finely defined and developed set of procedures that make the vertical and horizontal connections within the system highly interactive and organized without being overtly coercive. Lacking a history of the MOE's development, but knowing of its prewar and wartime abuses, one can only assume that over the last 50 years it has perfected this intermediate approach that relies on a complex of mechanisms designed more for consultation, persuasion, and participation than for executive direction or legal intervention. A 30-year tug of war, only recently ended, with a once very popular and entrenched Japan Teachers' Union certainly helped shape this style (Duke, 1973). But this cannot be the whole story for it resonates across a range of Japanese organizations, some of which experienced little or no union challenge to existing authority. Specifically, it is common to find consultation, local participation, and group processes playing a significant role between executive and lower levels in many private and public organizations.

Does this description mean that the MOE is unwilling to use its power or that the lower levels of education can ignore MOE initiatives? Clearly, this is not the case. No administrative system, first of all, has only one style or posture. The MOE has extensive legal and budgetary powers and ultimately it has the backing of the state. The potential to use these powers is ever present. Recent history has shown that under certain political circumstances, the MOE and prefectural authorities are willing and ready to move forcefully against an entrenched opposition unwilling to play by the normal procedural rules (Duke, 1973; Rohlen, 1984a). If typically the MOE moves carefully and patiently, this does not preclude it from acting swiftly or running out of patience on occasion, especially if its ultimate authority is threatened. Even more to the point is the possibility of focusing its coercive power in a carefully targeted manner on the most recalcitrant of locations (Duke, 1973; Rohlen, 1984a). The MOE has indeed developed a refined system that delegates a great deal to other levels and seeks a consensual response, but it never relinquishes direction or initiative, and, ultimately, it retains the option (albeit, a high-stakes one) of a more coercive approach.

Returning to the topic of procedural character, the various studies presented here provide new insights into how the middle ground works. By portraying change from the teacher and district-level perspective they clearly articulate what occurs in response to MOE initiatives. Without reiterating the details, it is apparent that many classroom teachers are not simply obliging functionaries, but are, rather, actively engaged participants in some aspects of the change process. That the MOE intentionally leaves a great deal to lower-level discretion and initiative when it comes to implementation is patently evident. This is possible, first, because as Chapters 1,

4, and 7 illustrate, the MOE operates by framing a very general set of guidelines and a set of vaguely phrased goals, rather than by insisting on highly specified standards. Second, some experienced teachers regularly evaluate and contribute to textbook redesign, while others help write teachers' manuals, and most are enrolled in local efforts to perfect instructional practice within a general framework. Stevenson in Chapter 6 underscores other areas of potential local flexibility in applying the national guidelines to the actual diversity of abilities encountered. The case study by McConnell (Chapter 8) shows how the acceptance of change in a system that is minimally coercive requires a great deal of time and local initiative. The term *glacial* seems particularly apt regarding most efforts at reform during the last 3 decades whether that be in changing the entrance examination system, shortening the school week, introducing computers, or improving foreign language instruction. McConnell's statement that success must be evaluated in terms of decades rather than years is particularly interesting. On the one hand, this seems very reasonable given the scale and complexity of what must change for even small advances in education. The patience and steadiness of purpose required in this approach are stunning and can be taken as signs of administrative wisdom. Yet, on the other hand, the appropriateness of such an approach must be judged relative to the necessity of change as measured by social needs in general, as LeTendre makes clear in Chapter 2. A "slow but sure" approach, which, incidentally, has been the hallmark of corporate Japan as well, can mean "too little, too late" depending on the necessity for change involved. The atmosphere in Japan, after over a decade of post-bubble recession, is one of near desperation to transform society from a highly articulated and disciplined, but cautious, one into a more flexibly loose and innovative one. In the eyes of the Japanese today, the very qualities discussed here as virtues in the perception of outside scholars appear as part of the country's fundamental malaise. I will return to this issue later in this epilogue.

The current system, like so many other examples of organization in Japan, is designed around a small set of fundamental principles that, while not hidden, are locally taken for granted. I wish to underscore two qualities in particular that are essential to comparative understanding. The first is the pivotal concept pointed out in Chapter 4 by Lewis, Tsuchida, and Coleman of an organizational design focused on and respectful of the *genba*— meaning the fundamental work site of an organization, the classroom in this case. We find this term widely applied in Japan. Studies of the organization of Japanese firms, for example, have long emphasized the important place of *genba*-level realities and worker participation. It is there that the crucial tailoring of collective tasks is done and from there that feedback about implementation problems should be encouraged. The *genba*, in other words, is where the rubber hits the road because if things don't work there the system fails. In any organization, obviously, change cannot move forward without compliance at this level. But given the Japanese emphasis on the *genba*, compliance is not enough. The educational system's expectations for the local level is a mix of informed acceptance, of testing and improvement in the details, and of feedback up the organization as to problems encountered. Little of this can be forced from teachers and local leaders, but must be generated primarily by on-the-ground processes. Initiatives and guidelines may come from above, but acceptance and implementation must be generated below. Viewed from above, then, both control and change appear to involve a lot of patient coaxing and behind-the-scenes manipulation by local school supervisors, as McConnell (Chapter 8, this volume) observes. Viewed from below, on the other hand, they center on a variety of group and peer activities among teachers, a point to which I will return.

In addition to being responsive to political directives from the ruling political party, a successful MOE, then, is one that carefully crafts its new initiatives to allow for local and particularly *genba*-level representation and participation. It is not surprising to find experienced teachers recruited to work within the ministry. Nor is it unusual to find teachers on the myriad MOE consulting committees. In this respect it is worth noting that compared with other ministries the MOE has a larger number of class II bureaucrats—persons not hired directly out of elite universities (particularly law departments), but recruited in the MOE's case from among the ranks of experienced teachers and subject experts. Not only is the experience of veteran teachers important to the process of crafting the details of textbooks, guidelines, curricula, and subject content, but their presence also helps to legitimate the procedural framework and thus its products.

The second fundamental characteristic of this and many other Japanese organizations is the centrality of peer-group activities that work across the horizontal dimensions within schools, districts, and prefectures (Smith, 1983). The details of many of these are discussed in the preceding chapters, and here I wish only to underscore their crucial importance in making this middle-range approach effective. Anyone who has ever done field research in Japanese schools discovers a world of stunningly active teacher relations. Committee meetings and class supervisory meetings seem to be almost a constant aspect of school life. Certainly intrateacher communication and coordination are on a level much higher than that in most American schools. Then there are local subject study groups, and larger meetings for district- and prefecturewide display and discussion of study group results. Teachers also socialize informally a good deal and even travel together on holiday. To be sure, some teachers are much less active than others in these activities, and some resent the constraints and pressures this pattern imposes on them as individuals. But socialized from childhood (and particularly in their own schooling) to participation in peer-group activities, the average Japanese teacher finds it difficult to refuse to participate. Put differently, the average Japanese teacher is very susceptible to peer pressure and very inclined to engagement as long as it is through participation in a peer group. We think of peer groups in the United States as essentially homogeneous in terms of age and status, but this is not the case in Japan, where such groups include new and seasoned teachers and where a degree of authority resides with those possessing experience and initiative. At every level of the system, in other words, there are those with some degree of formal or informal authority who orchestrate the activities we are discussing.

Were this not true, it is unlikely that the MOE's approach would succeed as it does. That is, without the peer-group activities, there is little guarantee (1) that the *genba* level would be actively engaged in tailoring the implementation process, and (2) that across the nation there would be as much coordination and uniformity as in fact occurs. The MOE's framework setting and delegation approach, in other words, would prove to be woefully inadequate to such key tasks without the active response from below described in the chapters in this book.

Understanding that the Japanese system rests on certain assumptions and institutional procedures that operate at the local level helps us grasp why the transfer from one system to another of particularly successful techniques and mechanisms is more difficult than first meets the eye. Rather than Japanese practices serving as ready options for Americans to consider, it is wiser to grasp the overall structure of the system and the place within it of particular practices. Such an inclusive and systemic perspective on Japanese education would then serve as a convenient foil, helping us see more clearly the nature of our own system.

AMERICAN EDUCATION IN LIGHT
OF THE JAPANESE EXAMPLE

Currently there is strong interest in establishing and raising educational standards in the United States. This interest is a major reason to see the work presented here as useful beyond the understanding it provides about Japan. Presumably, what appears to work so well in Japan to maintain high average levels of achievement (with smaller standard deviations in test results) could provide instructive insight for Americans seeking the same ends. Perhaps. But first we need to take another look at the American system. If in the past we have erroneously stereotyped the Japanese approach as centralized and hierarchical, we also have some rethinking to do about the nature of reform in the American system.

What is clear to the point of almost being a truism is that in its origins, and still very largely today, the American system is one that rests squarely on the assumption of local school board autonomy. The centralized qualities that have developed in our system are relatively recent developments that have arisen separately in each state and in an *ad hoc* fashion at the national level, resulting eventually in the creation of the U.S Department of Education, which is given the task of administering a hodgepodge of congressionally mandated and largely peripheral programs. The U.S. Department of Education is hardly even comparable to the MOE. Nothing is more indicative of this state of affairs, to my way of thinking, than the fact that private textbook publishers in the United States occupy a more central ground in the shaping of instruction nationally than does any single government organization.

The nature of our educational system has built into it another kind of autonomy as well. The American teacher in his or her classroom has a degree of autonomy that is inconceivable to a Japanese teacher used to fitting in and working in highly interactive peer situations, as the preceding accounts have so vividly shown. American teachers generally decide for themselves how they will use the textbooks, what supplemental materials they will introduce, at what pace they will proceed, what they will cover, and how they will conduct instruction. Lee and Zusho (Chapter 5) confirm this fundamental difference, reported by a generation of comparative studies of the two systems.

It should come as no surprise that in the American educational system the degree of disconnection on both the vertical and horizontal dimensions is much greater than in Japan, and, as a result, the organizational fabric of the American system seems weak and unwieldy by comparison. The fact that there are regular calls from the political right for the elimination of the Department of Education is but one illustration of this condition. The complex and confusing process of state and local textbook adoption is another. That we cannot find common ground on which to establish standards in even mathematics is also telling. In fact, we have entered the 21st century with what is essentially an early 19th-century system, one that grew unplanned and largely from the bottom up. Our system predates the rise in Japan and Europe and elsewhere of the state-centered constructions arising as part of the ideology of the strong nation state. Japan's basic system was developed in the 1880s as part of a powerful nation-building agenda.

The fit between our locally funded and locally controlled system and American social reality is curious and quite different from that in Japan. It is deeply allied with cultural and political forces here that have an enclave mentality, protecting various kinds of class, regional, and religious differences from outside forces representing something like the national common denominator. Wealthy and middle-class suburbs, religious sects, and agricultural communities, for example, believe they find protection in this highly diffuse system. One result is the perpetuation of a degree of socio-economic and cultural diversity unimaginable in Japan. The current level of residential mobility in the United States, on the other hand, puts our system in a very different light. Most Americans are not being educated today in a single local system. Rather, the typical educational career is one that embraces at least several, if not many, school districts. Nor are local investments in education likely to pay off in reliable human capital pools, given the way we Americans move around. Whether we are considering textbooks or standards or teaching methods, local authority appears sadly anachronistic in this light. Geographically mobile parents, strongly interested in their children's schools, are a common aspect of the educational landscape in both Japan and the United States today, yet the choices offered by the two systems are not the same. In the United States, without a national system in terms of budgetary equity, standards, or regulatory authority, parents struggle to find viable levers to effect broad reforms. In other words, opinion polls and electoral rhetoric may imply that our public concern is with education as a "national" problem, but the essential nature of our institutional arrangements makes centralized solutions exceedingly difficult.

Our efforts to reform education appear to follow two quite different paths, neither of which is at all like what we find in Japan. On the one hand, we are experimenting with standards and testing as something new and forceful that works top-down and across the board, and on the other, we continue at the local level to experiment in a massive way with every kind of initiative that holds out some kind of promise of improvement. Because of the disconnected nature of our system, we have few convenient institutions in the middle that might connect the two kinds of efforts.

This explains, I think, why when we seek to raise average achievement or raise the level of poorly performing districts and schools, we end up relying heavily on what are basically very coercive methods. We do not typically define these as coercive, but when compared with the Japanese approach they certainly have such a character. Take the many cases of legal intrusion into school system management as one example. Whether mandated by the U.S. Supreme Court, some state court, or a lower federal court, these intrusions have little or no real teacher input; almost intentionally ignore the realities of school and classroom; and force change primarily with threats of dismissal and closure. Also typical of this approach is close, aggressive, and often naïve supervision by the courts. The will of the courts, and their impatience, becomes central to reform once it is determined that the law is being broken. That judges could decide educational policy is unthinkable in the Japanese context.

A second common form of top-down intervention in the American case is the effort to legislate systemwide improvements by establishing universal standards coupled to standardized tests and other mechanisms of measurement and enforcement. Again, this kind of leverage can be found at all levels from the local to the national, and again without any clearly coordinated teacher input or consensus. Standards without tests have no teeth, obviously, and even tests without penalties are a weak form of coercion. Naturally, then, the movement to leverage average achievement by these means seeks to tie such things as graduation requirements, teacher pay, tenure, and other incentives and punishments to test results. The problems with this approach are so well known as to require no more than a brief list of its major defects: teaching to the test, debasing content, perpetual political disagreement on standards, issues of equity, ideological squabbling, the absence of critical skill development, widespread teacher resistance, and so forth. As with the case of legal intrusion from above, the time frames mandated tend to be too short for concerted reform, the consultation with teachers tends to be minimal, and the unintended consequences turn out to be quite large. In both cited instances, and this is the basic point, the middle ground where goals and means are adjusted and where teachers collectively join in the process of improvement and change hardly exists. One reason is that the institutions of consultation between national policy discussions and school-level change, so central to the Japanese approach, are absent. Instead, we delegate such communications to scholars, academic and professional journals, schools of education, district training sessions, and the like, areas very weakly developed in the Japanese system.

What have been the results of the American movement to establish a standards-based approach? Compared with Japanese students, American students certainly take more standardized tests annually. This may be surprising, but between testing at various grade levels and practicing to take such tests (not to mention teaching-to-the-test activities), American students are increasingly focused on tests imposed from outside the district. Eventually this will result in improved test scores, but probably will not lessen inequality or significantly improve general levels of skills or knowledge. The critical tests in Japan, those governing entrance to high school and university, cluster at the secondary level. These put enormous muscle behind the textbooks and the curriculum, as DeCoker shows in Chapter 9, and they also give a prominent role to private tutoring schools. Russell in

Chapter 10 illustrates how these are organized to fill the gap between the national guidelines and the competitive realities of the much condemned university entrance exams. Japanese secondary students are also thrust into practice test taking in a major way by the prospect of entrance exams. And, no doubt about it, entrance exams have all of the flaws just mentioned in regard to American standardized tests. The differences are, first, when the exams occur in the developmental process, and, second, that in Japan students are individually differentiated and ranked by their efforts (LeTendre, Chapter 2, this volume; DeCoker, Chapter 9, this volume), whereas in the American case the teacher and the school are likely to be punished for low results. The one emphasizes positive motivations; the other, negative ones. The Japanese approach makes students accountable; the American one makes teachers accountable. It is not surprising that in the United States the standards movement is often pushed most strongly by persons who harbor suspicions about teachers' qualifications and commitment. Furthermore, in Japan, it is the more talented and socioeconomically better off two-thirds of the population that are most affected by the entrance exam system, whereas in the United States, the effort to raise standards targets the lowest-performing one-third of the population. Most of our coercive efforts are aimed at the districts, schools, and teachers working with low-income, ethnic, rural, and disadvantaged students.

Standards per se are not the essence of our problem. Of course, there will be controversies when standards are first imposed, especially for easily politicized matters of language and social studies. Far more critical is the problem that any system designed to enforce standards contradicts the historic nature of American education. The attempt to establish strict accountability, furthermore, confronts some of the most basic organizational realities of education anywhere. Schools are limited instruments of social change, and accountability is a highly flawed concept when judgments are made simply on the basis of testing. Teachers, furthermore, are not motivated primarily by monetary or other easily manipulated incentives. Nor can accurate calculations be made of the appropriate time frames and support requirements needed to effect the levels of change intended.

Having arrived at a point in the United States where we as a nation have identified our greatest educational failures and acknowledged that they are intolerable, we still rely heavily in the policy realm on very crude top-down methods of change, ones that generally alienate most teachers and local administrators—the very people central to actually effecting the improvements needed. It is telling that Japanese high standards and high average achievement levels are not accomplished in the manner we have been inclined toward in public debate. Despite a few superficial similarities stemming from the fact that Japan is a centralized system, the fact remains that in Japan teachers and political policy meet in the middle. History has dealt us a notably poor hand when it comes to administrative approaches to reform. It is not that standards and tests are inherently bad, but that alone they are woefully inadequate.

The second path I identify as characteristic of American efforts to improve education is marked less by a desire to create systemwide change than simply to demonstrate that there are "better ways" to accomplish education. Thus we witness a constant flow of new experimental programs and initiatives, most at local levels, funded by an amazing variety of private and public sources of support. These are largely disconnected from one another and philosophically as heterogeneous as one can imagine. In the same district and even in the same school there can be conflicts among them, but typically a state of churn and flux prevails. At one extreme, we find home schooling becoming popular—the ultimate in American-style autonomy. Perhaps as many as a million children are currently schooled by their parents. Also reflective of parental choice and the autonomy of private initiatives are the many kinds of "alternative" schools arising and disappearing on the educational landscape. If we include the full range of religious schools, charter schools, Montessori schools, Waldorf schools, cultural and language preservationist schools, and so forth, they number perhaps in the tens of thousands. The largest category of experimental schools, however, is comprised of public schools enrolled in one or more experimental programs. Who knows how large this category really is? It is unusual to visit an urban public school at any level that is not involved in an innovative program of some kind, whether in math teaching, values education, bilingual instruction, citizenship, community involvement, teacher collaboration, back-to-basics, sex education, abstinence education, drug education, or one of literally hundreds of other types of initiatives. Most of these efforts, we know, prove to be short-lived, so highly dependent are they on teacher enthusiasm, short-term funding, and extra effort. When the leadership changes, or the money goes away, or burnout arrives, or teachers transfer, the momentum typically wanes. Yet nothing about American education is more impressive to Japanese visitors than the lively innovation and teacher optimism exemplified by this vast array of local-level change efforts. Such diversified, exuberant, and uncoordinated innovation is unimaginable in Japan.

Seen in this light, voucher schemes, while generally discussed as systemwide and policy-driven initiatives, actually turn out to be an ingenious, if deceptive, mix of the two typical American approaches to reform. They are proposed by legislators and officials at the top, yet speak to the spirit of local autonomy and the promise of independent innovation. A major shift in the direction toward vouchers would greatly amplify our already massive inclination to piecemeal innovative diversity. While national stan-dards and formal testing offer a highly specified if awkward and limited approach to reforming education, the "let a thousand flowers bloom" ex-perimentalism path of vouchers is formless, but actually closer in spirit to what teachers and many parents take education to be. Combining the two, as is now commonly proposed, speaks to both inclinations.

Whether, if such proposals were followed, we would get the best of both or the worst of both is the essential question. It is worth recalling that before the formation of the Meiji state in 1868, Japan, too, had an educa-tional landscape of great diversity and little if any inclusive organization. It chose a centralized, nation-state-oriented path, which has been modified considerably, but not fundamentally changed (Hall, 1973; Lincicome, 1995). Interestingly, the voices in Japan calling for a reorientation of edu-cation cite the American example as the ideal. It seems, ironically, that the grass is readily seen as greener on the other side of the Pacific, a point we shall take up in the next section.

Returning to the perspective granted us by this comparison, we can see that America's several paths to educational reform ignore the adminis-trative middle ground. We have precious few *noncoercive* means of effec-tively coordinating instruction in the schools and classrooms across the nation. There are few national curricular guidelines of real merit, but many national laws regulating a host of peripheral and trivial matters. Nor are our textbooks the product of consultative processes arising from interac-tion in the administrative middle. The erratic way they are received at the local level and used by teachers reflects this. We also lack plausible mecha-nisms for significant (as opposed to token) teacher participation in our larger reform processes. Our policymakers, like our textbook writers, rarely come from within the system. The trust in and respect for teachers is low. Public impatience and ideological polarities arising outside educa-tion tend to determine our policy agendas and, given the enormity of the task, almost guarantee that systemwide efforts will fail. We have been in a chronic state of "crisis" for decades with little to show for all the reform rhetoric and "new" and creative programs. Is this evidence that the absence of an institutional middle ground in American education is a fundamental flaw? The contrast with Japan so clearly set forth in the previous chapters suggests precisely this.

The weakness of an institutional middle ground where adjustment and improvement efforts are routine and nationally coordinated certainly helps explain why our two kinds of responses, coercive and centripetal, tend toward the extremes of the range of administrative options set forth at the beginning of this discussion. Ironically, if both options continue to be pop-ular, they are likely to become, in theory at least, increasingly interdependent. On the one hand, the heterogeneity of experimentalism will require a central core of standards if there is to be any framework legitimizing public expenditures. On the other hand, a system of standards and testing will have to discover reliable models of instruction and improvement to be dynamic. Perhaps this potential for interdependence is a key ingredient of a new design for American education.

Clearly, America is not Japan. The authors of the previous chapters are properly reluctant to make recommendations or to claim that Japan has something to teach America. It is not hard to see in their accounts, however, an admiration for Japan's approach and accomplishments. Implicit is the message that when it comes to the challenge of organizing and moving a large national system of instruction toward improvements and high achievement, Japan is worth studying, since it appears to have learned a great deal from a century of experience. The only way this experience will be of value to American policymakers, however, is if they become concerned with our lack of a viable middle ground, whether at the national or the state level. That concern is not much in evidence at present.

Our two distinct American paths to change could take us to a place far more unlike Japan than where we currently are. Whether we are engaged in the accidental invention of a quite new system is anybody's guess at present. Trends point, however, toward a circumstance in which public standards, standardized tests, and continued public funding form a kind of general context for a growing diversity of schools (increasingly private) and an accountability system that rests primarily on parental choice. Elements of this have been in place for a long time, but what is far from clear is whether this approach will actually address the hard core problems of the underperforming bottom third of the population any more effectively than the system we currently operate.

ON THE POPULAR COMPARISON OF JAPANESE AND AMERICAN EDUCATION

We do not regularly compare our education system with those of very many other countries despite the range of interesting examples abroad in the world and despite the fact that achievement test data now make comparisons among so many developed nations possible. We focus on top performers and especially on top performers that do things differently from the way we do them. Neither the media nor our politicians have shown much interest, for example, in Italy or Canada, but we have regularly made Japan a point of great educational interest. Nor have other national examples raised as much emotional heat as Japan regularly has in American educational circles. During the Cold War, of course, there was interest in education in the Soviet Union, but no suggestion that we need emulate it. With that partial exception, it is fair to say that no country comes close to Japan in being a focus of media interest or in the amount of exaggerated praise and criticism its school system has received. It seems that each newly arriving correspondent for the *New York Times* in Tokyo, for example, feels obliged to write about exam pressures or bullying or student anomie, if not all of these. If he or she places a child in a Japanese school, we are sure to have a report of how supportive and interesting schooling in Japan can be. The news services show similar inclinations. And the periodic announcement of international achievement test results typically starts a new cycle of such interest. It would not be too far off the mark to say that Japanese education has found a routine place in American educational discourse, sometimes idealized and sometimes demonized, but increasingly a predictable, if modest, part of the whole. Japan is embedded in what might be vaguely labeled our national psyche as far as education goes.

But our media accounts, being exaggerated and mixed, offer little clear guidance. The implication, the subtext if you will, is that something important is being revealed, otherwise why the particular report or special attention. But nothing important actually emerges for us (the public), because the sum now consistently contains a confusing jumble of pluses and minuses. There was a time in the late 1980s and early 1990s when the balance tended to reports of Japanese practices as though they might be important keys to improving U.S. education, and more recently, one can detect a shift toward emphasizing what is perceived to be Japan's problems (borrowing from the Japanese media stories on rote learning, authoritarian teachers, harsh conformity, school violence, and so forth), but generally the total picture has been a mix of black and white accounts that leave a grey confusion. It appears the recent negativity, furthermore, is consistent with a new media focus on a vulnerable and troubled Japan trying to escape the post-bubble depression. The American public can make very little of the pastiche of selected virtues and faults that has emerged, and it is probable that the findings of this book will experience the same fate.

The recent history of our schizoid, but keen, interest in Japan goes something like this: (1) Japan does remarkably well economically, while the U.S. economy stagnates; (2) utilizing the interest of an alarmed public, the media seek answers, even in the arena of educational comparison; (3) with some academic help, the media find much to praise in Japan while simultaneously noting the lower performance of the home team; (4) policymakers pick up on this and praise for certain putative Japanese practices crescendos; (5) this produces a defensive and mildly paranoid response within other sectors of the public, which then seek to underscore what is wrong with Japan; (6) a grey stalemate ensues; (7) the economic bubble bursts in Japan and this negative angle becomes dominant; (8) the positive and negative stereotypes develop a life of their own; (9) eventually interest wanes. I recite this hypothetical history only to underscore the inherent difference between scholarly studies like those contained in this book and the course of popular interest in Japanese education in this country.

Today, however, it is Japan that is the most interested in educational comparison, not America. This is a return to the situation in the 1950s and 1960s when America was also viewed in Japan as the world's most successful and powerful country. In fact, since the Occupation, the American model of education has been held up as an exemplar of progressive education by reformers in Japan. In the 1980s, of course, the economic incentives for what might be termed educational envy shifted the focus to the Japanese side. The end of the bubble has led to a decade of self-recrimination in Japan in which education has been a major target. Viewing a vibrant American economy centered on new areas of technology, the Japanese now perceive themselves trapped in less innovative institutions that served them well when the country was developing, but are ill adapted to the current global situation.

Ironically, for all their interest in and use of the American model in shaping the Japanese educational debate, the Japanese media and their scholarly informants actually pay only superficial attention to the realities of American schools. Accounts of American educational ideals, assorted anecdotes, and quick observation tours have generally sufficed to paint a rosy picture. In neither country, in other words, has it taken very much for the public to be interested in the contrasting "other." Each has become an inherent element of the cultural construction of meaning for the other. The peculiar mutual fascination has gained capacity for self-replication. Both nations have been economic rivals for most of the last half century, but it is the cultural and social contrasts and their symbolic centrality that sustain the mutual fascination. A fundamental opposition and attraction exists. Under stressful circumstances, it has taken very little for the one to be convinced that the "other" has the right medicine for its current ailment. But this reaction is also predictably countered by citation of the negative stereotype. This seesaw is virtually a perpetual-motion machine.

What is interesting is how each nation has used the other in its domestic debates on education. The two have come to the point where popular stereotypes of the other play a significant role in the formation of national educational debate. The United States and Japan have thus inadvertently joined in developing an interesting variant of what in interpersonal relations might be labeled co-dependency. The two, that is, are rivals who dwell (obsessively at times) on the other's strengths and weaknesses. They use the other to feel both bad and good, to motivate domestic reform and argue against it. Japan and America make strange bedfellows, no doubt, but it is the very fact of strangeness that gives the dynamic to this pairing.

Ironically, the politics of this are topsy-turvy. Advocates of progressive reform in one country find themselves allied by an odd symmetry with conservative opinion in the other. That is, praise for the other serves the purposes of change at home, but puts one in agreement with those advocating against change in the other country. By praising Japan's accomplishments as a means of urging American reform, for example, I am aligning myself with conservatives in Japan who favor the status quo. By underscoring Japan's failings, on the other hand, in arguing against change in the United States, one would be putting oneself in agreement with Progressives in Japan who are pushing for reform. In this regard, international conferences of reform-minded experts from the two countries make for a strange but predictable pattern: Each praises the other's approach and denies the other's praise of their own system. While it may appear that polite humility has become a substitute for debate, the fact is that a good deal is at stake politically in each asserting the virtues of the other's system.

The two public discourses basically talk past one another, unable to rise above their respective domestic preoccupations and the stereotypes that serve them. This results in another particular irony—that popular thought on both sides of the Pacific has become invested, albeit unwittingly, in the maintenance of the stereotypical "other," each having learned to symbolically use the other in a particular fixed mode. To Americans, for example, the Japanese will remain group-oriented, well organized, meticulous, and homogeneous, while to the Japanese the Americans will persist in being individualistic, flexible, innovative, and heterogeneous. Math and science are certain to be topics representative of Japanese strengths, while America's strong points are destined to be creativity and individuality as found in social studies and verbal arts. And, in fact, such differences do and will continue to exist *to a degree*, and they do and will affect educational outcomes *to a degree*. But they are far from the whole story. During the last half century, for example, there has been considerable convergence in many fundamental aspects of the two systems. The similarities are easily lost, and the differences are regularly dwelt on.

Is there a way out of this now rather predictable pattern? Or is it inevitable that research of the kind presented in this book, when picked up by the public, will be transformed to fit the already established symbolic arrangement? In thinking about this dilemma, it helps to keep in mind the three very separate forces and levels involved: scholarly work, media storytelling, and the policymaking processes.

There is little reason to expect the three to interact as scholars would want, that is, that scholars discover the "truth," which media faithfully report and which policymakers effectively utilize. In fact, the media feast on controversies, on moral tales of good and bad, of success and failure, and on stories of conventional understandings overturned. Policymaking, on the other hand, is a momentum game, one certainly fickle regarding something like learning from Japan's experience when it comes to education.

This does not mean, however, that research as represented here need be viewed as entirely isolated or of no ultimate practical use. The media need high-quality ingredients for stories, to begin with, and, second, occasionally the persuasive comparative example fits with the momentum surrounding some policy deliberation. It is my impression and hope that the research reported will have relevance to one or both of these larger processes.

It would help, of course, if some organization existed to amplify the scholarly voice with authority. Interestingly, in Japan the educational establishment (a cautious elite that includes some teachers) is more unified and has a larger role in policymaking than any such group in the United States. As a result, it is safe to say that, despite a less impressive comparative research tradition, the Japanese generally make more of comparative learning in shaping policy. On the other hand, we have no consensual voice of scholarly authority with a consistent pipeline to policymakers. The telling exceptions are the science and engineering academies that periodically publicize the need for better math and science teaching along lines demonstrated to work in Japan. Our decentralized approach and weak Department of Education preclude the sort of pipeline one finds in Japan. The perpetual fountain of reform proposals we generate is sufficient, furthermore, to maintain our characteristic national self-absorption in the realm of educational research.

As a longtime observer of Japanese education, I can attest that American research on Japanese schools and teaching practices has been of a consistently high caliber. The collective achievement is to have produced what is easily the most thorough and best-analyzed study of any non-Western school system known to comparative education. This research (some of the best represented by authors of these chapters) has stood up well to the many tests of time and is internally very coherent. That it has not had more of an impact on American education reflects the larger forces just discussed. Tellingly, superior Japanese factory management techniques (TQM, just-in-time, and so forth), while also confronted by considerable initial resistance and skepticism, have advanced much further in this country and this, I think, is because the general institutional framework is different. Here again, what turns out to be important is an area of society that is little discussed, an intermediate area between "local"-level actors (schools, teachers, and in this case researchers) and national-level ones.

WILL ANY OF THIS BE RELEVANT 20 YEARS HENCE?

The beginning of the new century is a time filled with near breathless predictions and prognostications. Not surprisingly, the new information technologies are regularly being trumpeted as central to virtually every aspect of our future lives. Particularly relevant to the topics of this book are the predictions that the next major areas to be impacted by the Internet are government and education. This is also a time marked by many changes that fall under the rubric of globalization. I would include under this category early challenges to the nation state's legitimate monopoly or near monopoly on educational agendas worldwide (Meyer & Ramirez, 1992). Japan is a very good example of this, of course, and it is worthwhile to speculate on the future of textbooks, national standards, curriculum, classroom instruction, even collegial activities among teachers, if the state's central role in education is increasingly called into question by such changes (Tyack & Cuban, 1995). Readers of this volume must wonder about the future of both the characteristic Japanese and American approaches to education given the scale of potential technological change on the horizon.

I must first indulge in something of a confession. My reaction to much of the futuristic enthusiasm for a technological revolution in education has been stubbornly skeptical, especially when it comes to claims for intellectual and spiritual progress arising from computers, the Internet, the globalization of information, and so forth. This resistance to the hyperbole about a bold new world has lately become the source of some personal embarrassment for me when talking with students, my children, and adult converts to the new vision here in California. Exclamations of what seem to me to be misplaced joy regarding the impending demise of books, libraries, and even schools (as we know them, at least) coming from the mouths of young entrepreneurs and engineers has a way of provoking in me a most curmudgeonly reaction. Decidedly not a convert, at least not at this stage, I find the prospect of a world comprised of people isolated night and day in front of blinking machines performing what up to now have been the critical social tasks of civilization—namely, communicating, learning, and thinking—decidedly sad and disturbing.

This confession made, I think it is very important to note that the future is not going to be like the past as far as education is concerned. In both the United States and Japan the institutions of education are heavily burdened by the weight of over a century of expansion without much change in their essentially 19th-century formulas. Universal public education has demonstrably become tired and inflexible in both countries. While public education is not on life support or anything so dramatic, the fact that reform is all that is talked about in both countries is indication of serious health problems. How little change has arisen lately from within public education is another notable sign of aging. It appears that forces outside education are likely to prove to be far more dynamic. The elements of the two education systems discussed in this book share in this uncertain future.

We should not think only about technology as shaping the future, but rather about the intersection of technology with the weakening of the nation state, and the increasing influence of global market capitalism. Viewed in this light, I would argue that national standards and curricula, textbooks and teachers' manuals, and the other central gearing mechanisms of national systems of education, Japanese or otherwise, face an uncertain future for a variety of interconnected reasons (Harvey, 1989; Reich, 1991; Waters, 1995; Wriston, 1997).

Looking back, it is helpful to remember that public schooling in Japan is very largely a late-19th-century phenomenon, part of a massive effort by government to build a nation of literate citizens as part of the urgent project of strengthening Japan in the face of foreign colonial power. The increasing level of government authority over everyday life that this effort entailed was legitimated by virtually the entire disparate range of visionary promises of the time. In Europe, a similar effort was occurring. American education certainly appears to have been an exception in terms of the centrality of the nation state, but here as well nationalism and the ideology of building a unified and democratic society greatly motivated the push for universal education at local levels.

If technology is our current preoccupation, social engineering as part of modernism was its late-19th- and early-20th-century equivalent. All of the ideologies of the age justified, in fact hinged on, universal public education as the key agent of uplift and unification (Ramirez, 1997). Naturally, given these intentions, such notions as standards and curricular requirements and such vehicles of standardization as textbooks and teachers' manuals became important elements of social transformation. This was a period of great general expansion in the area of government regulation in both countries. Whole new areas of social existence came under monitoring and control. The same impulse that gave rise to universal public education gave rise, for example, to the regulation of labor practices and to the supervision of food and drug production. It was equally a time of general uplift as evidenced by such things as the rise of organized youth movements and major efforts in public hygiene. What shaped education as we now know it, in other words, were forces of enormous power whose momentum are only now on the wane. Social engineering was a pivotal intent behind the rise of universal public schooling, and our interests in standards and textbooks and national testing continue to reflect this kind of aspiration. In the United States, this fundamental impulse has been somewhat muted and disguised by our unusual system of decentralized educational authority, but it is patently at the heart of the Japanese system.

I recite this well-documented background only to underscore the fact that much is taken for granted in the research for this book. Our assumptions, researchers and readers alike, begin with the notion of a national population that needs and wants compulsory education defined as a basic public good. In the United States this is not a contested notion. What is contested are the details of how uniform that education should be and what level of public authority has the right to determine the details. It is also generally assumed, even in this country, that most educational standardization is normal and desirable. Witness the activity in this regard at the state level. It is further assumed that governments are the authorities best placed to set standards and curriculum for compulsory education. Again, what is open to public debate are the details and the room for individual choice. In both countries the key agents for coordinating the educational enterprise are thought to be government agencies susceptible to political intervention rather than teachers or parents or employers or university admissions offices, or private companies. The central authority, in other words, is government and the target population is everyone. This apparatus, furthermore, is targeted at an imagined average child. Finally, the design of education in both countries is to achieve the efficient mass delivery of instruction using legions of classroom teachers working in thousands of largely public buildings. The fixed costs are enormous, and the labor content of this effort is very large.

In the 18th century, before the rise of the modern nation state, however, the content of learning was not so very different, but it rested on a framework very different from the one just described. Avenues to education were remarkably diverse in both Japan and the United States—from public and private academies of classical education for children of the elite to apprenticeships of every kind and ultimately to the idiosyncratic self-tutoring programs exemplified by the well-known educational careers of people like Ben Franklin and Ninomiya Sontoku. The distributional pattern may not have been so terribly different from today either. No one then could have imagined that there was only one path to knowledge or that the government should have a near monopoly on content or that one set of standards would apply to an entire generation of youth or that an imagined average student would be the pivot of an entire system. If broadly applicable standards existed in America, they came from various church hierarchies and applied only to religious instruction. In pre-Meiji Japan, in every realm of instruction, there existed a multitude of competing instructional philosophies and standards. If the Meiji state and the American school board in the 19th century could expropriate the job of setting standards from employers, guilds, professional groups, and churches, is it not possible that the role of government could be expropriated by newly emergent forces based in information technologies, global capitalism, and related developments? Patently, the question is somewhat different in the case of Japan than in the United States, but the general set of external forces for change is the same.

Apart from education, trends toward a dilution of centralized authority are much in evidence around the world. We hear a good deal about deregulation, decentralization, and privatization. Pointedly, in post-bubble Japan the search for a more flexible and innovative economic order leads generally away from government control and national uniformity. On many fronts the effort is to reduce regulation and central influence. Virtually everywhere in the developed and much of the developing world, the trends are much the same. The impact of globalization also is forcing a retreat of the state in many areas where national boundaries are concerned. The international flows of capital, goods, information, and people are simply more and more difficult to control. That American and Japanese high-tech industries need significant flows of skilled labor (educated, for example, in India or China) is indicative of the shifting international landscape as far as human resources are concerned. The rapid rise of global nongovernmental organizations is a further illustration of the ground shift away from specific national agendas and toward global issues that cross national borders (Mathews, 1997). New communication capacities have also made largely unregulated, electronically based markets increasingly central to many areas of our lives. Neither Singapore nor the Chinese People's Republic, for example, is able to stem the rapid rate of social change arising from travel, trade, and telecommunications. In a world where, thanks to the Internet, buyers and sellers can transact across most borders with ease (obtaining drugs or trading stocks or peddling pornography), the day will come when instructional content will also flow internationally along similarly unrestrained channels. Where will government, national or local, be in this world? Will it remain primarily a regulator? Will it be a major consumer? Will it learn to be a producer effectively competing with globally organized private generators of educational content?

Commercial impulses have been central to much of this early development of global flows, and they may well be central to the evolution of instruction via the same channels. Already provisioned electronically with vast amounts of cheap information and clear evidence of future markets, we appear on the brink of possessing tolerably good interactive instructional packages that will couple individuated record keeping, feedback systems, exciting graphics, and more, all targeted at particular kinds of learning and categories of learners. And we are told that this is only the beginning of what will be a veritable revolution in machine-aided learning that will apply to every subject and age group. It is true that the track record of computer-based learning has been disappointing so far, but that should not be reason to discount the possibility of considerable future advances. We certainly have evidence on the home front and in business of major changes arising with the advancing use of computers. That education is an area that has been slow to experience the impact of the new technology is evidence of just how difficult it is to construct high-quality instructional formats, not that this is inherently impossible.

Assuming such progress, questions abound. Who will assemble the best instructional packages at the lowest cost—government, universities, media companies, private firms in the teaching business, or some combination of these? Who will buy them—school systems, parents, or some other kinds of consumers? Companies could conceivably make them a major purchase for their employees and their employee's children. Ford Motors, for example, has recently announced a plan to offer PCs and connections to the Internet free to all 350,000 of its workers worldwide. Will some packages like math or science or English composition quickly find international audiences and thus become free of the debilitating constraints of national curricular authority and the limitations of poorly prepared, average public school teachers? Will other commercially available packages in fields such as literature and history become segmented by socioeconomic status or aptitude factors or ethnic preference? Will various ethnic niches arise that link members of one or another global diaspora via educational packages such as Bengali History or Korean Ethics and Etiquette? Will unresponsive governments end up holding what will increasingly be the short end of the stick if they hide behind their current monopolies? Free of political/ideological controls and inspired by potentially very large markets, commercial developers appear poised to have a field day in the area of selling not only university preparation products, but content of many kinds.

Such packages will eventually be evaluated by market mechanisms, presumably, but shaped by what influences—those based on university admissions criteria and results, or by the choice of elite consumers (who will shape early demands), or the opinions of education specialists, or the admonitions of religious and political groups? All are almost certain to enter the picture and make for greater complexity of choice and confusion in the general public realm. One can readily envision competing secondary-level science packages for the gifted, the religiously conservative, the environmentally sensitive, the medical school candidate, the aspiring farmer, the visually oriented, the native speaker of Spanish, and so on. What will happen to textbooks? Will they be translated, so to speak, into the new format, or will they be unbundled into extensive lists of lesson modules capable of being flexibly assembled by individual teachers or school boards or parents? Might each student in a school district one day receive a personalized curriculum? If so, what is the likelihood that a government or a teacher corps would be the source of such a project? What kinds of self-paced, at-home applications might develop as essentially antischool in nature?

Standards may themselves become more diverse and refer to a greater range of learning realities. Conceivably, measurements of learning could be calibrated quite readily to individual talents and limitations, for example, as is already a goal of some reform efforts. Similarly, it will almost certainly be no problem to measure progress against past individual performance, rather than solely against national or other averages. It is equally conceivable that by using more refined and complex computer-based systems, standards could be developed to fit individual ambitions and career plans. It is possible that just as textbooks and teacher manuals and guidelines have been state-driven means to standardize instruction across whole populations over the last century, so in the next century, a new set of forces will offer greater variety within nations at the level of the learner, while, on the other hand, increasing many forms of transnational standardization.

Even if the current national standards remain in place and achievement testing continues, what will give them teeth under conditions of increasing diversity? Certainly certification and graduation requirements come to mind immediately. Yet these represent minimum standards only. The majority of parents are likely to be preoccupied by information regarding the relative efficacy of commercial products in relation to university admission, particular kinds of employment, or narrow specialized fields. As increasingly informed consumers, many parents are likely to pressure schools in new ways to arrange their children's learning as they now arrange sports experiences or music lessons. Will teacher accountability mean less and less if teachers are no longer as central to instruction and if textbooks give way to more individuated offerings? So much of what we take for granted in the current system could begin to fall apart as the internal logic weakens.

What about teachers and schools? Whether public schools will be the nexus of the perfected learning systems (when they arrive) or be made to seem obsolete by them is impossible to know at this point. But the question is a serious one. Several times recently graduate students of education have argued in my class that public schools will disappear in the foreseeable future. They were answered by others who agreed that schools may not be needed as much for the cognitive part of human development, but would survive nonetheless by evolving into places specialized in peer socialization, civics, community work, sports and music training, and, most telling, glorified public baby-sitting centers for busy parents. It is sobering to hear future teachers offer such analyses based on their own reading of the future impact of computer-based learning. Given the high costs currently involved in maintaining public education, furthermore, one wonders whether at some point in the future, as instruction shifts more and more to electronic media, the value added by teachers and schools will lose public support altogether. I am not suggesting this as an immediate prospect, but as something that in the longer run is far from impossible.

No one can doubt that in both Japan and the United States there has been a gradual loss of legitimacy for the existing public monopoly of K–12 education. The Japanese government's role is being questioned in education more seriously than at any previous time in the last century. I was surprised to find that there is already considerable interest in charter schools in Japan, for example. And certainly in this country the voucher idea has achieved a currency that is surprising. We can note also that universities in both countries have been experiencing a gradual globalization of faculty, along with graduate and undergraduate enrollments. The degree of change in this respect is far greater in the United States than in Japan, but the trends in both nations point in the same direction. Europe is even further along this path now that the European Union has removed barriers to university access among member countries. The world's top schools (private and public) are now so sought after on an international basis that they are, in effect, setting global standards for educational excellence, for an emerging global elite (Ilon, 1994).

Nancy Russell in Chapter 10 notes the rising influence of private cram schools in Japan and how they confound the MOE's efforts to regulate the pace of instruction. This case seems indicative of a potentially much larger set of possibilities that are emerging globally. If we could survey the entire range of private commercial developments in the education field in Japan and the United States, we would, I think, discover a surprisingly dynamic, profitable, and expanding world of private enterprise in education. Currently it centers on adult vocational training and preparation for entrance exams, but recently it has expanded dramatically into university- and graduate-level for-credit offerings in many occupational fields. Names like the University of Phoenix, DeVries, Edison, Kaplan, Princeton Review, Sylvan Systems, and Kumon Juku in the United States will soon be joined by many others arising from the intersection of media and communications companies well positioned to develop educational products, if not entire alternative educational systems. What is to prevent companies in India, China, and Europe from also entering the sweepstakes in categories where they might have creative or cost advantages? These possibilities appear most likely to converge first in the marketing of practical content to adult learners and to ambitious parents of the global upper middle class seeking special advantages for their children.

We are witnessing, I sense, the beginnings of something that could eventually snowball commercially. It is too early to grasp the extent of its ultimate impact, but as the critical technological basis for such systems expands demographically, commercial education markets will grow, assuring that giant companies like Disney and Time Warner or Murdoch's media empire or Sony or Star TV will soon be seriously engaged. If we equate the effort and money needed to create a powerful Internet instructional package to making a full-length commercial movie, it is obvious that only when the volume of prospective demand grows quite large will the underlying economics become attractive. It is also obvious what kinds of organizations will be best positioned to respond. In education this demand has so far been largely controlled by government, but it is quite plausible that a global marketplace and powerful commercial players may come to dominate in the future.

The likelihood of this happening more rapidly in the United States than in Japan is great for some of the reasons presented in the previous chapters. Teachers in Japan are more engaged in the process of perfecting instruction, to begin with, and as computers become more available in schools in Japan, it is predictable that teacher input will assist greatly in the development of effective instructional packages. Second, the central budgetary power of the MOE and the efficiencies of developing instructional products for a unified national school system will probably allow the MOE to stay abreast of private commercial development efforts. On the other hand, decentralized and inclined to piecemeal experimentalism, the American system is likely to change more rapidly and with far greater private commercial influence. The coercive inclinations associated with standard setting and accountability may prove viable as a minimal structure of evaluation for public accounting purposes, but appear increasingly inept at the same time. Loyalty to the public system among American teachers could erode further under such conditions. In other words, the differences between the two education systems illustrated so well by the studies presented here could well serve to define two very different future courses of adaptation and reform in the face of these new external forces.

It is my assumption, furthermore, that while many of the conditions behind the research presented here will diminish in the coming decades, the profound value of the experience that skilled teachers bring to an understanding of how learning can be improved will actually be more, rather than less, valued. Instructional packages are likely to be compared and scrutinized more carefully in the future and eventually this means that those that are well informed and well designed will gain wider recognition. The consultative processes leading to such improvements will also gain in importance, even if the organizing entity is a private one rather than a governmental one. New interactive communications, furthermore, could be of positive assistance in furthering interactive processes among teachers, as emphasized in the Japanese case. This is to say that the educational "middle ground" could assume more, rather than less, importance as a result. There is hardly any guarantee of this, of course.

In sum, the basic knowledge and mechanics involved in improving learning and teaching—the topics of this book—are far more immutable than the current public delivery systems to which they belong. Certainly there will be a continuing need for this knowledge regardless of future delivery format. To begin with, what skilled teachers have learned about effective instruction will not be disregarded or supplanted, but will be critical to the future design process. The range of quality and degree of teacher idiosyncrasy is certain to decline (as it has with the rise of national systems in the first place), but instruction, especially in a competitive environment, will remain only as good and as viable as the basic understandings on which it is designed. One also can suppose that continuous improvement will be an important part of such a future marketplace for instructional packages. We know that artificial intelligence will not begin to be up to this kind of challenge for all but the most routine aspects of feedback and analysis. In Japan teachers are likely to continue to be crucial to the improvement process, but what about in the United States? Will our state systems discover the importance of the middle ground in seeking to develop better packages? Will private firms learn this lesson faster and capture the best teachers for their own more efficient methodologies? Will market forces turn out to reward organizations that adopt Japanese-like approaches to meta-learning? Continuous improvement will arise not from feedback from thousands of computers, but rather from creative use of teaching experience. As with today's textbooks and instructional practices, improvement will still rest on such basics as careful attention to the details of learning, a practical grasp of developmental sequencing, and the astute evaluation of instructional options. Teachers will remain central, but will their numbers shrink eventually? Or will the majority of teachers find their job descriptions changing radically from the current focus on routine delivery of academic content to one of supervising and monitoring a set of perfectible processes in which most of the routine instruction will be assumed by digitally based packages? The burden of actual teaching (in terms of time and attention) could shift from being overwhelmingly centered on academics to other currently slighted matters like social development and civic values. Teachers could become managers of the delivery system. Teacher feedback and evaluation would then actually increase in importance. This kind of future evolution could capitalize on ground-level (*genba*) teacher experience and understandings, but there is no guarantee, especially in this country, of such an outcome. Presumably, the tailoring of instructional packages in the future will be made easier than is the current case with textbooks. If so, the issues we have seen being considered by Japanese teachers in their interaction with one another—such as too much versus too little information, or the appropriate amount of time to accomplish a particular lesson, or the means to greater clarity of expression, or which modes of thinking and knowledge construction to emphasize—could be more, not less, important in the future. Much of what is so interesting about the current state of teacher-based improvements in Japan, as described in this book, will be of growing relevance in both countries, as they face the new challenges of this century from their very different institutional perspectives. It will be important to follow and carefully compare them in these terms. This book will serve that purpose well as a baseline by which to examine change. And despite the problems of comparability and the pitfalls of popular comparison, each nation will have much to learn from the other's voyage through these uncharted waters.

Acknowledgments. I would like to express my gratitude to the Canadian Institute for Advanced Research for its support in the form of a fellowship. I would also like to acknowledge the crucial role played by Robbie Case in the development of my thinking about the impact of technology and globalization on our state-based systems. I have missed his intellectual friendship since his untimely death.

REFERENCES

Cole, R. (1989). *Strategies for learning.* Berkeley: University of California Press.

Cutts, R. (1997). *The empire of schools.* Armonk, NY: M. E. Sharpe.

Duke, B. (1973). *Japan's militant teachers.* Honolulu: University of Hawaii Press.

Hall, J. P. (1973). *Mori Arinori.* Cambridge, MA: Harvard University Press.

Harvey, D. (1989). *The condition of post-modernity.* Oxford: Oxford University Press.

Horio T. (1988). *Educational thought and ideology in modern Japan: State authority and intellectual freedom* (S. Platzer, Trans. & Ed.). Tokyo: University of Tokyo Press.

Ilon, L. (1994). Structural adjustment and education: Adapting to a growing global market. *International Journal of Educational Development, 14*(2), 95–108.

Itô, C. (1969). *Shûdan shûgi no saihakken* [A reexamination of Groupism]. Tokyo: Daiyamondosha.

Lewis, C. C. (1995). *Educating hearts and minds.* New York: Cambridge University Press.

Lincicome, M. E. (1995). *Principle, praxis, and the politics of educational reform in Meiji Japan.* Honolulu: University of Hawaii Press.

Mathews, J. (1997). Power shift. *Foreign Affairs, 76*(1), 50–66.

Meyer, J. W., & Ramirez, F. O. (1992). World expansion of mass education, 1870–1980. *Sociology of Education, 65,* 128–149.

Ouchi, W. (1982). *Theory Z.* Reading, MA: Addison-Wesley.

Peak, L. (1991). *Learning to go to school in Japan.* Berkeley: University of California Press.

Ramirez, F. O. (1997). The nation-state, citizenship, and educational change: Institutionalization and globalization. In W. K. Cummings & N. F. McGinn (Eds.), *International handbook of education and development* (pp. 47–62). Oxford: Pergamon.

Reich, R. B. (1991). Who is them? *Harvard Business Review, 69*(2), 77–88.

Rohlen, T. P. (1975). The work group in Japanese organization. In E. Vogel (Ed.), *Modern Japanese organization and decision-making* (pp. 185–209). Berkeley: University of California Press.

Rohlen, T. P. (1984a). Conflict in institutional environments: Politics in education. In E. S. Krauss, T. P. Rohlen, & P. G. Steinhoff (Eds.), *Conflict in Japan* (pp. 136–173). Honolulu: University of Hawaii Press.

Rohlen, T. P. (1984b). *Japan's high schools.* Berkeley: University of California Press.

Smith, R. (1983). *Japanese society: Tradition, self, and the social order.* New York: Cambridge University Press.

Stevenson, H. W., & Stigler, J. W. (1992). *The learning gap.* New York: Summit Books.

Tyack, D., & Cuban, L. (1995). *Why the grammar of schooling persists.* Cambridge, MA: Harvard University Press.

Waters, M. (1995). *Globalization.* London: Routledge.

Wriston, W. (1997). Bits, bytes, and diplomacy. *Foreign Affairs, 76*(5), 172–182.

Yoneyama, S. (1999). *The Japanese high school: Silence and resistance.* New York: Routledge.

About the Editor and Contributors

Gary DeCoker is Professor of Education and Director of East Asian Studies at Ohio Wesleyan University. He received an M.A. in Japanese Studies and a Ph.D. in Comparative Education from the University of Michigan. His publications include translations and analyses of medieval Japanese treatises on the teaching of calligraphy and studies of contemporary Japanese education. During the past quarter century, he has lived in Japan for 7 years as a student of the Japanese traditional arts, a graduate student at Kyoto University, and a visiting professor at Waseda University.

Hiroshi Azuma is Adjunct Professor of Psychology at Bunkyo Women's University and Professor Emeritus from the University of Tokyo. He received his undergraduate degree in psychology from the University of Tokyo and his doctorate in educational psychology at the University of Illinois. Founder and president of the Japanese Society of Developmental Psychology, he is currently the president of the Japanese Psychological Association and the Japanese Union of Psychology Societies. He had been an active member on advisory councils to the Japanese Ministry of Education and also on a number of international organizations and editorial boards. His research areas include educational, developmental, and cultural psychology. His publications include *Child Development and Education in Japan* (co-editor with H. Stevenson and K. Hakuta, 1986).

Samuel Coleman is pursuing a Master's in Social Work at California State University, Long Beach. He holds a Ph.D. in Anthropology and Certificate of the East Asian Institute from Columbia University. His recent book *Japanese Science: From the Inside* examines the organizational barriers to creativity in the laboratory sciences in Japan. *Nature* hailed the book as "a profound and insightful critique of scientific organizations in Japan." Coleman is now conducting research around areas of concern common to anthropology and social work, including a study of epistemological issues in the evaluation of clinical interventions.

Shin-ying Lee is Associate Research Scientist at the Center for Human Growth and Development, University of Michigan. She is a developmental and educational psychologist. Her research focuses on the cultural contexts that facilitate the attainment of academic achievement. She is particularly interested in understanding the Asian school settings that may be conducive to effective mathematics teaching and learning. Based on findings from cross-cultural comparative research, Lee is also working with several American schools to develop an elementary mathematics curriculum and a model of professional development to enhance effective mathematics instructions in American classrooms.

Gerald K. LeTendre is Associate Professor of Education Policy Studies and Chair of the Comparative and International Education Program at the Pennsylvania State University. He specializes in educational decision making, adolescent schooling and adjustment, and comparative research methods. Dr. LeTendre was a primary researcher on the Third International Mathematics and Science Study (TIMSS) and has served as a methodological consultant to the International Association for the Evaluation of Educational Achievement (IEA) Civic Education Project and the Board on International and Comparative Studies of the National Research Council. His publications include four books comparing Japanese and U.S. school systems (Cambridge University Press, 1996; Falmer Press, 1999; Yale University Press, 2000; and Routledge/Falmer, 2001).

Catherine C. Lewis received her Ph.D. in developmental psychology from Stanford University in 1979, and is currently a member of the Education Department at Mills College in Oakland, California. Her book *Educating Hearts and Minds: Reflections on Japanese Preschool and Elementary Education* was named outstanding academic book of 1995 by the American Library Association's *Choice*. For more than a decade, she directed formative evaluation of the Child Development Project, a school renewal effort designed to build school communities rich in intellectual challenge and in close, supportive human relationships. Her research in Japanese elementary schools over the past 20 years has focused on how Japanese teachers educate heart and mind simultaneously, and on how they continuously improve instruction through collaborative "lesson study." She currently directs a National Science Foundation–funded study of promising U.S. and Japanese models to "teach for understanding" in elementary school science. More information about this project can be found at http://www.lessonresearch.net.

David L. McConnell is currently Associate Professor of Anthropology at The College of Wooster in Wooster, Ohio. He received his Ph.D. from Stanford University in 1991 and was a postdoctoral research fellow at the

Program on U.S.-Japan Relations at Harvard University. A Fulbright scholar, he has spent over 5 years living in Japan and has published numerous articles on Japanese education. His book *Importing Diversity* received the 2001 Masayoshi Ohira Memorial Prize for its contribution to furthering understanding of educational and cultural interactions in the Pacific Basin.

Thomas P. Rohlen is a Professor Emeritus at the School of Education at Stanford University and a Senior Fellow of the Institute for International Studies at the same university. He is also a Fellow of the Canadian Institute for Advanced Studies. The author of numerous books and articles on Japanese organization, culture, and education, he is currently working on a project studying the urban dynamics of East Asia.

Nancy Ukai Russell is an independent researcher. She lived in Japan for 14 years where she studied different aspects of Japanese education as a Fulbright English Fellow at the Toyama Prefectural Board of Education. She was also a reporter for the Tokyo bureau of *Newsweek*. Russell is presently studying private-sector education in Japan and the United States. Her publications include "The Kumon Approach to Teaching and Learning" in the *Journal of Japanese Studies* and "Lessons from Japanese Cram Schools" in *The Challenge of Eastern Asian Education*.

Nobuo K. Shimahara is a professor of education and anthropology at the Graduate School of Education and a member of the faculty of the Graduate School, Rutgers University. He has taught at Rutgers since 1968 and has served as a visiting professor at several Japanese universities including Nagoya University, Naruto University of Education, National Institute for Multimedia Education, and Tokyo University. He has published many books and articles. His recent publications include *Learning to Teach in Two Cultures: Japan and the United States* (with A. Sakai, 1995), *Teacher Education in Industrial Nations* (co-editor with I. Holowinsky, 1995), *Politics of Classroom Life: Classroom Management in International Perspective* (editor, 1998), *Teaching in Japan: A Cultural Perspective* (2001), and *Ethnicity, Race, and Nationality in Education* (co-editor with I. Holowinsky and S. Tomlinson-Clarke, 2001).

Harold W. Stevenson is Professor of Psychology at the University of Michigan. He has served as president of the Society for Research in Child Development and of other related professional organizations. He is a Fellow of the American Academy of Arts and Sciences, a member of the National Academy of Education, and among other activities is the author, with

James Stigler, of *The Learning Gap*, a widely read summary of the research conducted by the Michigan research group and colleagues in the United States, China, Taiwan, and Japan.

Ineko Tsuchida is a San Francisco–based educational researcher and consultant. Since earning her doctorate in education at the University of California, Berkeley, in 1990, she has conducted qualitative and quantitative studies comparing U.S. and Japanese school systems. Her research has examined student responsibility and learning, student-teacher interactions, teachers' instructional and management statements, research lessons, and differences between U.S. and Japanese elementary science textbooks. Recent works include "A Look at the Other Side of Japanese Education: Student Responsibility and Learning" (with C. Lewis, 1999) in *Competitor or Ally? Japan's Role in American Educational Debates* (G. LeTendre, Editor, 1999) and "A Lesson Is Like a Swiftly Flowing River" (with C. Lewis, 1998) in *American Educator*.

Akane Zusho is currently a doctoral candidate in the Combined Program in Education and Psychology at the University of Michigan, Ann Arbor. Her research interests include the achievement motivation and self-regulated learning of ethnic minority students, cross-cultural research on academic achievement, mathematics learning and instruction, and curriculum development and professional development in the area of mathematics.

Index